PRAISE FOR *NAVIGATING BEHAVIOR CHANGE*

"This engaging and practical book offers educators powerful strategies that are easy to implement in the classroom. Whether you're a general or special education teacher, a behavior support professional, or a school or district administrator, the insights shared by the authors—based on their own experiences—will enhance your ability to create a more positive, supportive learning environment. It's a must-read for anyone committed to strengthening universal supports and improving school climate for students and staff alike."

—Dawn Spurlock
Director of Special Services,
Caldwell School District in Caldwell, Idaho

"*Navigating Behavior Change* is a gem! It's brimming with relatable wisdom and practical classroom strategies rooted in evidence-based practices focusing on universal supports for all students to enhance learning. Teachers, university faculty preparing teachers, and others supporting teachers will undoubtedly find the perspectives, strategies, and tools valuable in real-world situations and immediately actionable."

—Michael F. Giangreco
PhD, University Distinguished Professor Emeritus of Special Education,
University of Vermont

"*Navigating Behavior Change* provides a step-by-step roadmap for teachers, school psychologists, and other educators to effectuate positive behavior change in classrooms. It is a must-read for current school professionals as well as pre-service educators in higher education training programs."

—Katherine A. Dockweiler
Assistant Professor of School Psychology and
President of the Nevada State Board of Education

"Teachers, school leaders, educational consultants—this book is ideal for anyone who needs user-friendly tools and a framework when navigating behavior change to improve student progress in classrooms. Busting myths with evidence-based strategies, Amanda and Danielle break down components of quality instructional practices with solid rationales and guiding questions to apply effective tools and strategies the next day!"

—Alison Lovelace
PhD, BCBA-D

T0398285

Navigating Behavior Change

Navigating Behavior Change

Change

Strategies to Minimize Challenging
Behaviors in Your Classroom

AMANDA WILSON, Ed.S., NCSP, BCBA

DANIELLE LINDQUIST, M.Ed., BCBA

JB JOSSEY-BASS™
A Wiley Brand

Published by John Wiley & Sons, Inc., Hoboken, New Jersey.
Published simultaneously in Canada.

ISBNs: 9781394282692 (Paperback), 9781394282715 (ePDF), 9781394282708 (ePub).

For general information on our other products and services, please contact our Customer Care Department within the United States at (800) 762-2974, outside the United States at (317) 572- 3993. For product technical support, you can find answers to frequently asked questions or reach us via live chat at **https://support.wiley.com**.

If you believe you've found a mistake in this book, please bring it to our attention by emailing our reader support team at **wileysupport@wiley.com** with the subject line "Possible Book Errata Submission."

Wiley also publishes its books in a variety of electronic formats. Some content that appears in print may not be available in electronic formats. For more information about Wiley products, visit our web site at **www.wiley.com**.

Library of Congress Control Number: 2025023096 (print)

Cover Design: Wiley
Cover Image: © porcorex/Getty Images
Author Photos: (Wilson) by Joshua Wilson, (Lindquist) Courtesy of the Author

SKY10117526_061625

To my husband, Josh, and my parents, Pam and Gary, for your unwavering support and belief that I can achieve great things.
– Amanda

To my parents, and extended family, for your fierce support throughout my journey. And to my daughter, Isla
– stay curious, be open, and never stop learning.
– Danielle

To our past students, you have motivated us to do better and to support others in doing better as well.
– Amanda & Danielle

Contents

Foreword

I walked into my first classroom on a hot August day, carrying only a roll of paper towels and a bottle of cleaning spray in a grocery bag. The classroom, located on the fourth floor of a 150-year-old building, had been empty for years, with high stacks of furniture covered in even higher stacks of dust. I was wildly unprepared for my first year of teaching, both literally and figuratively. That year transformed my understanding of the immense challenges that teachers face. Teaching in a self-contained special education classroom, I quickly realized I lacked the skills and strategies necessary to manage it effectively.

An undergraduate degree in education cannot fully prepare a teacher for the complexities and diverse challenges of the job. Beyond content knowledge, effective teaching requires a deep understanding of developmental psychology and behavior. The limited coursework in classroom management does not adequately prepare educators for the varied challenges they will encounter.

Being a great teacher isn't just about mastering content and knowing how to teach it. It's about fostering connections, engagement, and growth. To achieve this, we need a strong foundation – one that classroom management provides. I often refer to the analogy of a house's foundation when describing classroom management. Imagine a house being constructed: clearing the site, pouring concrete, framing the structure. These initial steps are crucial for building a sturdy home. Similarly, classroom management consists of the essential steps needed to create a successful learning environment. Just as a foundation is not optional for building a house, effective classroom management is critical for successful instruction.

In *Navigating Behavior Change*, Amanda and Danielle offer the foundation and framework necessary for establishing a thriving classroom. This resource was the missing piece in my grocery bag all those years ago when I first stepped into my classroom. It took years of trial and error, plus a master's degree, to fully understand the core components of a solid classroom foundation. Now, this knowledge is beautifully summarized in this blueprint. Amanda and Danielle present actionable strategies for success in a practical and approachable way.

Sasha Long, MA BCBA
Founder and President
The Autism Helper, Inc.

About the Authors

Amanda Wilson, Ed.S., NCSP, BCBA is a nationally certified school psychologist, board-certified behavior analyst, and educational consultant with extensive experience in the public school system. Her unique background as a military wife has allowed her to work in various regions across the United States, exposing her to diverse educational settings and experiences. Throughout her career, she has served in a variety of roles, including school psychologist, behavior analyst, consultant, coordinator of behavioral supports, and curriculum and professional development.

Amanda is passionate about equipping educators with the knowledge and skills necessary to prevent challenging behaviors in their classrooms. Recognizing that student behavior is a common difficulty in the classroom, Amanda empowers educators to implement universal practices effectively, enhancing their competence and confidence in intervening at the classroom level, regardless of building supports. As the cofounder and owner of Navigating Behavior Change, Amanda offers workshops, consultation, and coaching in universal supports, positive behavior intervention frameworks, and effective behavioral strategies. Through her work, she aims to create impactful learning experiences for all educators. You can connect with her at **NavigatingBehaviorChange.com** or on Instagram @ navigatingbehaviorchange.

Danielle Lindquist, M.Ed., BCBA is a certified elementary education teacher, special education teacher, and board-certified behavior analyst. Upon the start of her career at a therapeutic day school, she quickly developed a passion for the population of students who many deemed too difficult to reach. Her work as a consultant in a wide variety of educational settings has assisted leaders in revamping procedures and processes surrounding inclusion, data analysis, restraint and seclusion, and the implementation of evidence-based positive behavior interventions and supports. Danielle has extensive experience providing professional development and coaching for individual educators, classroom teams, schools, districts, and state-run and global organizations.

Though passionate about supporting at-risk students and those experiencing severe challenging behavior, her goal is to build capacity around universal supports for all learners in order to prevent and reduce the need for more intensive, individualized interventions. Her work is focused on trauma-informed and dignified teaching practices that create a classroom environment that is both motivating and conducive to learning.

Introduction

How It All Began

Danielle here, your fellow teacher. When I was first starting out, I knew what I knew, and I didn't know what I didn't know. As the Greek philosopher Socrates once said, "The only true wisdom is knowing you know nothing." So, according to him, I was quite a wise educator. That being said, it didn't help me sleep any better at night. After all, I still had to learn how to effectively teach a group of students with a wide range of skills, cultural backgrounds, learning histories, caregiver dynamics, diagnoses, and adverse childhood experiences. Like most educators, I went into the field to teach. But I never stopped to consider what teaching truly meant. Nor did I consider that without certain needs being met, our students aren't even available to learn.

It was a Tuesday afternoon, and I was spending my time on something I truly thought was a priority; I was putting together a binder to help me track all the math standards my multi-age class within a therapeutic day school was expected to meet that year. Amanda (my co-author) walked in and asked me what I was working on. I told her, and instead of immediately responding, she paused. She relaxed her posture and looked me dead in the eyes. To this day, I share her words with every educator I meet. She said, "Danielle, how are you supposed to meet the math standards if your students are struggling to even get through a lesson without engaging in challenging behavior?" *Ah-ha!* Someone who understood! But before I could spew out my next thought, she continued: "No matter their age, they can always be taught how to read and do math – but they have only so much time before the system gives up on them due to their behaviors." I put down the binder and sat down, stunned by this idea. She wasn't arguing the chicken or the egg; she was arguing the fact that I had to prioritize helping them achieve behavioral success just as much as I was prioritizing academic success.

Now, I could have done what most of us educators do on a weekly basis. I could have saddled up and ridden up the mountain of blame. I could have blamed my student's parents. I could have blamed my administrator for giving me all the "difficult kids" because she thought I was so good at teaching. I could have quit (it's not like I hadn't thought about that daily). I could have spent that weekend trying to come up with a list of harsher consequences for when challenging behavior occurred. But I knew all those options were dead ends. Sure, coming down on parents, admin, or students might result in some type of uncomfortable, short-term gain (or not!), but I wasn't naive enough to think that those would produce the outstanding, long-term results I was looking for or the results my students deserved. Plus, that wasn't me. I valued self-development and curiosity. I didn't set out to be just a teacher. I wanted to be an effective teacher – I wanted results.

However, effectiveness can be a tricky thing. Why? Because to achieve results, one first must get clear on *what* those results are. For many of us educators, the results we often yearn for end up being a compliant group of students who do what they are told without dispute. However, this didn't feel quite right to me. I had to determine what a truly successful class full of students looked like, sounded like, and felt like. At the end of the day I wanted my students to *want* to come to class and to cooperate. I also had to figure out *who* would be responsible for determining those results. I knew I would be back to square one if I solely focused on everyone but myself. That would back me into the coercion corner faster than I could exclaim, "Don't make me call your parents!" No, to be effective, I had to have my students (and at times some additional players) on board.

Not only that, but I also had to identify *how* those results would be achieved. You see, anyone can walk into two side-by-side classrooms and, at first glance, they may look and sound the same. The students might be following directions, completing their work, and using respectful language. But, there are different ways to achieve this outcome, and some of those ways are detrimental to the students' overall mental health and well-being. I knew this process would entail taking a long, hard look at what I personally was doing and not doing that was either moving us further from or closer to our goals. I learned early on in my career what most go their entire teaching career without recognizing – *that for student behavior to change, one must change how they think about student behavior*. It was time to redefine what it meant to be an effective educator.

I (Amanda) remember that conversation with Danielle clearly. I was new to the building that year and was quite shocked by many of the practices and procedures in place, or lack thereof. As a school psychologist and behavior analyst, I desperately wanted to begin the process of improving programming for our students. To do so, I first had to build relationships and gain staff buy-in. Change is difficult, especially when I'm asking staff to reflect on their practices, to consider alternative approaches, and ultimately to change *their* behavior. That's daunting for even the most motivated staff!

Danielle wasn't deterred. That one conversation changed the trajectory of not only that school year but her career as well. Ultimately, because of her unwavering goal to be as effective a teacher as possible, her students benefited greatly. Danielle and her classroom team met that hard truth, that to ensure her student's academic success, she first needed to prioritize their behavioral needs. From there on out, each time I entered her classroom, I was met with a list of "Questions for Amanda" filling portions of the whiteboard and clipboards. Together we embarked on a collaborative journey to ensure her students' social, emotional, and behavioral success through implementation of core universal supports, teaching of behavioral skills, and effective responses to both desirable and challenging behaviors.

Ultimately, Danielle was able to teach those math standards. In fact, because she spent the time supporting the behavioral needs of her students, she was able to teach far more academics over time – and significantly more than any other classroom in the building! Her students felt successful. They *were* successful. And several were even able to transition back to their neighborhood schools by the end of the year.

Why We Wrote This Book

Google any educational buzzword, term, or strategy that has to do with "classroom behavior" and you will get a million different hits – from books, to blogs, to curriculums, to Teachers-Pay-Teachers resources, to courses, to Tik-Tok videos. Tools for our toolboxes are constantly being thrown at educators, administrators, and related-service providers, and quite frankly, it's filled with too much useless crap to lug around anymore. Let us be clear, there are many fantastic resources out there, but here's what we've noticed: most of them are very one-sided. There are books on basic classroom management. There are PDFs on the steps of effective lesson delivery. There are workshops on trauma-informed care. There are guides on the executive functions. There are full-blown college degrees in applied behavior analysis. But what we couldn't find was a resource that brought everything together in a cohesive and actionable way that educators can easily understand.

Teachers don't just need basic classroom management. They don't just need to know how to deliver an engaging lesson to 25 kindergarteners. They don't just need to know how to tactfully interact with five unruly high schoolers in sixth period. They don't just need to be able to consider Sally's trauma history. And they sure as heck don't just need to understand what to do about their student with ADHD and it's not even 8:30 a.m. They need strategies to support *all* their learners!

Over the course of our careers, we've spent countless hours implementing individualized, intensive behavioral interventions for students. Danielle has been the one in the classroom trying to implement "all the individual plans," and we've both been the consultant suggesting individualized strategies to classroom teams. Guess what? It was exhausting, not only for the teaching staff asked to implement these strategies, but also for us, as we worked to support staff in implementation. What we didn't initially realize, though, was the significant adverse impact of missing tier 1, universal supports. *Without these supports in place, the students struggled and looked like they needed higher levels of support, when in reality, they didn't.*

So why did we find it a stellar idea to write yet another resource to answer the question: "How do I prevent challenging behavior in my classroom?" Our classrooms are diverse, and our goal is to help you effectively teach any group of students that come your way while reducing the need for individualized interventions. Regardless of how well your school building or district is implementing multi-tiered systems of supports (MTSS), *we want you to be able to understand and implement universal supports to prevent challenging student behavior within the walls of your classroom, to ultimately lead to student success and decreased frustrations for you.*

At this point, you may be wondering, "What are these universal supports you're speaking of?" Plain and simple, universal supports are free, low-to-no-prep, time-efficient evidence-based strategies that should be implemented across all ages, grades, abilities, settings, and subjects. The U.S. Department of Education describes universal supports as prevention services that support students' academic and behavioral needs by providing equitable conditions for all learners while simultaneously limiting discrimination (Weeks et al., 2019). Further, universal supports are considered the foundation of MTSS and align with legislation surrounding the Individuals with Disabilities Education Act (IDEA), the Civil Rights Act of 1964, and Title VI (Weeks et al., 2019).

> *Yet even though universal supports are aligned with MTSS and federal legislation, are preventative, and are appropriate for all students, the actionable strategies and the adult behaviors required to implement them aren't well known by most educators. In this book, we aim to remedy this skill gap by providing knowledge and actionable strategies that every educator can implement!*

How to Use This Book

We recognize that educators spanning a variety of grade levels, disciplines, and roles may utilize this book. Therefore, we want to highlight the different ways this resource can be used to meet your individual needs:

Individual classroom use: As the leader of your classroom, regardless of what supports are or are not in place within your building, you can use this book as a guide to ensure you are implementing universal supports with fidelity.

Consultation, training, and coaching: As a consultant, instructional coach, administrator, or related service provider, you can use this book to assess for gaps in implementation and strategically target areas of need with your mentees.

Professional learning committees: Together as a team, you can learn, reflect, and plan for implementation.

Book club: Get a small group together to expand your knowledge and skillset. Take actionable steps to implement universal supports within your classroom and share your new knowledge with staff by leading by example.

Professional development: Assess for strengths and weaknesses, map out a plan for training, problem-solve barriers to implementation, and build staff capacity in implementing universal supports.

Format

This book is formatted to provide the rationale for how universal supports assist students in effectively navigating the school day. Within this, we provide you, the reader, with background knowledge to better understand behavior, executive skills, and motivation – both your students' and your own! From there, we take a deep dive into universal supports and how they relate to classroom management. The core content within this book covers the essential components of universal supports. For each support, we have provided a description of it, evidence of its effectiveness, and step-by-step information on how to implement it. We have also included additional considerations such as how to differentiate the support, when to use versus not use, and examples and nonexamples.

Activities

Throughout this book you will find activities embedded to assist you in understanding and applying learned content. We encourage you to take the time to complete the activities as doing so will increase your understanding and aid you in planning for implementation. Activities will focus on the following:

Specific skill practice: Following discussion of a specific universal support, scenarios are provided to assist you in discriminating between examples and nonexamples of the support, identifying where and when a strategy would be beneficial to implement, and problem-solving scenarios for missed opportunities to use a skill.

Reflection activities: Some of these activities will ask that you reflect on your current implementation of a specific support. Others will ask that you consider your classroom's specific challenges and consider how you can use the discussed support to set students up for increased success and decrease challenging behaviors.

Common classroom challenges: In Chapter 8, you will find several scenarios that likely occur in classrooms across the country. Here we ask you to consider the scenario and (a) identify which universal supports you would implement if this were occurring in your classroom and (b) the specifics of how you would do so (what it would look like and sound like). This activity allows you to build on all that you have learned throughout the text and put it all together.

Resources

Appendix: To assist you in implementing universal supports, we have included an appendix of reproducible forms. These include implementation checklists, planning guides, and reflection forms.

References: Here you will find information on other works we have referenced.

Glossary: Here you will find an alphabetical list of all the terms we have defined throughout the book.

CHAPTER 1

Foundations of Behavior

What Does Behavior Have to Do with Universal Supports?

Behavior. It's everything that we think, say, or do. We often hear things like, "Ugh, Johnny had *another behavior* today." And our internal thought response is "Well, I hope he is engaging in behavior. Otherwise, he's dead." There's this misconception that behaviors are just the problematic things that students do when, in reality, it's everything that we do . . . all day, every day.

Another common misconception is thinking of behaviors as only being observable, meaning anyone around the individual can see or hear the behavior occurring. While we do engage in external behaviors that can be seen or heard by others, this does not encompass all forms of behavior. We also engage in internal behaviors like thoughts that can then drive our external, observable behaviors.

Here are two examples of behaviors a student may engage in within the classroom when presented a task that is difficult for them:

> *They may think "I'm so stupid; I can't do this."*
> *And they may say "This is dumb!"*
> *And what they may do is swipe their textbook off their desk.*

> *They may think "I hate writing argumentative essays."*
> *And may say "This is hard, but I can do hard things."*
> *And what they may do is type the assignment on their Chromebook.*

The first example demonstrates behaviors that we may label as negative, disruptive, inappropriate, undesirable, unexpected, or challenging. The second example demonstrates behaviors we may label as positive, appropriate, expected, or desirable. To keep things simple throughout this text, we will be using the term *challenging behavior* to describe distracting, disruptive, or dangerous behaviors that interfere with the student's learning or the learning of others in some way. We will use the term *desirable behavior* to describe behavior that meets classroom expectations or is generally considered appropriate for the situation or setting.

> ### Challenging Behavior:
>
> Distracting, disruptive, or dangerous behavior that interferes with the student's learning or the learning of others.

While it is important to discriminate between challenging and desirable behaviors, we'd be remiss if we didn't pause to talk about the difference a bit more to reframe our thinking.

Let's consider the following two statements:

> "I want my students to engage in these behaviors less so that I can actually teach!"

> "What behaviors can my students and I do more of so we can accomplish our goals?"

Typically, as educators, when we discuss student behavior, we consider our needs and the behaviors that we want to see less of. These very well may be distracting, disruptive, or dangerous behaviors that interfere with our ability to teach. However, when we focus solely on *our* needs, this places responsibility on the student to change their behaviors without considering why they are occurring. And this sets ourselves and students up for failure.

If we reframe our thinking to consider what we need to do, what students need to do, and how we can support them in doing so, we are more likely to achieve long-term positive behavior change. *It is important to recognize that for student behavior to change, adult behavior must also change.* We are part of the environment. We set the stage for success or failure within the walls of our classroom through our relationships, our structures and routines, the use of effective strategies, and our responses to both desirable and challenging behaviors.

As we move through this text, you will notice that we continually highlight the adult behaviors we must engage in to support our students. We propose that any interventions to create long-term behavior change be implemented with the goal of increasing a student's skills, their overall functioning, their ability to form and maintain relationships, and/or their independence. This is what behavior analysts refer to as *social significance*, and ethically, all interventions should consider this. We must look beyond "compliance" with adult instructions and expectations as the singular goal. If we operate under the mindset that they just need to suppress challenging behaviors, do as they are told, and meet expectations, we *will not* achieve long-term behavior change.

To understand our and our students' behavior, we need to understand four core truths of behavior:

- **Behavior is circumstantial:** It does not occur in a vacuum, out of the blue, or without reason. Everything we do is directly influenced by the environment in which the behavior occurs. If we fail to consider the context under which the behavior is occurring, we will fail to effectively support our students. We will also see the challenging behavior continue. For example, if Johnny is an angel in Mr. Smith's class, following all classroom expectations and completing his work, but engages in disruptive behaviors in your class, then the context is different. There is something different within the environment that is setting the stage for the disruptive behavior. It may be that you interact differently with Johnny. Your classroom routines may be different, or your subject requires different skills (academic, social, or behavioral). Or, perhaps, the peer group or instructional format is different.

- **Behavior has underlying influences:** There are a wide variety of factors that impact individual human behavior. For example, genetic disorders can predispose an individual to engage in certain behavior. Likewise, medical conditions can result in behaviors that increase an individual's sensitivity to environmental stimuli. Medical conditions can also cause pain and discomfort for which a behavior, once engaged in, decreases or eliminates that pain. Traumatic experiences, both acute and chronic, impact an individual's future behavioral responses to events or stimuli within their environment. Being without access to something that is desired, such as food, can influence behaviors that assist the individual in getting what they need. Conversely, having too much of something (having eaten and being full) can decrease engagement in behaviors that result in obtaining food. Finally, we can generally consider factors that influence behaviors as setting events as they increase or decrease the likelihood of certain behaviors occurring when in play. For example, missing daily medication, poor sleep the night before, or feeling unwell may increase the chance of challenging behaviors occurring. Underlying influences are important to consider because when we are aware of them, we can make adjustments to support ourselves and our students more effectively. A note of caution: while it is important to consider and identify underlying influences of challenging behaviors, it is important to move beyond admiring their occurrence. Just because an underlying influence is present doesn't mean we can't implement strategies to lessen their impact.

- **Behavior is functional:** All behavior serves a purpose or meets a need for the individual engaging in it. This is true even if the behavior seems odd, out-of-context, or disproportionate to the situation. This behavior may be the only behavior the student knows how to engage in, in a moment of stress, to meet their needs. We can categorize all behaviors as either helping us to "get" more of the things that we want/ like or "get away" from the things that we don't want/like. It's important to note that, sometimes, we do consciously think about what behavior we are going to engage in to meet a particular need in the moment. However, most of the time, we behave "automatically" because in the past certain behaviors have helped us to get or get away from things. This learning history influences our behaviors, as does our skill level, and the overall need for safety and quick outcomes. It's imperative that we consider the function or purpose of a behavior because simply trying to eliminate it without addressing the need it is meeting is unlikely to increase more desirable behaviors.

- **Behavior can be changed:** What we do or don't do has the potential to influence behavior, leading to an increase or decrease in challenging behaviors over time. To effectively change behavior, we can and should consider the circumstances under which it occurs, the factors that are influencing it, and the purpose or need it is serving. We can implement preventative strategies, including the universal supports outlined in this book, teach and reinforce desirable behaviors, and respond effectively to challenging behaviors to increase student independence, grow engagement, and improve quality of life.

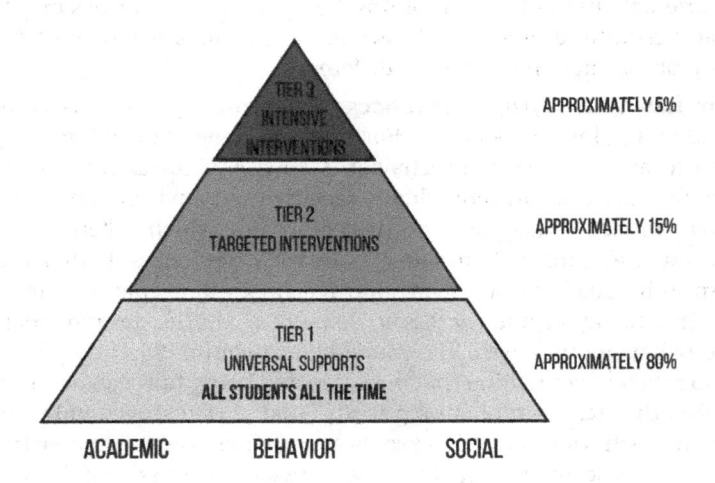

At this point, you may be wondering how behavior, universal supports, and classroom management link to create optimal conditions for learning. More than likely, you are familiar with one or more of the following terms: Positive Behavior Interventions and Supports (PBIS), Response to Intervention (RTI), and Multi-Tiered Systems of Supports (MTSS). These frameworks share a similarity in that they all include supports and interventions within a three-tiered approach. The lowest tier (tier 1) is considered the universal support tier, wherein all students receive the same core supports. Statistically, most students (approximately 80%) will be successful with these supports in place and will not require additional supports. However, approximately 15% of a student population may require additional "targeted" tier 2 supports, and another 5% may require "intensive" tier 3 supports.

The key component we are focusing on within this book is tier 1 universal supports, which are provided to all students all the time, with the following goals:

- Promoting positive and effective learning environments
- Preventing challenging behaviors
- Limiting discrimination
- Supporting all students

This is a big goal, without a lot of details of what strategies to utilize. In fact, ask any educator, and you are likely to hear many different interpretations and understandings of what these tiered levels include. For example, within the PBIS framework, many educators believe that the universal support level is simply a school store to reinforce student behavior. While a school store may be included within a PBIS framework, it is certainly not the only component and in reality isn't even necessary.

Effective classroom management plays a significant role within the implementation of universal supports as well. If you search for a definition of classroom management, you are likely to find a variety of definitions. Key phrases may include "Procedures," ". . .an environment conducive to learning," "Actions a teacher takes," ". . .successful instruction can occur," "Skills and techniques teachers use. . .," and ". . .keep students on-task."

Overall, implementing universal supports, which include effective classroom management strategies, requires that adults engage in specific behaviors that then increase the likelihood of our students engaging in specific behaviors that increase their engagement and overall learning. However, to be able to implement universal supports effectively, we must know what strategies to implement and why and how to implement them.

The Brain: The Not-So-Big Elephant in the Room

To better understand behavior, both that of our students and our own, we want to provide you with a basic understanding of how our brain impacts our behaviors, because remember, our behavior is directly impacted by our environment and underlying influences, and it serves a purpose to us. Additionally, we learned that behavior includes internal or private behaviors that may not be observed by others but can drive observable external behaviors. Gaining an understanding of the role of the brain in behavior will assist you in effectively supporting your students (as well as yourself) *and* lead to increased engagement.

Our brains contain three main divisions: the cerebrum, cerebellum, and brain stem. The cerebrum is the largest of the divisions, making up approximately 80% of our brain, and its different parts are responsible for interpreting our environment and regulating our emotions, reasoning, and learning. Of most importance to what we are talking about is the role of the prefrontal cortex within the frontal lobes. Located behind our foreheads, this upper front of our brain can simply be described as our "thinking" brain. When all is well within our environment, we can use our prefrontal cortex (thinking brain) appropriately. We can be considered rational; we are generally available for learning, social interactions, and completing tasks; and we are typically able to place a bit more space between our internal thoughts and our observable behaviors. In addition, we are better able to access and utilize our executive functions to assist us in getting things done (Professional, 2024).

> ### Executive Functions:
>
> The cognitive processes that enable us to regulate and direct our behavior in order to begin tasks and achieve goals.

It's common to consider the prefrontal cortex as being like the cockpit of an airplane. It's essentially the control system for all that we need to accomplish. When we are flying and all cockpit controls are working properly, we can process information, communicate our wants and needs, regulate our emotions, utilize good judgment and reasoning skills, plan for what is coming up, and think before we act. Essentially, executive functions are the foundation of everything that we do, and our use of our executive functioning skills allows us to keep our plane safely in the air moving toward our destination.

There are many executive functioning skills that support our overall abilities to regulate our behavior through selecting, problem-solving, persisting, and ultimately achieving goals. A list of these, as described by Dawson and Guare (2018), is shown here:

Core Executive Function Skills

- **Response inhibition:** The ability to think before you act, to resist the urge to do something
- **Emotional control:** The ability to manage your behaviors under stressful circumstances
- **Working memory:** The ability to retain and draw upon information when needed
- **Attention control:** The ability to attend to relevant stimuli despite distraction or a decrease in motivation
- **Task initiation:** The ability to begin tasks efficiently and in a timely manner
- **Planning:** The ability to create a roadmap to complete a task or navigate a routine
- **Organization:** The ability to create and maintain systems to keep track of information and materials
- **Time management:** The ability to accurately estimate the time one has to complete a task and then allocate that time accordingly
- **Persistence:** The ability to follow through on the completion of a task or goal
- **Flexibility:** The ability to revise a plan and adapt to changing conditions
- **Metacognition:** The ability to self-monitor and self-evaluate one's own behaviors

See the appendix's Form 1.1 for a one-page cheat-sheet of these executive skills.

As you read this list, did it strike you how important each of these executive functioning skills are to each of us every single day? Did you perhaps recognize some of these executive functioning skills as a strength or weakness for you? Did you think of a student who struggles with one or more of these?

Having strong, well-developed executive functioning skills positively impacts our mental health, physical health, performance in school/work, and overall quality of life. Underdeveloped executive functions adversely impact these areas and may make it more difficult to form and maintain relationships. The good news is, executive functioning skills can be taught and strengthened over time, as they are behaviors that we can learn, practice, and master.

While we are born with the ability to develop and utilize executive functions, our environment heavily impacts their development. If we live in a chaotic home with individuals who struggle to regulate their emotions and use other important executive functions, there will likely be minimal modeling and opportunities to practice these skills. Individuals with autism, ADHD, certain genetic disorders, as well as those who have experienced chronic childhood trauma, often have underdeveloped executive functioning. This then adversely impacts their educational success and can result in school feeling extremely stressful and difficult to navigate. Many times, challenging behaviors are due in part to underdeveloped executive functioning skills.

As educators, we often fail to recognize the impact of both developed and underdeveloped executive functioning skills. Daily, we observe our students either meeting expectations or not meeting expectations and engaging in some form of challenging behavior. We often assume they have the necessary knowledge, skills, and motivation to do what is expected of them within the classroom and school setting. This assumption leads us to take their challenging behavior personally or even blame the student. However, when we make this assumption, we are neglecting to consider that the student may be lacking a particular set of skills that would help them be more successful and engage in desirable behaviors more often. Because the routines, activities, and related executive functioning skills required of students are constantly changing throughout the day, it's critical that we engage in a set of core practices that support the ongoing development of these skills.

It's also healthy to consider your own strengths and weaknesses (your potential areas of improvement) when it comes to executive functioning as this impacts your classroom leadership, structure, and environment. Remember that behavior has underlying influences. If we are disorganized, struggle to plan and prepare instruction, or respond emotionally to challenges, we are going to see that reflected in our students' challenging behavior. It truly takes a skilled educator to reflect on the part of the day that results in the most challenging behavior and reflect on what skills they need to improve upon in addition to the student. Form 1.2 in the appendix will assist you in reflecting on your own strengths and weaknesses.

Activity: Spot the Skill

 **Executive functions:** Response inhibition (impulse control), emotional control, working memory, sustained attention, task initiation, planning, organization, time management, persistence, flexibility, metacognition (monitoring and evaluation)

Read through the following scenarios. Identify which executive skills may be impacting the success of both teacher and students.

Scenario 1: Mrs. Johnson's small group tables are often covered in miscellaneous papers, books, and personal belongings. She has been noticing that students are quick to start fooling around when they sit down as she searches for the lesson materials. She also observes that her groups typically take a while to start the activities after her mini-lesson, save for her three "brightest students."

Related **student** EF skills(s): _____

Related **teacher** EF Skill(s): _____

(continued)

Activity: Spot the Skill (continued)

Scenario 2: Mr. Peterson prides himself on his engaging lessons. He states that he and his students end up having "so much fun" that he usually ends up running out of time at the end of each activity. He notices his class struggles to "rein it back in" as they rush out the door to next period. Some of his students often forget to write down their homework and as a result are close to failing the class. "They just need to start being more responsible; I can't do everything for them," he often states.

Related **student** EF Skill(s): _____

Related **teacher** EF Skill(s): _____

Scenario 3: Ms. Thompson often finds herself raising her voice and out of frustration removing minutes off her class's recess due to frequent off-task behavior during writing. She complains, "I tell them over and over again what to do – they are in fifth grade, they know how to write a paragraph! This is the laziest class I've had in my teaching career. I'm not going to coddle them and hold their hand through the entire activity. If they don't want to pay attention, they can suffer the consequences."

Related **student** EF Skill(s): _____

Related **teacher** EF Skill(s): _____

Let's now return to our airplane analogy to continue our discussion of the role of the brain in behavior. When we are flying and our environment is safe, there is good weather, and all our equipment is properly functioning; our cockpit, the prefrontal cortex, is in control of our behaviors. However, when we encounter a stormy environment, our cockpit no longer works as efficiently, and we are required to implement our safety protocols.

The same is true when we encounter individual triggers or stressors that we perceive as a threat. When this happens, our thinking brain turns control over to our limbic system, specifically our amygdala, with the goal of maintaining safety and ensuring our survival. Our limbic system accomplishes this by releasing cortisol and adrenaline, increasing our respirations to increase oxygen, increasing our heart rate to improve blood flow, and tensing our muscles – all to prepare us to keep ourselves safe.

When these triggers occur, our response to them occurs like a reflex. In that moment, the threat of consequences such as losing recess, missing out on a PBIS buck, or parents being called doesn't matter. At this point, we have very little space between our thoughts and our actions, and it's difficult to focus. Our ability to access and utilize our executive skills decreases significantly, as does our ability to communicate and reason. We are essentially no longer able to access our rational brain, and we are in survival mode. When students are in this place, they are not available for reasoning, rationalizing, or teaching. Our job is to keep them safe and assist them in regulating so that they can return controls to their prefrontal cortex.

Usually, when we think of the need to maintain our safety, we think of the obvious need to maintain our *physical safety* such as when the house is on fire or someone is physically hurting/threatening us. So, when we observe our students engaging in behaviors such as refusal, eloping, screaming, cursing, hiding, or destroying property, we don't always recognize it as a way of maintaining physical safety for themselves. Rather, we might see it as lazy, as manipulative, as provocative, or even as a choice. However, our limbic system will also take over controls when we perceive threats to our *emotional* and *psychological safety*.

The interesting phenomenon here is that this safety response will occur due to both real and perceived threats in our environment. Often, without context or knowledge of our students' histories, their responses may appear disproportionate or unwarranted for the situation. However, this occurs because something in the immediate environment shared some similarity (sight, sound, smell, tone, body language) with a past experience in which their physical, emotional, or psychological safety was threatened. Over time, these triggers can generalize and occur frequently, essentially tricking the brain into thinking there is a threat. The more time that our brains spend operating in a state of perceived threat, the more threats we are likely to perceive, which increases the safety responses from the limbic system.

For many of our students, and ourselves, a little stress here and there isn't going to lead us to heightened perceptions of threats and engagement in challenging behaviors. However, bad stressors can accumulate, resulting in chronic stress. When this occurs, it impacts our brain in the current moment and brain development over time. This is why chronic stress has such adverse implications for brain development and functioning. When we don't have the skills to work through stressors effectively, our nervous system and behaviors adjust to maintain a vigilant and reactive state. This means we are never fully relaxed, and teaching and learning feel impossible.

Environmental stressors will always be present as there is no way to fully eliminate them for our students or ourselves. *However, when we implement universal supports effectively, we have a far better chance of helping our students spend more of their time with their prefrontal cortex in charge.* This means they will be available for learning, and we will have more opportunities to provide uninterrupted instruction. Further, when they do perceive a threat and their limbic system takes over, we will have the supports in place to regulate and return to learning sooner.

Why We Do What We Do

Throughout the school day, our students are presented with instructions, tasks, and activities that they may or may not be all that interested in completing. The same is true for everyone. We don't always love all the tasks and chores we do throughout the day. This begs the question, "Why do we do what we do?"

Take a moment and consider three things you likely do each week: buy groceries, fill your vehicle with gas, and spend time with people you care about. Now, consider three reasons that you do each of these things. When considering why you engage in these behaviors, are your reasons similar? We are guessing that you may have indicated one reason you spend time with people you care about is that you have fun when you are with them. Was having fun also a reason for buying groceries or getting gas? Probably not. However, your reasons for buying groceries might have included getting food for your family, having increased energy by having healthy food choices available, and getting out of the house. Some things must be done. And while these things aren't necessarily fun, the act of doing them results in outcomes that benefit us in some way.

There are two primary factors that influence why we do what we do: *motivation* and *reinforcement*.

Motivation:	Reinforcement:
The underlying want or need to get or get away from something. This can be an immediate or a delayed want or need.	The outcome that occurs after the behavior that increases the likelihood the behavior will be used again in the future.

Students and adults are motivated to engage in specific behaviors because of the immediate or delayed outcomes they produce. Individually, we have ongoing, underlying wants and needs at all moments of the day, which motivate us to engage in behaviors that get us access to the things we want or want to get away from. When those behaviors are effective in meeting our needs, then those behaviors have been reinforced, and we are more likely to engage in those behaviors again.

Getting or getting away from things can be accomplished with the use of desirable behaviors as well as the use of challenging behaviors. Whether an individual uses a desirable or challenging behavior in any given situation to meet their needs is determined by efficiency and skill.

Efficiency. Students and adults alike tend to use the behavior that is the most efficient in effectively meeting their needs. When we refer to efficiency, we select and use the easiest, fastest, and most reliable behavior to get or get away in that moment. We also tend to select the behavior for which we have the most muscle memory or history of using.

For example, Susie has a strong dislike for long-division worksheets; therefore, she is motivated to avoid (get away from) completing them. When presented with a worksheet, she swipes the paper off her desk and shouts "I'm not doing this." When Susie does this, her teacher consistently responds by pointing to the door and saying, "Go to the office." Susie quickly leaves, leaving her worksheet behind. In this example, Susie's disruptive behavior is easy, requiring little effort to engage in; is fast as it takes very little time to swipe and shout; and is reliable as her teacher responds the same way each time by sending her to the office. This behavior would be considered efficient for Susie in getting away from her math task.

Skill. Students and adults alike also tend to utilize behaviors for which they have the skills to do so. When we can engage in desirable behaviors to efficiently meet our needs as well as cursory skills, we are more likely to do so. However, when we lack skills such as the ability to tolerate frustration, wait, or communicate our needs, we are less likely to use the desirable behaviors in that moment to meet our needs.

For example, Wesley has a strong need for assistance and reassurance, especially when he is struggling to understand a math concept due to his significant skill gaps. When Wesley raises his hand to gain assistance from an adult, he is often told to wait or keep trying on his own until the adult can get to him. However, waiting and re-attempting on his own are cursory skills that are difficult for him. Instead, Wesley leaves his desk and begins running around the room. This consistently results in an adult guiding him back to his desk, sitting one-to-one with him, and helping him through the task. In this example, Wesley engages in the desirable behavior of raising his hand but does not have the skills to wait or try another problem. Therefore, he instead uses the more efficient behavior of leaving his desk and running around the room to efficiently gain one-to-one adult assistance.

Through the consistent implementation of universal supports, we will be able to create a classroom environment that supports all students in consistently and effectively meeting their fundamental needs. When these needs are met, motivation and appropriate behaviors increase naturally.

> ### Fundamental Needs:
>
> Basic, innate human psychological needs, which, when met, ensure optimal functioning.

While many different theories exist, two resonate with us as being the most impactful within the educational setting and beyond. The first is Maslow's Hierarchy of Needs (1943), which posits that one's basic needs for food, water, shelter, and safety must be met before an individual is available to move up the hierarchy and meet more complex social needs such as belonging, esteem, and eventually self-actualization. As educators, we play a vital role in meeting these basic needs day in and day out for our students, no matter their background or socio-economic status. There is no argument that student basic needs must be met for learning to occur. It's awfully difficult to care much about spelling or trigonometry when you haven't eaten since yesterday's school lunch or slept in the park the night before.

The second relevant theory is Self-Determination Theory (Niemiec & Ryan, 2009), which describes three additional innate, psychological needs – autonomy, competence, and relatedness – and their role in student learning. Reflect for a moment on these three needs and their importance for you as an adult. Do you value having choice within your day? Are you more motivated to do the things that you feel knowledgeable and confident in? Are you less motivated when you lack the skills to do something as well? Do you value connections with family, friends, and co-workers? Do these connections motivate your behavior in some way, shape, or form? Reflecting further, how might these three areas impact your students' motivation and behavior?

As educators, we have the power to set the weather, not only within the walls of our classrooms but also within our school community. Therefore, we should strive to ensure that these fundamental needs are met to the best of our ability as they support educators and students alike in optimal functioning. For our students, this is important because this means they are most likely to be available for learning with their prefrontal cortex in charge. Additionally, when we provide opportunities for students to meet these needs, their motivation to engage, participate, and attempt the hard things will also increase. Let's dive a bit deeper into each of these fundamental needs.

The basics: *The desire to obtain what we need for survival and daily functioning.* Many of our students arrive each day without having had enough to eat or drink or who are unsure when or how they will access food again. Some may currently be sleeping in a car, on a relative's couch, or in an apartment without a bed, a blanket, or heat. They may have slept poorly last night or the previous five nights. Another may have a toothache or an ear infection that has gone untreated. One may have been moved from one foster care setting to another unexpectedly, losing their few belongings in the process. They may be feeling over- or under-stimulated because of any of these reasons or for entirely different reasons. When any of these examples are at play, functioning is adversely impacted. Students aren't available for learning when they are starving, haven't slept, feel unsafe, or are dysregulated. Not only does their motivation to engage in expected behaviors and school-related tasks decrease, their executive functioning (working memory, inhibition, attention, cognitive flexibility, etc.) also decreases because of physiological impacts.

When considering your students' basic needs, you may consider daily probes and/or teaching your students to self-assess and to advocate for their needs. Potential probes could include the following:

Basic Needs-Probing Questions

- Does my body feel like it's had enough to eat or drink?
- Does my body feel tired?
- Am I too hot, too cold, or just right?
- Do I feel physically sick, irritated, or in pain?
- Do I feel physically and psychologically safe?
- Do I have the appropriate amount of energy and stimulation for this activity?

Autonomy: *The desire to exercise choice and have multiple degrees of freedom: the opportunity to be independent and free from the control and restriction of others.* Consider for a moment how many choices you make as an adult each day. Consider further how many choices you make each day before you even arrive at school. What about within the school day? Do these opportunities for choice increase your motivation to do the things that must be done? Now consider how many opportunities for choice your students have throughout their school day. Are they provided with opportunities to make meaningful choices, or are they simply provided demands and expectations to meet? If we are going to maximize student motivation, we want to maximize opportunities to exercise choice within their instructional day. Doing so increases their motivation to participate, helps them persevere, and teaches them a valuable life skill.

You may want to gain feedback from your students to determine whether you are providing ample opportunities to make meaningful choices and meet their need for autonomy. Potential probes could include the following:

Autonomy-Probing Questions

- Can I respond in a way that works for me? Do I have options?
- Am I given opportunities to share my thoughts and opinions?
- Is my communication honored or do people dismiss my message?
- Am I given the opportunity to engage in activities that incorporate my interests or are important to me?

Competence: *The desire to experience mastery and feelings of accomplishment.* When we feel that we have the skills to navigate a social situation, complete a challenging task, or solve a problem, we are far more motivated to attempt to do so. In fact, being able persevere when situations are hard or uncomfortable, even when one doesn't experience the typical feelings and emotions that help drive motivation, is a skill in and of itself! Competence is about skills, and we frequently make the error of assuming our students have mastered all the skills they need to do what we are asking them to do. However, we tend to focus on academic skills and forget about other important skills that assist them in navigating the school environment and meeting expectations. Think back to our discussion of the various executive functioning skills required for success: working memory, inhibition, task initiation, flexibility, time management, planning, etc. Weaknesses in any combination of these can easily tank motivation, as does continued failure. Weaknesses in self-advocacy, communication, and coping skills adversely impact motivation as well. Further, skill deficits are the reason that most reward or incentive programs are ineffective in increasing student engagement in expected behaviors. The student may absolutely be motivated to access the reward but lack the skills needed to effectively meet criteria to do so. Instead, we see our students giving up, avoiding tasks, or engaging in disruptive behaviors because they don't have the skills to do what they need to do. When we focus on building missing skills, especially executive functioning skills, we assist them in achieving competence, thus increasing their motivation.

Teaching your students to reflect on and advocate for their needs is a meaningful strategy that will assist them now and throughout life in achieving competence. Potential probes could include the following:

Competency-Probing Questions

- Do I have the skills and resources to do what I am being asked to do?
- How confident am I that I will succeed, or keep failing?
- Do I know what my goals are? Am I making progress toward my goals?
- Am I critical of myself or do I have a positive outlook?
- Can I recover from mistakes or negative experiences?
- Can I accept these uncomfortable feelings for what they are and work through them to reach my goals?

Relatedness: *The desire to experience meaningful connections with others.* As educators we are frequently reminded of the need to build relationships with our students. But why? Consider someone who is very important to you. Why are they important to you? Do they make you feel safe, cared for, loved? Does spending time with them make you happy or bring you joy? Do you engage in activities of interest together? Do they help you to learn things? When we are truly connected to others, we can access so many things that we like and need. We feel valued, important, and that our thoughts, feelings, and voice matter to others.

Disruptions in relatedness can adversely impact our biological, psychological, and social functioning. Think about the students who are withdrawn and whom nobody seems to notice. Think too about the students who seem to use acting out as a means of being seen and connecting with others. While it may seem counterintuitive, acting out may produce predictable, sustained, high-quality attention. These interactions, sometimes taking the form of lectures or scolding, may be more efficient in gaining attention and connection than appropriate behaviors in the classroom. Students will seek connections in many forms because the need to relate to others is powerful.

Being connected and accepted by others in our environments is a protective factor that increases motivation and leads to emotional independence. Potential student probes to assess needs could include the following:

Relatedness-Probing Questions

- Do I feel accepted, well-liked, loved, noticed, and included?
- Do I feel as if people truly care about me and my needs?
- Do I feel supported during my most difficult moments?
- Am I recognized for my efforts or progress?
- Do others join me in doing things that bring me joy?

You may now be wondering how you achieve this? Or, perhaps, you're thinking this isn't real life – you can't possibly create a utopia where we effectively meet all these needs. However, you are likely already doing more of this than you think. In addition, when we intentionally plan our room design, instruction, and interactions with our students around these four fundamental needs, we transform our classroom into a space where challenging behaviors aren't necessary!

To move toward this, begin with considering your students' motivation to cross the threshold into your classroom. Do you want them entering only because they fear something bad will happen if they don't? Or do you want them entering because life is good in your classroom? Specifically, is life good because they know there is a high likelihood many of their needs will be met? Are they stepping in because they are being taught to advocate for themselves? And when they do so, you attempt to honor their attempts? Is life good in your classroom because you've worked to build a community and they feel connected to peers and staff? Do you frequently provide opportunities for autonomy and independence, increasing their motivation to participate each day? Are they excited to learn because staff focus on building competence by teaching in a way that is explicit, is engaging, and breaks things down so that they can understand? All of this is good teaching. All of this will result in creating a classroom where students enter each day with increased motivation to not only be there but engage in learning. Your students will be more likely to persevere when tasks are hard and less likely to require resource-heavy tier 2 and tier 3 support.

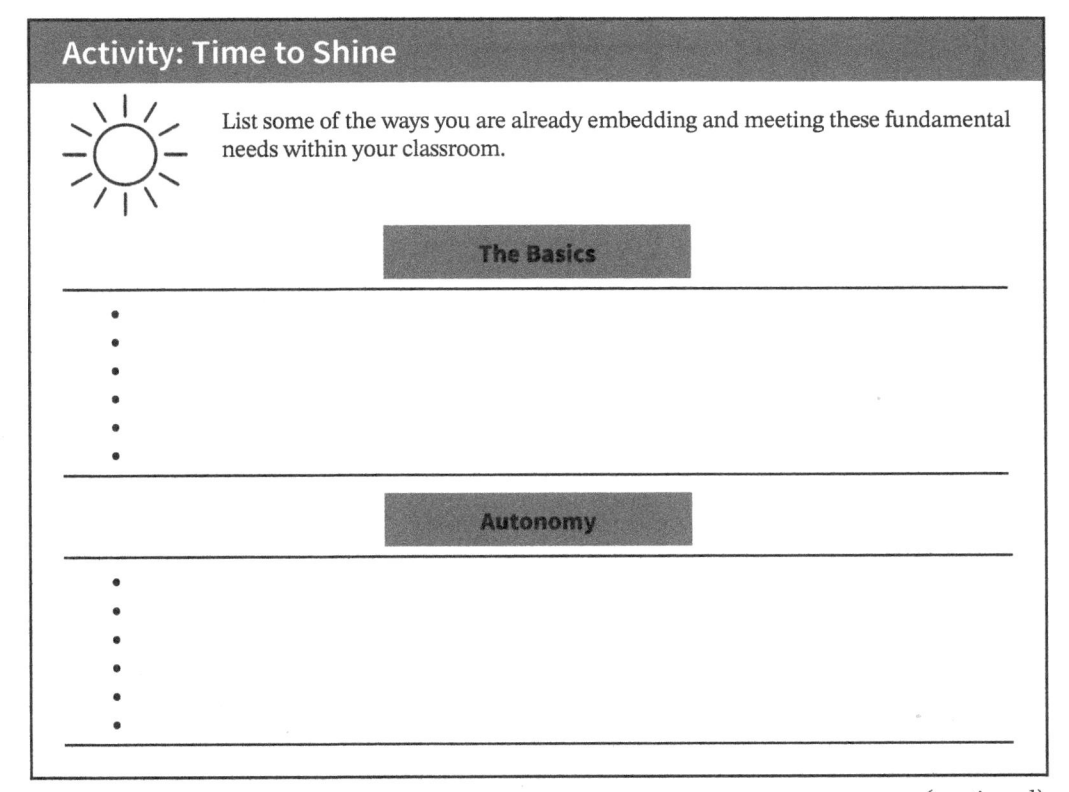

Activity: Time to Shine

List some of the ways you are already embedding and meeting these fundamental needs within your classroom.

The Basics

-
-
-
-
-
-

Autonomy

-
-
-
-
-
-

(continued)

Activity: Time to Shine *(continued)*

Competence

-
-
-
-
-
-

Relatedness

-
-
-
-
-
-

CHAPTER 2

So You Want to Manage a Classroom?

Debunking Common Classroom Management Myths

As we previously stated, universal (tier 1) supports include effective classroom management strategies, which are behaviors that adults engage in to increase student engagement and overall learning.

You have likely heard another educator tell you, "Here's another tool for your toolbox." We've constantly had teachers, mentors, and consultants giving us tricks and tips to add to our overflowing bucket of classroom strategies. The problem was, we were provided with so many "tools" over the years that we felt completely overwhelmed. The content in this book is not about adding more unnecessary tools to your toolbox. It's about identifying the tried-and-true, universal tools that can be used to build or renovate any classroom. We want to have the tools that have been proven repeatedly to contribute to high rates of student success. So, let's take a closer look at some common misconceptions in the big old education toolbox.

Consider for a moment some things you have heard, or things you may personally believe, about classroom management. What have you read on social media? What have you been told by others in the field?

Myth: *Classroom management and tier 1 supports are necessary only in the general education setting.*

Truth: Classroom management and tier 1 supports apply to all classrooms, no matter the program or level of tiered support. No matter what age students you are teaching, no matter what grade, no matter what type of school or classroom, you need to have solid classroom management practices to have your classroom run as smoothly as possible. Just because a student receives special education services doesn't mean we don't put in place classroom routines. Just because a student is diagnosed with a learning disability or emotional disturbance doesn't mean we don't have classroom expectations. In fact, it could be argued that there is an even greater need for strong classroom management if you work with students who receive special education services because they often benefit from more structure, crystal clear expectations, explicit teaching of missing skills, and more. Even the students who don't engage in challenging behaviors still have emotional, social, physiological, and academic needs. We aren't just putting these things in place for our students who struggle; we are doing it for all students – so those who are struggling can do well and so those who are doing well don't start to struggle. We commonly hear, "Well, Amanda and Danielle, I need behavior management strategies for kindergarten or high schoolers, or I need something that works with autistic students or those with mental health issues." Just because these supports are universal doesn't mean you don't differentiate them. The principles and science behind all these strategies are the same. You can use different language or visuals for different grades, for example, but this is a universal support – that means all our classrooms should have core classroom management components in place to help students be successful socially, emotionally, academically, and behaviorally.

Myth: Challenging behaviors mean the student needs a behavior plan – this is not a classroom management/universal support issue.

Truth: The fact is, many, if not most of the distracting, disruptive, and dangerous behaviors can be prevented with strong universal supports. Remember, behavior serves a purpose. When we conduct functional behavior assessments and develop behavior intervention plans, we are not only identifying the purpose or functions the behavior is serving for the student, but why the *need* for those behaviors exists in the first place. What needs are they trying to meet, and why are they trying to meet them? We can effectively prevent challenging behaviors from occurring by meeting these common needs ahead of time at the class-wide level.

Myth: Classroom management is a consequence system for challenging behavior.

Truth: When asked "What's your classroom management plan?" many educators will start to talk all about their plan to deal with the challenging behavior when it's occurring or what they do right after it occurs; this is often in the form of an intended punishment system. We cannot punish students into doing better, or simply just keep "managing" the behavior on the back end, when the reason they are struggling isn't accounted for. In addition, responding to challenging behavior should be only a small part of the behavior-change process. There will be times where you need to respond to disruptive behavior, but the key word here is RESPOND (more on this later).

Myth: Classroom management is a type of reward system.

Truth: Though an important part, acknowledging and reinforcing desirable behavior is only part of it. Classroom management that relies on rewards to ensure "good" behavior is not classroom management. It's not always but often code for "I'm not sure what else to do, so I'm going to try having them earn stuff." Reinforcement systems *can* create behavior change, no argument there. But they don't get at the root of most classroom behavior issues and, therefore, *often* are not effective long-term.

Myth: All these supports are just more things to add to my plate. I don't have time for this.

Truth: You likely already implement many of the strategies we discuss in this book to some extent. These supports may *feel* like extra work when they are new and we struggle to conceptualize how and when to use them. As we previously stated, teacher preparation programs and available resources often don't walk you through implementing these strategies, leading to feelings of overwhelm and inaction. However, we can guarantee you that implementing universal supports is 10 times easier, less time-consuming, and less stressful than working through challenging behavior day after day, week after week, month after month. So, stick with us as we demystify universal supports.

Myth: Classroom management is a single strategy that you use to get behavior under control.

Truth: Classroom management is a wide variety of practices used together to increase engagement and learning. You cannot simply establish and teach classroom expectations without establishing and teaching common routines. Likewise, you cannot simply utilize behavior-specific praise without having previously taught the expected behaviors you are calling attention to. It wouldn't make sense to use active student responding techniques during a lesson without having a plan for how to respond if students become off-task during said lesson. Using some universal supports while neglecting the rest is like building a house and leaving out critical parts of the foundation – it's sure to crumble.

Starting with the End in Mind

So, we get the job, and we start to teach. But, if you've been around the block, you know teaching comes with its daily challenges. We get into the throes of an activity and then. . .we lose 'em (either that or we never had 'em in the first place). We start to experience a flood of emotions and thoughts and often get "hooked" on them, or we may start to spiral. And we get it! When we try to manage our classroom and it doesn't produce the results we want, it's discouraging.

Think about some of your emotions that pop up when you encounter challenging student behavior. What are some of the thoughts that show up alongside these emotions?

Maybe you feel frustrated, overwhelmed, or anxious? Do your thoughts include "I can't take this anymore" or "What am I doing wrong?" Whatever comes to mind are all perfectly normal and common emotions and thoughts. But that's just it – they are just emotions and thoughts. Yet, because our body is physiologically ramped up as Thursday's math lesson gets hijacked by someone in the third row, we many times end up acting on those emotions and what is often faulty thinking. These physiological responses in our bodies, along with these emotions and thoughts, often drive our reactions to student behavior when we don't have a handle on what's happening inside of us. The problem is that when we get hooked on certain thoughts and emotions when things feel difficult, we do what most immediately helps relieve those feelings of discomfort. All too often this looks and sounds like raising our voice, threatening, getting in the student's space, taking away recess minutes, sending them to time-out, or making sarcastic comments. The problem is that whatever "relief" we may have experienced is typically only temporary. . .and many of the things we might end up doing and saying are things that don't really align with who we really want to be as a teacher.

So, what else do we tend to do when things aren't going the way we envisioned in the classroom?

We Ride "The Blame Train"

"It's the system/parents/students that need to change, not me!" This train does not end up in some lovely place; it goes around and around in circles. There will always be someone you can blame for life's problems. If you're living and breathing, you can still do things to serve your students in a way that promotes class-wide positive behavior. If we think back to our big behavior concepts, we already know that behavior has underlying influences: lack of sleep, medical issues, neurodevelopmental disorders, poor staff-student rapport, and the list goes on. But let's not forget that other behavior concept: behavior is circumstantial – if it's happening in our classroom, something within that environment is contributing to its occurrence. It can be a hard pill to swallow, but we may inadvertently influence challenging behaviors. We may neglect to implement some important practices that can often prevent them, we may trigger them, we may escalate them, and we may do things that strengthen them over time. We obviously don't do these things on purpose, but it happens when we don't recognize that we are a very big part of our students' environment. When we own this, then we are in a position to be able to change it. But, we cannot positively influence student behavior and create an exceptional learning environment if we don't first examine our own practices.

We Make Assumptions

It's one thing to hold all students to high expectations and convince them (and yourself) that they can succeed no matter their unique circumstances. It's another to always assume they have the skills to *be* successful under all circumstances, and thus, if they don't meet expectations, they simply must not be motivated. A lot is required from students during a school day: from writing essays to listening to 30-minute lectures to navigating unstructured play to remembering all materials for seven different classes to doing a packet of math problems within a set amount of time to transitioning between preferred and non-preferred activities to independently dealing with bullies during passing time, all the way to holding an uncomfortable seated position in a chair for one hour (only to do it again in the next class). We often assume our students have the skills to tackle these tasks and navigate these situations calmly, independently, and with ease. Yet, underdeveloped skills are one of the primary reasons challenging behavior exists. Instead of assuming all problems are issues with motivation, we need to be asking, "What skills are required to do this activity, navigate this situation, or meet this expectation? Might my students struggle with some of those skills? How can I support, build up, and reinforce those skills so they *can* succeed?"

We Opt for Compliance or Bust

Ah, the compliance corner. Yes, having a class full of students who follow directions without hesitation makes teaching a lot easier, but we need to consider *why* they are following directions. Humans are complex; likewise, behavior is complex. We are not robots programmed to blindly follow repeated commands. Yet, this is often the expectation (or a phone call to the principal soon follows). We say "Jump"; they say, "How high?" Those who don't jump then get to spend their choice time or recess, well. . .jumping (or rather, commonly, sitting there still refusing to jump while the consequences double-down). Compliance-based approaches will often reach roughly 80% of your class. Sure, there are kids who live to please adults (which is not always a good thing) and take no issue with anything they are told to do. Then there are those kids who fall in line mainly to avoid punishment. They may not present desirable behaviors externally, but internally they might be falling apart. Fear-based compliance wreaks havoc on mental health, skill development, motivation, and self-worth. Why force compliance only for it to "work" with *most* students, when you can shift toward gaining cooperation and reach *all* your students? No one is 100% compliant. Not you, not us, not our students. We promise you will get more cooperation when you adopt a "Let's work together and problem-solve" frame of mind instead of a "Do what I say or else. . ." frame of mind.

We Get Cozy in Consequence Land

It has to be said – we spend far too much time pondering what to do when challenging behavior occurs. We think, "What consequence should I give them?" or "They need a harsher consequence because clearly they don't care about this one." This is the wrong place to put what little time and energy we have. Living in consequence land (we are referring to the type of consequences or outcomes intended to decrease challenging behavior) is a time suck and quickly leads to feelings of frustration because you signed a teaching contract, not a firefighting one! The problem with living here is that the problem behavior has already happened. When here, we aren't putting our efforts into strategies that will result in significant change. As we alluded to earlier, intended punishments don't meet needs and they don't teach underdeveloped skills. But we can create safe, engaging, and supportive classrooms that proactively address those needs.

Activity: Self-Reflection

 Think about the past few times challenging student behavior has occurred. Remember, physical sensations, thoughts, and emotions will naturally come with situations like this – that's normal! But, sometimes to "fix" or "escape" these uncomfortable situations, we do and say things that are unproductive and only further the struggle.

Think about (notice) whether you have done any of the following when the challenge occurred:

Hopped on **the blame train**.

Have you ever gotten caught up in placing blame?

Whom have you blamed?

(continued)

Activity: Self-Reflection (*continued*)

Got caught in the **assumption trap**.

> What assumptions about your *students* have you made?
>
> What assumptions about *yourself* have you made?

Strived for **compliance or bust**.

> Did you want your students to do things one specific way, a way that *you* decided?
>
> If so, why do you think you lean toward this?

Spent too much time in **consequence land**.

> What consequence(s) have you tried?
>
> Were they effective long-term?

Values

The path of least resistance isn't always the path that helps us reach our goals.

When we blame, make assumptions, force compliance, and focus too much on punishment-based consequences, we escape the uncomfortable thoughts and feelings that flood us when challenging behavior occurs. We are human, and by nature we use behaviors that meet our needs in the most efficient way possible – just like our students. However, dealing with student behavior in traditional ways such as these often momentarily makes us feel better. Threatening to call parents or take away privileges, raising our voice, spending half of our meeting talking about how their behavior is due to their parents' lack of "parenting" – it all gives us an odd sense of control when things feel so much out of our control. . .but, the key word is "momentarily." It's the smaller, sooner reward. In the long run, we typically end up feeling just as frustrated and overwhelmed as we did before, if not more.

Doing the hard stuff? Reflecting on our own practices? Taking accountability for *our* behavior? Analyzing our instruction and interactions? Making changes to the way we are doing things around here? That takes more time and effort, and the results often come later down the road. It's the larger later reward. But make no mistake, the results are worth the wait.

Values are our guiding principles that describe how we, as individuals, want to act. They serve as motivation for doing things that push us out of our comfort zone.

Take a moment right now and consider the following:

What words describe the type of educator I want to be?

- How do I want staff and students to view me?
- What am I doing and saying when I feel like the best version of myself as an educator?
- Is the way that I act around my students in alignment with the type of educator I want to be?

Come back to these questions when the going gets tough. Let these serve as the true motivation to make change.

We now ideally can appreciate how much work goes into taking charge of one's mind and one's behaviors. This is hard for us as adults, yet we often expect our students to change their behaviors immediately, without issue, and all on their own. To change our behaviors, we first need to have awareness of them. We need to be able to both recognize and accept the uncomfortable thoughts and feelings that surface for us. Then we need to create space between those thoughts and our actions, to essentially defuse or unhook from them. We also must keep our values front and center to prevent us from being pulled into engaging in unhelpful classroom practices that drive us further away from the educator we want to be and drive our students further away as well.

Are You Ready?

Are you ready to work on staying present and not ruminating in the frustrations?

Are you ready to accept that you will continue to experience uncomfortable thoughts and feelings no matter what? You can never escape those.

Are you ready to work on noticing your thoughts and feelings and creating space between them and your actions?

Are you ready to focus on acting in accordance with the teacher you want to be for yourself and your students?

Are you committed to learning new skills, setting goals, and working through hurdles when the going gets tough?

☐ Yes, I'm Ready   ☐ No, Not Yet

If so, make that commitment. If not, that's okay. Maybe by the end of this book, you'll feel differently.

Maybe you won't. That's okay, too. Behavior change is a process, for both students and staff.

Components of Effective Universal Supports

Universal supports are free, low-to-no-prep, time-efficient evidence-based strategies that should be implemented across all ages, grades, abilities, settings, and subjects. The U.S. Department of Education describes universal supports as prevention services that support students' academic and behavioral needs by providing equitable conditions for all learners while simultaneously limiting discrimination (Weeks et al., 2019). Universal supports are considered the foundation of MTSS and align with legislation surrounding the Individuals with Disabilities Education Act (IDEA), the Civil Rights Act of 1964, and Title VI (Weeks et al., 2019).

The goal = to create the most optimal conditions for learning

Now, at first read that might feel like a lofty goal, and likely we are making "professional dog-walker" seem like a very viable backup career plan. But hold up and practice that psychological flexibility – remind yourself of the educator you want to be. We are creating the most optimal conditions for learning *you* can. We already examined "the blame train" and we hope you decided not to buy a ticket. This is all about what we, the educators, can control in this present moment. That is, our practices. With the overwhelming pressure to effectively teach a generation of young students impacted by a world-wide pandemic and a mental-health crisis, it often feels like our job extends outside our classroom walls. For the remainder of this book, we want you to focus on just you, your classroom, and your students that fill it. *Your one true job is to simply do the best you can with the knowledge, skills, and ideally newfound motivation (and resources).* And if you lie in bed each night and think, "Today, I created the most optimal conditions for learning I could," then you are right where you need to be. And as you drift off to dream land, you remember a moment in which you could have done something a little bit differently, knowing that you can wake up and create an even *more* optimal learning environment tomorrow.

> ### Universal Tier 1 Supports:
>
> Universal supports are free, low-to-no-prep, time-efficient evidence-based strategies that should be implemented across all ages, grades, abilities, settings, and subjects.

We know you've been waiting with bated breath to hear what are these illusive practices that make up tier 1. When we first started in the field many moons ago, we thought of Big Foot every time someone mentioned "universal supports" or "tier 1 practices." We *heard* about them but never really *saw* them or knew exactly what they were. We want to note that there are various ways to categorize the various universal supports and practices. For the sake of simplicity, we have categorized them into seven core areas that reflect across the literature and research:

1. Physical space
2. Expectations
3. Routines
4. Schedules
5. Instructional practices
6. Reinforcement of desirable behavior
7. Responses to challenging behavior

You will find most, if not all classrooms touch upon these to some extent.

"We have classroom expectations; they just don't care."
"The schedule is posted. They just don't follow it."
"I've tried praising them. It doesn't work."

Simply having classroom expectations won't be enough to get students to follow them. Having a schedule posted won't be enough to increase adherence to it. Telling a student "Good job" won't be enough to increase their participation in math class. Please know that long-term, positive behavior comes from *how* each of these is targeted.

We also find it critical to point out that just doing *one* or *two* of these things effectively is not enough of a determinant to say that a student isn't responding to tier 1 interventions. The whole point of universal support is to ensure *all* components are implemented with what we have coined "flexible fidelity" – meaning, we are following the core steps of each practice while still being responsive to our students' needs and adapting them as we see fit. Saying "Johnny requires more intensive supports or a more restrictive environment" when only a handful of universal practices have been in place, is like building a house, but neglecting to lay all parts of the foundation – then getting frustrated that the house is now requiring expensive repairs that take an excessive amount of time, energy, and money. When this is the case, school-wide data will often show an astonishingly high ratio of students *looking* as if they require tier 2 and tier 3 support, when they don't. The last thing a teacher needs is a pile of unnecessary (and often infeasible) behavior intervention plans when they have enough on their plate. Based on our experience supporting administrators, coordinators, and student support teams, we have found that high numbers of at-risk students often *really means* that a high number of teachers need high-quality training and coaching at the universal/tier 1 level (not that the students need more restrictive interventions). Legally speaking, functional behavior assessments assume universal practices are already in place – but if teachers aren't effectively trained and continuously coached in how to implement these practices, well. . .you can see the ethical conundrum.

The motivated and cooperative class you long for will come if you are ready to put in the work. If the goal is to increase desirable student behavior and, as a result, decrease challenging behavior, we must first increase our own desirable behaviors (micro-steps of universal practices) and decrease our own outdated, ineffective, and potentially harmful current practices. To start, complete the Universal Supports Core Components Checklist (on the next page and also in the appendix labeled Form 2.1) to generate baseline data with regard to your present level of performance of universal practices. The checklist outlines each of the seven core areas of universal practices and their subcomponents. Consider if each practice is consistently in place, sometimes in place, or not in place. We must reiterate that this is not a checklist in terms of a one-and-done, but rather a check for consistency with implementation. And don't worry, no one is looking at this! We are all at different points of the spectrum in terms of the knowledge, skill level, and motivation necessary to carry out all steps. Next, review the checklist and identify one of the seven components you would like to improve upon (e.g., reinforcing desirable behavior). Don't try to tackle everything at once (that never helped anyone feeling the burnout!). Then, choose one (or a handful) of educator behaviors that you are going to work on related to that component and set a goal (e.g., increase my ratio of positive to corrective interactions with Student A, from 2:1 to 3:1). Cross-reference any behavior data you are already collecting in the classroom and keep referring to the checklist to see where you might need to focus next. If you are using this form to support other educators, please ensure you communicate that this is *not* evaluative, but rather an effective tool to help inform practice, as well as plan and track training and coaching.

Activity: Gathering a Baseline

 Since competency is one of those fundamental reinforcers, it's time to start goal setting and tracking our progress! Fill out the following checklist to give yourself a visual of where you are with regard to each component. Be honest with yourself – it will only help you and your students.

Universal Supports Core Components Checklist
No = not in place **Partial** = somewhat or inconsistently in place
Yes = consistently in place

Physical Space	No	Partial	Yes
Instructional spaces are clearly defined			
Allows for ease of movement and limited crowding			
Students can be seen at all times			
Furniture arrangement matches instructional approaches			
Students have a clear view of the source of instruction			
Materials are organized, labeled, and easily accessible			
Wall displays support instruction and promote a positive culture			
Distractions are minimized			

Expectations	No	Partial	Yes
Developed with students			
Between 3 and 5			
Aligned to school-wide expectations (if applicable)			
Positively stated			
Equitable (reflective of student culture, needs, characteristics)			
Supported by visual cues			
Posted within clear view			
Explicitly taught across common routines			
Reviewed prior to routines and activities (precorrection)			

Routines	No	Partial	Yes
Critical routines (e.g., attention signal, entry/exit routine, transitions) are established			
Routines are supported by step-by-step visual cues			
Explicitly taught			

Schedules	No	Partial	Yes
Posted in clear view			
Consistently followed			
Advanced notice when changes are made			
Referenced throughout the day			
Lesson agendas are posted and reviewed			
High allocation of instructional time (minimal downtime)			

Instructional Practices	No	Partial	Yes
Curriculum is differentiated and appropriate for ability level			
Materials are prepared and ready to go			
Teaching method is varied (discussions, partner work, project-based learning, independent, etc.)			
Lesson length is appropriate for age and ability			

(continued)

Activity: Gathering a Baseline (continued)

Lesson includes a discussion about the rationale (the "why")

Lesson targets and success criteria are reviewed

Active supervision is used (moving, scanning, interacting)

Students are provided frequent opportunities to respond (ASRs)

Student interests and experiences are tied directly to lessons

Instruction is delivered at a brisk pace

Students are given frequent checks for understanding

Instructional choice is provided when possible

Skills are taught explicitly (instruct, model, practice, feedback)

Lesson is closed out

Reinforcing Desirable Behaviors	No	Partial	Yes
Behavior-specific praise is utilized following target behaviors			
4:1 ratio of positive to corrective interactions			
A variety of strategies are used to meet students' basic needs to the maximum extent possible			
A variety of strategies are used to help students feel connected to and related to staff, their peers, and activities			
A variety of strategies are used to help students increase their skill set and feel competent			
A variety of strategies are used to meet students' need for freedom and choice			

Responses to Undesirable Behaviors	No	Partial	Yes
Pre-determined to the maximum extent appropriate			
Explicitly taught			
Calm, brief, private, and unemotional			
Applied responsively and with flexibility as needed			
Void of the following: threats, lectures, sarcasm, inappropriate gestures, raised voice			

CHAPTER 3

Structuring Your Way to Success

An Organized Classroom Supports Organized Behavior

Surprise! You have yet another meeting to attend. You don't know when it is. You don't know where it will be. You don't know how long it will last. You don't know what it will entail. You don't know who will be there. You don't know if it will be engaging. You also don't know what will be required of you. Will you be put on the spot? What if you don't have all the answers? Will you have all the skills to do what will be asked of you in the meeting? Will you be able to leave if you need to? Now, take a moment to stop and think about your level of motivation when it comes to attending this meeting. Are you feeling pumped to go? Most folks we pose this hypothetical question to give us a resounding, "No."

For students, a classroom that lacks organization, structure, and predictability will almost certainly contribute to challenging behavior – not because students don't *want* to do well but because they *aren't being set up* to do well. So that "defiance" you're seeing? It may be due in part to not having enough structure. However, this is something within our circle of control.

Structuring the conditions under which we teach is a critical part of the framework for positive behavior. So, how exactly do we ensure our classroom provides a solid structure under which students feel safe, motivated, and more relaxed? We have found that putting systems in place that *proactively* answer the following (though nonexhaustive) list of questions for students will put you and them on the fast-track to increasing desirable behaviors:

- **Who:** With whom is it being done?
- **What:** What do I need to do to get ready? What do I need to do now? What do I need to do next? What might get in my way? What do I do if this happens? What will happen as a result?

- **Where:** Where will it take place? Where should it go?
- **When:** When is it happening? When does it need to be done?
- **Why:** Why does it need to be done? Why should this matter to me? Why might this matter to someone else?
- **How:** How does it need to be done? How do I know when it's completed or that I have met the criteria? How long will it last?

We now know that classroom structure focuses on minimizing the unknown by increasing predictability and clarity with regard to expectations, activities, interactions, and routines. But how exactly do we answer these questions for our students in a way that is doable and sustainable? To do this we turn to some key target areas to help build a strong frame to our classroom "home": physical layout, visual aids, schedules and lesson agendas, expectations, and routines. Keep in mind, there will be many other ways we will add structure and predictability to the day with other practices we discuss in this book, but first we need to start with a solid blueprint or else, you guessed it, our house will start falling apart. You cannot slap paint on the walls of a house and expect it to fix a crumbling foundation.

Activity: Cue the Questions

 When it comes to the unknown, do you have students who seem to ask questions all day (e.g., "When is lunch? What do I do? How much longer?")? Take a moment to write down some of the questions your students regularly ask you. How can you clarify some of these questions proactively?

-
-
-
-
-
-
-

Arranging the Physical Layout

One might describe school as a second home – and for some students, it feels more like home than the place they actually live. It can be tempting to devote less time to this piece, especially at the secondary level. The physical environment of a classroom speaks without saying a word. It can say everything from "This is a cold, negative, unthoughtful, and unwelcoming place" to "This is a warm, positive, and welcoming place that was mindfully created to nurture success." Devoting time to creating classroom spaces that are conducive to learning is a worthwhile service for those who learn there (teachers and students included).

What message do you want your classroom setup to send your students?

What It Is

The physical layout of a classroom refers to the arrangement of the pieces within the space. The layout should not only bring clarity to the types of activities that occur but directly support predictability, safety, and engagement. It is within the physical layout that we examine how furniture is placed, how materials are stored, and how the walls are furnished in a way that promotes positive behavior.

Why It's Effective

A well-thought-out classroom layout sets the stage for desirable behavior in so many ways. Engagement will increase substantially through the strategic placement of furniture and minimization of distractions. Feelings of safety and comfort are more likely when opportunities to proactively meet students' basic needs, as well as their need for connection, competence, and autonomy, are embedded within the physical layout as well. An environmental configuration that considers our students' strengths, struggles, and interests is a strong blueprint for everything that comes after it. Of course, every classroom will look different – as it should. There is no single way to arrange a room. Your classroom also might look different year to year; this can be a good thing because it means you are tailoring it to your group of students. There will be benefits and limitations to whatever type of setup you decide on. However, there are some common features we need to deliberately account for no matter what grade or subject you teach.

How to Do It

Zoning

Zoning the classroom is an important first step in mastering the art of physical structure. Creating zones brings clarity to the different activities and routines within the setting. We recommend first considering the instructional approach that would be best suited for your group of students.

Will your learners benefit most from whole group instruction? If so, arrange desks in a way so all students can see you and the board yet allow you a clear route to move about the room using active supervision to keep students engaged. Do you do a lot of collaborative small group work? If so, you may want to consider grouping desks together or at least creating spaces where students can gather as a small group. Do you do a lot of paired work? This may lend nicely to desks in rows of two. Perhaps you find center-based instruction is ideal to differentiate or work on IEP goals. In this case, you will want to brainstorm a list of centers and create zones for each. If you do a lot of movement-based activities, ensure you zone space for this. And if you are using a wide variety of instructional approaches within your day, list them on a piece of paper and start thinking about how you can set up your furniture to allow for each approach.

We wouldn't be very good behavior analysts if we didn't also consider the physiological needs of all students. We are constantly considering the reasons students require behavior intervention plans and what can be proactively done to support all students in meeting those needs. Think basic needs: Is there a designated space for food or drink and are students taught how and when they can access these? Is there a zone where students can take a power nap if they are truly tired? (We have seen this make a night-and-day difference for many students, so don't be quick to write it off.) Is there a space to chill out and regain composure during times of stress? Are there designated areas or tools students can access to help them regulate sensory input and maintain appropriate levels of alertness? Though not all classrooms have the room to support certain spaces, think about basic needs and brainstorm a variety of ways you can set up and organize your room to help students meet these needs in advance.

When it comes to zoning, make it very clear where all activities and routines take place, as well as where all materials live. It can be helpful to make a list of all the activities and routines that will take place during the day or period. Then, think about what you will use to clarify where these take place. Think about the different ways to use filing cabinets. Tables and desks. Bookcases. Partitions. Rugs, tape, placemats, bins, you name it. Hunt for furniture around the building. Trade with other teachers if possible! You'd be amazed at how putting $20 used bookcases around instructional areas helps students maintain calm and focused behavior. Label everything (e.g., tables, journal bin, cubbies, sharpened pencil bucket, you name it) in the beginning to ensure students know exactly what goes where and what happens in each space.

But wait, there's more. The room should be arranged in such a way that students can always be seen. This might mean positioning adult chairs so that you can see out into the classroom while providing instruction or moving shelves so that students are in clear view. Students should also have a clear view of the source of instruction without having to do a full 180 in their chairs.

We also need to design the room in a way that we can easily move about the room during instruction. Ask yourself, "Can I get to all students quickly and easily?" This is going to be essential for active supervision (more on this practice later). Equally as important, students need to be able to move about and pull out their chairs without bumping into one another. Teach traffic patterns. Which way do you want students to go when they come in? Transition to another location? Get up to sharpen a pencil?

Also, consider how your furniture arrangement can discourage track (running in circles) or parkour (climbing on and across furniture – and as tempting as it may be, you cannot put extra virgin olive oil or barbed wire on top of the bookcases). Good physical layouts minimize distractions. Cover items not in use, use curtains or solid-colored bins, and put things in cabinets or storage that you aren't using. Keep out only what is being used on a consistent basis.

In addition, certain materials should be easily accessible and labeled. Many students struggle to infer and recall where things go and where things happen. And this is a big one: materials are organized and easily accessible. Nothing good happens when downtime occurs. We need to be able to grab materials and get going rather than spending precious moments searching through piles of papers and drawers for each lesson. So, start brainstorming an organizational system for each center or main area of instruction to ensure materials are ready and within arm's reach.

Lastly, check and ensure equipment is in working order to the best of your ability. Do the doorknobs work? Do all headphones work? Computers? Know whom to contact and what their contact information is if something breaks. Have extras of materials whenever possible. Make a Plan A, B, and C so you aren't left scrambling.

"I try, but my students don't keep things clean and organized! It looks like a tornado hit!" Sound familiar? We hear you loud and clear. If you are finding yourself spending time cleaning up after students, it's time to pivot. We *oversee* our classroom here, so we must make keeping the space clean and organized part of the classroom culture and expectations.

For starters, take one day to have a lesson on what it means to keep the room clean and organized. Review where everything goes and have students practice putting things away. Organization is an executive skill and one that many students need to be explicitly taught. Then, schedule in the time for cleaning and organizing. This might be 5 minutes at the end of the instructional block. One teacher we worked with put "Home Edit" as a magnetic schedule piece as part of the schedule on the board! This was their predetermined time of the day to stop and make sure everything was in its place before recess and before packing up. Use active supervision here. When materials are being used, make sure you are up and moving around the room. Don't be afraid to provide feedback such as, "Oops, look at the label. Did you put that in the correct basket?" or "Hm, I noticed the garbage landed on the ground. What needs to happen?" You cannot do this piece if you are sitting at your desk or yelling from across the room. Model staying organized using think-alouds. For example, "I'm going to push my teacher chair in so that you have a safe, clear path to move about." You can also use verbal scaffolding to get students thinking about organization on their own. For example, "Class, I notice something about our room that doesn't meet our expectations about safety. Put your thumb up when you notice it too."

Seating

We've discussed a lot thus far, but we haven't yet talked about seating. Many disruptive behaviors can be prevented by spending 30–60 minutes strategically planning where your students will sit (at least to start). To begin, take out your class list (you know, the one that students are constantly being added to up until the last week of school. . .). Come up with identifiers such as numbers or colors that represent the level of support or the specific *type* of support each student needs. Then, assign seats based on said needs. For example, highlight students purple if they need the highest level of support. Alternatively, write a one next to the students' initials who are mostly independent. You might write BA next to students who should be seated closer to the break area. Maybe you put a T next to students who benefit from being closest to the teacher so you can actively supervise, prompt, and reinforce behavior more efficiently. Then, on your map, place your students accordingly. It can be very beneficial to go sit in each seat to see what it will be like from the student's perspective. Additionally, ask yourself if anyone benefits from sitting:

- Further away from the door? Close to the door? Up against a wall?
- Near the bathroom?
- Next to a space containing specific materials, accommodation tools, or snacks?
- Closer to the chill-out zone? Movement space?
- Closer to the board?
- Away from furniture that could be used as a jungle gym?
- Next to specific visual supports on the wall?
- Away from areas that might serve as a distraction?

We also shouldn't be moving students around every time there is a problem. You do *not* need to create new seating assignments contrary to what many teachers think. That's too much work; it tends to be disruptive to the goal of creating predictability and doesn't teach them any skills. Plus, it can quickly turn into one giant game of Whack-a-Mole. Instead, take some time to identify what the true issue is and what else you can do to solve it.

Think about the last time you sat down to complete something at home. Did you sit on your couch? Your kitchen table? Your ergonomic office chair with stellar lumbar support? When given the opportunity, we often opt for seating that provides the appropriate amount of sensory input and comfort to support our attention for the task at hand. Having the autonomy to move one's body in a way that assists with regulation and attention is one critical way to increase engagement during lessons and activities; offering students a choice in seating options does just that. Flexible seating (and everything else we discuss in this book) is not an "elementary thing" – it's a human need. Remaining flexible and providing a variety of seating options helps create cognitive space for our students to focus on the assignment in front of them, rather than focusing on trying to regulate. Teaching students to choose options that help them stay engaged takes some trial, error, and feedback, but in the long run, your students will benefit. Here are some seating options you may consider: standing desks, lap desks, stadium seats, bean bags, gaming rockers, bar stools, Hokki stools, wobble cushions, balance balls, kneeling chairs, bathmats, pillows, and chair cushions.

Walls

Lastly, we turn our attention to the walls. There is a bit of an art to using wall space effectively. Typically, less is more when it comes to creating an environment that serves the purpose of helping students learn. When thinking about what to put on these big blank canvases, it can be helpful to first consider some of the overarching needs of your students. Do an overwhelming majority struggle with communication? Maybe you have a wall with a giant core board or language supports. Perhaps your students are working on a particular set of social-emotional skills so you create an interactive wall you and students can reference throughout the day. Conversely, you may have a class of students who need support when it comes to securing shelter, finding employment, or engaging in safe relationships. In this case, you may decide to dedicate a special bulletin board in the room to helping them access community resources that assist with these. We also highly encourage you to embed your students' interests on the walls in different ways. You can do this by infusing visuals with their favorite colors, using themed decor such as sports, putting up posters of certain icons they admire, or having cutouts of their favorite tv characters hanging around the room. But keep in mind, we don't want every inch of the walls to be covered; we want them to feel balanced, rather than too dull or too overwhelming.

Here are some other questions to ask yourself when thinking about your wall displays:

- What will the focus or theme of each wall, or section of the wall, be?
- Will certain sections be used to support a specific activity or center?
- How will I make sure students can clearly understand the displays and their purpose?
- How will I include students in the creation of the displays? (Do *not* have the wall displays fully built before students arrive! Build them *with* your students as the year goes on. This is one way to target autonomy and relatedness.)
- Which wall display will stay the same and which ones will I rotate out and when? (If certain displays will be rotated out weekly, monthly, or quarterly, it can be helpful to plan this ahead of time using a calendar.)

We will leave you with one last question to continually ask yourself any time you go to put something up on a wall:

Is this wall display, bulletin board, or poster TRULY going to serve a functional purpose and help my students be more motivated, cooperative, independent, and therefore successful? Or. . .is it just unnecessary fluff?

Activity: Considering Adjustments

How might the physical layout of your classroom impact student success and/or challenging behavior. Consider what you just learned and go through each area brainstorming what you can do to nurture desirable behavior.

(continued)

Activity: Self-Reflection (*continued*)

Zones and Spaces

_____

_____

Seating Options and Arrangements

_____

_____

Wall Displays

_____

_____

_____

Communicating the Message Through Visual Aids

Visuals are likely not a new idea to you if you've been in education for a bit. But to use visuals effectively we need to understand not only their purpose but also how to use them in a meaningful way to structure our classroom.

Visuals are all around us. They help us understand our world and figure out how to complete everyday routines, follow certain expectations, and navigate our environment. Visuals are not a special education thing – they are an "everybody" thing! Society would be a mess without visual supports. Consider what would happen if there were no numbers on apartment mailboxes, no street signs, no airport maps, no IKEA furniture directions. What does that leave us with? Lots of guesswork. And what does guesswork lead to? Frustration, anxiety, errors, and avoidance.

If you're like us, you have 10,000 sticky-note reminders, but when it comes to our students, we just expect them to remember everything and then get upset when they don't. Why can't they remember the steps of resolving peer conflict? Why can't they remember to hang up their backpack? Why can't they remember to bring their book to math class?

Our students need visuals to help them navigate their school day. It is inefficient and cognitively demanding to expect one to retrieve all necessary information on a dime. We are flooded with so much information all day long that the brain essentially says, "I need to forget all other information to consolidate only what I need at this very moment." Unfortunately, when stressed, we aren't always the best at this. That means a student may in fact be quite motivated to complete their math worksheet, but when they cannot spontaneously retrieve the steps of long division and feel embarrassed to request assistance, they shut down. When you observe behaviors such as this, get in the habit of being curious and considering what visuals could be put in place for them. When activities, expectations, routines, required skills, and information are constantly changing minute-by-minute throughout a six-and-a-half-hour school day, visuals help our students keep up.

What It Is

A visual support is a concrete object, a photo, graphic, written word, or combination that gives information about an activity, routine, expectation, or skill to be demonstrated.

Why It's Effective

The human brain does not magically retrieve every piece of information we need in a given moment, especially when it hasn't been properly encoded or stored in the first place. Visual supports help keep us on track and clarify all those questions we discussed earlier. Students can be shown what needs to get done by way of a checklist. We can show how something should be done by visually breaking down tasks or skills into steps. Visuals also delineate where things should happen, such as the location of activities or materials. We can use visuals to show when things will happen using schedules and timers as well. Visual supports assist individuals with conveying wants and needs, as well as increasing their ability to understand and process spoken language. All our executive skills (working memory, response inhibition, organization, planning, etc.) are supported using a wide variety of visual aids. Spoken words, directions, and reminders are far more difficult to fade over time than visuals are. So, if you find yourself feeling like a broken record, you should consider using visuals more intentionally. Thus, if desirable behaviors and independence are the goals, then leaning on visuals is key to helping your students navigate more challenging routines.

How to Do It

First, identify the situation or challenging routine where you believe visuals may be of benefit. Then, when considering the underlying reason why the students might be struggling, determine what behavior or skills you want your students to engage in. Are you wishing they would write their name on their paper because they always forget? Is it that they struggle to keep their desks organized? Perhaps it's that the morning arrival routine isn't going smoothly. Then, consider what type of visual (or visuals) would best assist them in making this time less challenging. Remember, visual supports can be written words, photos, graphic organizers, objects, colored tape, furniture arrangements, anything that conveys the necessary information in a way other than verbally telling them what to do. After determining what the visual support(s) will look like, it's time to make the visuals.

Now, before you get all color-printer happy and start throwing visuals all over the room, it's important to know that they should be explicitly taught. Students need to become familiar with the visual, where it's located, what it means, how to recognize situations in which one would need to use it, the steps of using it, etc. Whether it be a "What to do when I'm finished with my work" checklist, a break card, a script of how to respond to bullying, the steps of the restroom routine, or a simple breakdown of how to solicit help during independent work, create the time to teach it. Lastly, reference the visuals throughout the day. Turn attention to them during the times when students should be using them, rather than waiting until it's too late. Though a visual in and of itself is considered a prompt, students should be guided through the process of thinking about the visual on their own, rather than habituating on it and requiring endless reminders. So, right before the transition, activity, or opportunity to use a skill, draw their attention to the visual and use indirect questioning to get them thinking about the visual (e.g., "What do we need to do first? It looks like you're stuck – what tool can you reference? What tool can you use to show you where this belongs?"). Lastly, bring attention to the moments when you notice students referencing the visuals and following the expectations outlined by the visual. Any moment you can bring their awareness to the visual and reinforce students' usage of it will make it more likely they will become independent with it, and you won't have to sound like a broken record. You can find an implementation checklist in the appendix; see Form 3.1, "Visual Checklist."

Additional Considerations

If you remember one thing about visuals, remember this: *function over form*. Ditch the Pinterest-pretty vibe and focus on clear and easily understandable. Here are some additional criteria to keep in mind when developing a visual for your classroom:

Match their ability: Using schedules as an example, visuals with black-and-white written words might be effective for typically developing high schoolers. Conversely, preschoolers who are deaf or hard of hearing might require color-coded pictures paired with a representation of the sign. Once you have an idea of your students' strengths and areas of need, you can craft your visuals accordingly.

Keep it age-appropriate: Ensure visuals take into consideration student age. As cute as those kindergarten clip-art graphics might be, sixth-graders and high schoolers are likely to have a different opinion. This goes a long way when it comes to treating our students with dignity and respect.

Reflect student diversity: If using pictures, symbols, or colors, verify that chosen imagery avoids stereotypes and is representative of student race, ethnicity, religion, gender, values, etc.

Make it visible and accessible: If the classroom expectations are posted near the ceiling and printed on an 8.5″×11″ sheet of paper, they aren't visible or accessible. If there are so many visuals on the wall, desk, or other classroom spaces that students can't locate the ones they need, they won't use them. Less is more.

Keep things simple: Use no more than two or three inclusive fonts. A classroom covered in rainbow colors and hard-to-read fonts is overwhelming to many students, even if it may seem like it doesn't faze them. Ensure consistency by limiting the number of fonts being used and ensure they are fonts that all students can easily read. Additionally, ensure the colors don't detract from students' ability to understand the visual. Ensure that written words contain short, simple sentences or phrases and are large enough to read and interpret.

Activity: Communicating the Message

 Read through the following scenarios and determine what type of visual support would encourage desirable behaviors and help students meet expectations.

Scenario 1: Mr. Miller finds his high schoolers struggling to maintain focus and appropriate behavior during collaborative groupwork. He thinks that maybe he shouldn't let his students work with their friends anymore since they can't "handle it." Between the disagreements and off-topic discussions, he is at his wits' end. He has been told by two behavior analysts that creating opportunities for his students to work together can proactively meet their need for "relatedness," but it seems to be causing more issues than it was worth! Also, Mr. Miller is not one to get hooked on his thoughts and is committed to moving forward and be the teacher he wants his students to remember him as, one who values human connection and the great benefit it has on learning and motivation. He thinks some visual supports might be helpful, so he begins brainstorming.

(continued)

Activity: Communicating the Message (*continued*)

Possible visuals:

-
-
-
-

Scenario 2: Ms. Martin loves teaching. What she does not love, however, is the time period between 8:30 a.m. and 9 a.m. when her third graders arrive. Her stomach is in knots each morning when she hears them laughing in the hall. Though they seem to be in a pleasant mood each morning, they are certainly a loud, animated, and lively bunch. Mr. Gonzalez, the PE teacher, frequently jokes that they most definitely "sing to their own tune." Ms. Martin is one who frequently receives reminders to complete her attendance, but she is always so busy trying to get her students to focus on their entry routine that she often forgets. Some of her students who arrive earlier fly through their assignment and start distracting the other students. She taught the classroom expectations at the start of the year and her students complete the same routine every morning – how hard can it be? Lying in bed that night she wonders if visual supports might be one of the missing pieces to the entry routine puzzle.

Possible visuals:

-
-
-
-

Ensuring Predictability with Schedules and Lesson Agendas

Picture this: You're getting ready for the upcoming week, but you don't have a schedule. No calendar, no phone app, no lesson book, nothing. You must remember which subjects are at which times, which classes are when, how long each block is, what activities you are doing and in what order. On top of that, you know you have a meeting every day but are unaware of what is on the meeting agenda until it's happening in real time. How are you feeling? Now, if you were able to sit down in a quiet room without distractions with ample time on your side, you could likely retrieve a good amount of that information. But the hustle-and-bustle of the school day is not an ideal world and most of us perform best when we know what's happening next and in what order. Enter schedules and lesson agendas.

What It Is

A schedule is a sequenced list of events according to the date and time they will happen. A lesson agenda is a type of schedule that outlines the sequence of tasks to be achieved during that lesson or academic block.

Why It's Effective

Schedules and agendas increase predictability by showing when things will happen and in what order. This typically assists in reducing a large amount of anxiety. When we know exactly what's coming and when, and how much is left, we are more likely to persist through assignments and stay motivated. This naturally increases the amount of time students are engaged. When used effectively, schedules and lesson agendas can increase feelings of success and accomplishment (this is the reason we love crossing things off to-do lists). We can use schedules and lesson agendas to teach and improve executive skills such as flexibility, planning, and time management. Lastly, schedules and agendas help establish critical routines that are essential to a smooth-running classroom.

How to Do It

We find it most efficient to work from a large-scale schedule down to a smaller one. Meaning, start by building your weekly schedule and then your daily one. Downtime is the enemy, so try to have every minute accounted for. If you don't plan for what students should be doing, they will find ways to keep busy, and those ways won't always bring a smile to your face. Time is too precious to waste trying to get students back on track from too much unstructured time. From the moment they walk through the door, the schedule or agenda should refer them to a meaningful routine or activity. We want it to be crystal clear what every student should be doing at all times. Note, this is especially helpful when you have additional staff in supporting roles! Then, create the schedule in a way that all students can understand and easily refer to. A schedule is a type of visual, so it's important that it meet the visual criteria we discussed earlier. A schedule that is tucked away in the back of the room or too overwhelmed by pretty fonts and colors won't serve anyone. This goes for both class schedules and individual student schedules.

Most classrooms have a daily schedule, so this is where we really kick things up a notch and start to help our students feel at ease by breaking down each activity block into a lesson agenda or mini-schedule. There is no rule for how much you break things down! If anything, it's better to visually break down tasks too much and combine steps than it is to not break things down enough and have to respond to problem behaviors. Let's consider a math block, for example. You may display a lesson agenda for your math block that includes the following components: bell ringer, mini-lesson, partner work, exit task, homework, dismissal. You may then decide to increase predictability even further by breaking each of those tasks into its own mini-schedule (e.g., break down what students need to accomplish and in what order during partner work). An implementation checklist can be found in the appendix; see Form 3.2, "Lesson Agenda Implementation Checklist."

Schedules and lesson agendas, you guessed it, need to be explicitly taught, referenced, and reinforced. It pays dividends to have an actual lesson around schedules and agendas. Discuss their importance and how they can help students reach their goals. Teach students how to cross off items on the agenda and celebrate their achieved tasks. We know how good it feels to cross "wash dishes" off of our to-do list – give your students the same good feeling, even for the simplest of tasks. Remember, feelings of competency are one of the big sources of motivation and reinforcement. Refer to the schedule and the mini-schedules throughout the day. Keep referring to them aloud to get students in the habit of doing the same. "Okay, we finished our entry task – one thing down already! Caty, what's up next for us?"

Schedules and agendas are also great because they make things less personal and can reduce conflict. Instead of saying, "I need you to start your _____," you can reword to, "I understand, but the agenda says it's time for _____. Do you need help getting started?" In addition, catch your students using the schedule and draw their attention to it. For example, (Teacher): "Hey, how did you know to get your pencil and highlighter?" (Student): "I noticed editing was next on our agenda." (Teacher): "Nice work referencing that tool and being prepared." For your reference, see the lesson agenda implementation checklist can in the appendix (Form 3.2).

Additional Considerations

It feels silly to even mention it, but to truly increase feelings of safety and trust, we need to follow our schedules and agendas. Now, we know school schedules are ever changing (sigh. . .), but to the best of our ability, if science is scheduled for 10 a.m., we should be starting science at that time. We should use schedules to prime students with information about the upcoming day or activity by frontloading them with as much information as they need to feel at ease (this is especially true for students who have been impacted by trauma). It's also important to consider the types of activities within the schedule or agenda and order them in a way that is going to assist students in maintaining attention, regulation, and motivation. If you notice students start to tune out, determine at what point in the lesson they start to lose steam and plan to end or take a quick break right before that time. You also might notice that they are too energetic after recess so they struggle jumping right into writing. Instead of resorting to a punishment for their inability to settle down, throw in a neutral buffer activity (like. . .or. . .) to help them wind down and prepare for writing. Getting student feedback on the schedule and involving them in making adjustments is a great way to make meaningful changes that benefit them and you.

Creating Exceptional Expectations

When it comes to classroom expectations, there are two common traps educators often fall into:

The telling trap: "I've told them one thousand times; they are choosing not to listen."
The age trap: "They are in middle school now; they know how to act."

Many of us think or say things like this, but when we think or say these things, we need to pause. We are more likely to respond to violations of expectations with punitive practices that lead us away from the educator we ultimately want to be. It is poor practice to hold someone accountable for something they haven't been explicitly taught. Are you willing to suspend a student or take away their recess based on assumptions that they:

- Know what the expectation looks like and sounds like for the specific conditions?
- Have the skills to meet the expectation?
- Are motivated to meet the expectation?

Before we dive into how to create these expectations we speak of, let's first examine why students so often fail to meet school or classroom expectations.

- **Many students fail to meet expectations because they perceive they are an attempt at controlling them:** We are far more motivated to follow expectations when we have a say in them. This is why we vote and attend school board meetings. Not having autonomy when it comes to what we are expected to do and say under a variety of circumstances can feel stifling and increase the urge to push back against them.

- **For some students, they truly lack the full understanding of an expectation:** Let this sink in. Routines, activities, and situations are *constantly* changing through the day. Many students don't know what certain expectations look like or sound like under these different and often nuanced circumstances.

- **They don't see the value or importance of the expectation:** If we struggle to piece together how certain behavioral guidelines benefit us, both in the short term and long term, it makes it difficult to muster up the motivation to follow them. And receiving a punishment for not following them often decreases that motivation even further.

- **What the expectations look like or sound like may be too restrictive or rigid:** An example is allowing only two ways to sit on the carpet or requiring students to hold their hands one very specific way in the hallway or have a voice level zero. When we limit degrees of freedom so much that students have no option but to act one very specific way, we inadvertently create a high opportunity for failure.

- **There are competing distractors throughout the day:** Life is full of things that vie for our attention every single minute. If you recall, attention control is a high-level skill (heck, we struggled with it while writing this book). If Johnny gets sidetracked putting his backpack away because he noticed T.J.'s new iPhone, give him some grace.

- **The way the expectations are written and/or taught might be different from what the student experiences in their culture or family traditions:** The expectation "Treat others how you want to be treated" might mean something different to different students. Speaking in a loud or aggressive tone or talking over someone may be common in some families. For them it might be completely appropriate. Just because a student's family behaves differently doesn't mean the way they behave at school is "right." What it does mean is that many students may require more time to learn and discriminate between the two settings and groups of people. Additionally, it means we need to demonstrate understanding and support toward students who are learning to navigate different social norms.

- **They lack skills or generalization of certain skills:** Underdeveloped skills are one of the most common reasons students fail to meet expectations. This often looks like a sheer lack of motivation in disguise. Are students struggling in the hallway because their impulse control isn't strong enough? Are they failing to meet expectations during a mini-lesson because of an underdeveloped ability to sustain attention to what's important? Are they getting into trouble during independent work because they don't know how to initiate tasks or problem-solve when they get stuck? Maybe they lack the skills to self-motivate and tolerate feelings of anxiety or discomfort. All skills that impact behavior, yet all skills that can be taught and strengthened.
- **Poor teacher-student rapport exists:** This doesn't get talked about enough and is at the root of most classroom behavior problems. We are 10 times more likely to cooperate with someone's expectations when we feel a sense of relatedness to them. This is not a problem with the expectations, but rather the relationship. The problem is many traditional ways of "responding" to challenging behavior only worsen the relationship.
- **There are more global setting events at play:** Trauma, fluctuating anxiety, medical needs, incarcerated parents, and so much more – these all make following what we would consider a simple expectation almost impossible for some students.

What It Is

Expectations are the broad, general guidelines of how one is to act; they are the overarching behavior goals we are aiming for. Well-developed expectations recognize that human behavior is complex and cannot be stuffed into a black-and-white box. We know things that aren't black-and-white tend to make us feel uneasy but stay with us here. Expectations are not rigid; they are global enough to apply to all students yet flexible enough to approach behavior in an individualized, equitable way.

You may have heard the term *rules* thrown around in the field. Many somewhat mistakenly think that rules are a list of things one shouldn't do. This is due in part because society as a whole doesn't understand the research behind positively stating what folks should do, so you end up seeing lists of "No-stop-don'ts" everywhere you go in the community! The term *rules* is outdated and not a term we suggest entertaining.

A common mistake we find teachers make when developing classroom expectations is that they end up with a set of half expectations and half-expected behaviors. The reason we want classroom expectations to be broad is so that we can encompass all behaviors under them and have them apply to a wide variety of situations. For example, "Raise your hand to speak" is a commonly used classroom "expectation" – however, this is in fact not an expectation, but rather a specific expected behavior that only applies under certain circumstances. If we are using a lot of active student responding techniques to increase engagement and decrease off-task behavior (more on this strategy later!), then raising one's hand would not be applicable. Another example of a commonly used "expectation" is "arrive on time." Arriving somewhere on time is specific, measurable, and observable. This would not be an expectation but rather an expected behavior under a specific context. Expectations are made up of a set of expected behaviors. Both are necessary, but the development of expectations comes first and serves as the framework for which you then teach the corresponding expected behaviors under a variety of different routines (circumstances) throughout the day.

Expectations:

The broad, general guidelines of how one is to act within the environment.

Expected Behaviors:

The specific, observable behaviors that describe the broad expectation they fall under.

Activity: Expectation or Expected Behavior?

 Read the following statements. Determine if the statement is written as an expectation or expected behavior.

Statement	Expectation	Expected Behavior
In this class we act safely		
We respect body boundaries		
Walk		
Use a level-one voice		
Be a team player		
We value honesty		
Throw trash away		

Why It's Effective

Developing and teaching expectations (in a similar fashion to what we are about to describe) assists us in creating a safe and predictable environment. It not only makes sure students *truly* have substantial knowledge about each expectation but also ensures they are equitable. Expectations done well strengthen the teacher-student relationship, as well as student-to-student relationships. They not only increase our students' ability to modify their behavior under different circumstances but increase motivation to follow expectations as well.

How to Do It

Great news: it's never too late to establish, teach, or tweak expectations. So, don't let that pesky little thought in your brain saying, "Why bother? It's already December!" talk you out of it.

When it comes to starting with expectations, we find most folks get stuck here – racking their brain trying to figure out how to get students to buy into the expectations. It's time to change our business philosophy here, though – one doesn't have to sell a product to the designer; after all, they created it. Slapping a poster of prefabricated "Rules" that you found in the Staples back-to-school aisle up on the wall won't be effective, so save your money for the overpriced Starbucks drink instead. The whole "Here's the expectations and this is how it's going to be" often feels very coercive to students and is likely to start working against you in subtle ways. However, involving our students in this process will increase the likelihood they view them as fair and equitable and naturally increase their motivation to follow them.

Steps to Implementing Expectations:

1. Define what expectations are.
2. Provide the rationale (why they are important).
3. Develop the expectations.
4. Explicitly teach the expectations.

First, map out one (or a few) dedicated times in your schedule where you will develop the expectations in the context of actual structured lessons. You heard correctly – this is not a 10-minute conversation; this is a process. We must get out of the habit of flying through this just to get on with the curriculum. You will get to *more* instruction in the long run if you spend more time on establishing and teaching expectations in the beginning! Go slow to go fast.

When you are ready to develop the expectations and introduce the lesson, take time to define what exactly expectations are, as well as discussing the rationale for them. This is one of the most important parts of the entire lesson. Discuss where in the community expectations exist and why. What would happen if they didn't exist? How would it impede their ability to achieve their goals and live according to their values? Keep bringing the conversation back to how having classroom expectations will benefit *them* as the students – this cannot be overstated. Teacher-student rapport can quickly be harmed in this lesson if students perceive that you are attempting to control them rather than help them become successful members of society.

When it comes to creating the expectations, there are many ways this can be done. You might choose to have students create their own vision boards on a piece of paper. What do they envision the classroom looking like, sounding like, and feeling like? Then, develop the expectations based on these culminating visions in the form of a class-wide vision board and mount it in a prominent spot in the room.

Another way we suggest introducing expectations is by having students draw or write their values, goals, or things that are important to them (depending on level of understanding) and work backward. Once they have these things drawn or written out, have students start brain dumping a list of expected behaviors that they would need to engage in in order to live according to those values, achieve those goals, and access the things that are important to them. This is a powerful way to naturally target motivation and allows us to create a direct link from the expectations to the things our students find most meaningful, showing them that expectations are in place to help them succeed. These expected behaviors can then be sorted into themes, and each theme can be given an expectation name (e.g., safe, respectful, responsible). Another reason we recommend this activity is because it allows you to identify student preferences and start pairing yourself with things your students find meaningful and enjoyable, thereby establishing your sheer presence as the ultimate reinforcer.

If you are developing expectations with younger students, you may decide to have them write or draw what they think would be expected behaviors for the classroom on sticky notes. Your students will likely end up giving you a combination of both broad expectations (such as "Be safe") as well as expected behaviors (such as "Push in our chairs") – both are important. You can then sort the expected behaviors into like-groups and determine what the umbrella expectation would be. Many students will draw or write the behavior in negative terms (e.g., "No hitting" or "Don't swear"). Go through each sticky note as a group and flip any negatively stated behaviors or expectations into positive terms. No matter how you develop the expectations, a rule of thumb is to have no more than three to five classroom expectations. More than that and they become overwhelming, difficult to remember, and meaningless. So, if you have nine posters of classroom "expectations," chances are you have a combination of expectations and expected behaviors. If this is the case, it's time to pair them down.

Both expected behaviors and overarching expectations need to be phrased positively. This is a critical feature of well-established expectations. It's simple to identify what we don't want to see, but it takes more effort to think about what we want students to do instead. We end up working against ourselves here because negatively stated expectations and corresponding expected behaviors increase the chances of students "violating" the expectations for a few reasons:

- They end up being the last thing the student hears. When we say, "No running" the last thing they hear is "running."
- We end up highlighting the challenging behavior. We don't want to bring any more focus to that. It's like saying, "Don't touch the big red button. . .." We are naturally driven to want to touch it.

- They require our students to be able to make inferences and problem-solve on the spot, skills many of our students struggle with to begin with. They also require high levels of self-control.
- They promote paranoia, escape, and avoidance behavior because it creates an atmosphere of negativity.
- They make it more likely we get stuck in a negative interaction cycle because students are more likely to make behavioral errors.

(Winston n.d.)

Instead, when creating your expectations and teaching what they look like and sound like in the context of different routines, we want to highlight the observable, expected behavior the student should engage in. Stating them this way makes it crystal clear for students exactly what they need to do and say. It also makes it clear for staff because they now know exactly what behaviors to support the students in.

Once you have established the classroom expectations, then you can teach what they look like and sound like across the common routines or activities in your room. So, this is where we get more specific. Some students truly don't generalize expectations across a wide variety of people, places, and situations when we often assume they know. And even if they can verbally state what it means, doing it in the moment is a whole different skill set. If you ask any random student "What are the classroom expectations?" and they can't communicate (a) what they are and (b) examples and nonexamples across a variety of different routines, we haven't done a good enough job with this piece. What does "being respectful" look like and sound like during our exit routine? What does it look like during a transition? The expected behaviors that describe each expectation will be different depending on the routine or activity, so creating a matrix with the expectations down the left column and your most common activities across the top can ensure you don't miss anything.

This instruction should be done in the natural setting when possible. (For example, if you are teaching lunchroom expectations, bring the class to the lunchroom and teach the lesson there. Give clear examples of what the expectation looks like and sounds like, as well as what it does not look like and sound like. Then use the guided release method and model it. Describe and think aloud as you go. Then have a student assist in modeling the expectation. Have the other students provide feedback. What did you do well? Did you do anything that showed you weren't meeting the expectation? Then give the students a chance to practice. Do *not* have students practice nonexamples; they likely have already had enough "practice" with those, and we want muscle memory for the expected behaviors to strengthen.)

Allow all students the opportunity to practice and provide feedback as they do so – both positive and constructive. Have students work on that metacognition and self-reflect. What did they do well? Why? What were the associated outcomes of following the expectation? Which part do they need to retry and why? Always end with success and have them rehearse the expectation again if necessary. And yes, we even have our secondary level students up out of their seats and practicing the expectations around the school. Disregard the eye rolls, stay positive, and remind them (and you) that this will help them be successful in the long run!

We highly recommend posting the expected behaviors for various routines and activities in the location they take place (e.g., expected computer behaviors next to the computer, expected break area behaviors within the break area). You don't have to do this for every single one, but at least do it for your student's more challenging routines – the ones where you find yourself repeating directions, reminding them of things, or redirecting behavior often. So, classroom-wide expectations should be hanging up nice and big so all kids can see them no matter where they are because you want to be able to refer to them throughout the day. We also love projecting PowerPoint or Canva slides because you can easily change the visuals depending on the activity and they are visually located where everyone can see. See the implementation checklist in the appendix to assist you (Form 3.3).

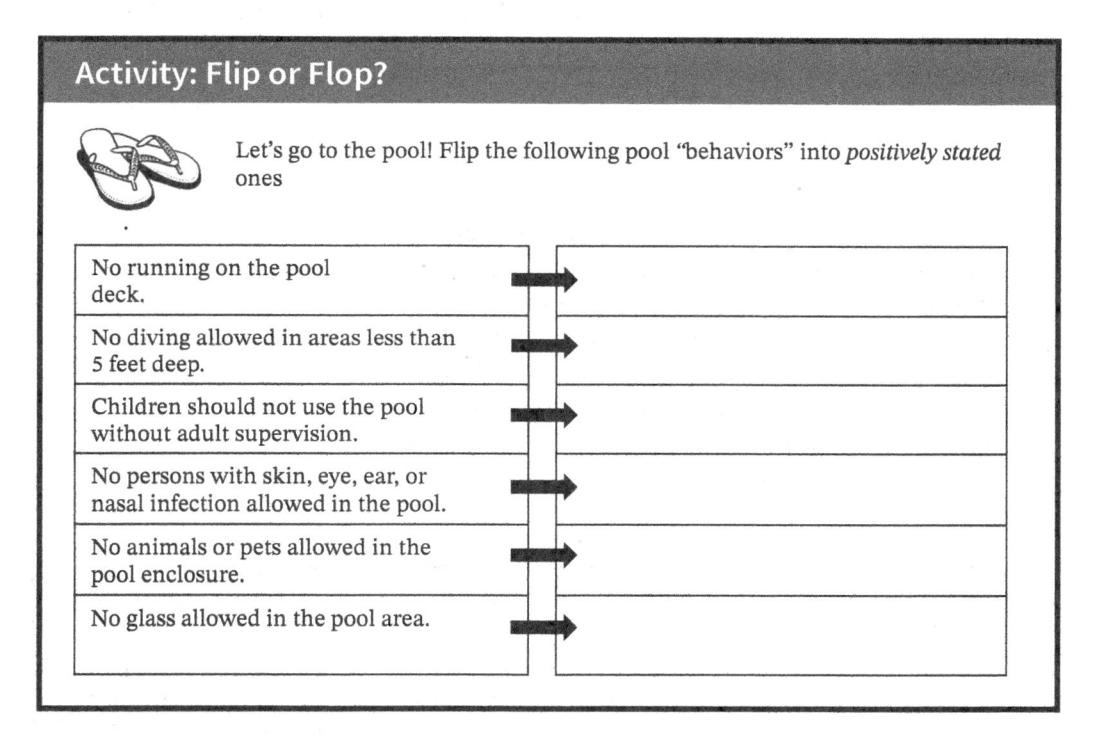

Activity: Flip or Flop?

Let's go to the pool! Flip the following pool "behaviors" into *positively stated* ones

No running on the pool deck.	→
No diving allowed in areas less than 5 feet deep.	→
Children should not use the pool without adult supervision.	→
No persons with skin, eye, ear, or nasal infection allowed in the pool.	→
No animals or pets allowed in the pool enclosure.	→
No glass allowed in the pool area.	→

Additional Considerations

For younger students, asking parents and guardians what types of expectations they have in the home or what types of behavioral guidelines their child responds best to can be helpful in developing classroom expectations that are both trauma-informed, neurodiversity-affirming, and culturally responsive. Collaborating with other professionals (e.g., your speech language pathologist or school counselor) who support specific learners can also provide insight into what types of behaviors would be appropriate or inappropriate to expect from certain learners based on student history, need, ability, etc. The generalization of behaviors across a variety of settings, people, and situations is key to durable behavior-change; thus, it's important to ensure all adults interacting with and supporting your students are on the same page when it comes to the behaviors we are expecting. In addition, if your school already has school-wide expectations in place, you should align your classroom expectations to these to ensure consistency across settings, people, and situations.

And we will now leave you with the secret ingredient to the expectations sauce: before developing expectations with and for your students, have them develop expectations for *you* and put them up on a poster next to the student expectations. This not only allows you to model how to develop expectations in a low-stakes context (because the focus is on you) but also helps avoid the power trip and eliminates the "me versus you" feeling within the room. Often when a student fails to follow expectations, we start acting in ways that also violate our own classroom expectations. We all need to be held accountable. If we are helping our students stay accountable, they should be able to help us stay accountable, too. Then before each activity, you can review both sets of expectations. After the lesson, take a minute as a group to reflect on how well *everyone* met their expectations.

Here are some additional ways to increase engagement and generalization of expectations:

- Have students create songs or raps about the expectations.
- Put together class skits (which can also be put on for the school).
- Have students create comic strips or a class book (you can make copies to send home for students to read with parents or guardians).
- Video tape or record the class following the expectations. (Older students can make and edit YouTube videos and create a school video channel.)
- Have students teach the expectations to younger students.
- Play games that test student knowledge of the expectations across a variety of routines (e.g., Jeopardy, Kahoot, Quizizz).

Activity: Reflecting on Your Needs

 Great news: it's never too late to establish, teach, or tweak classroom expectations. So, don't let that pesky little thought in your brain saying "Why bother? It's already December" talk you out of it! Do you have classroom expectations in place? If so, list them here.

-
-
-
-
-
-
-

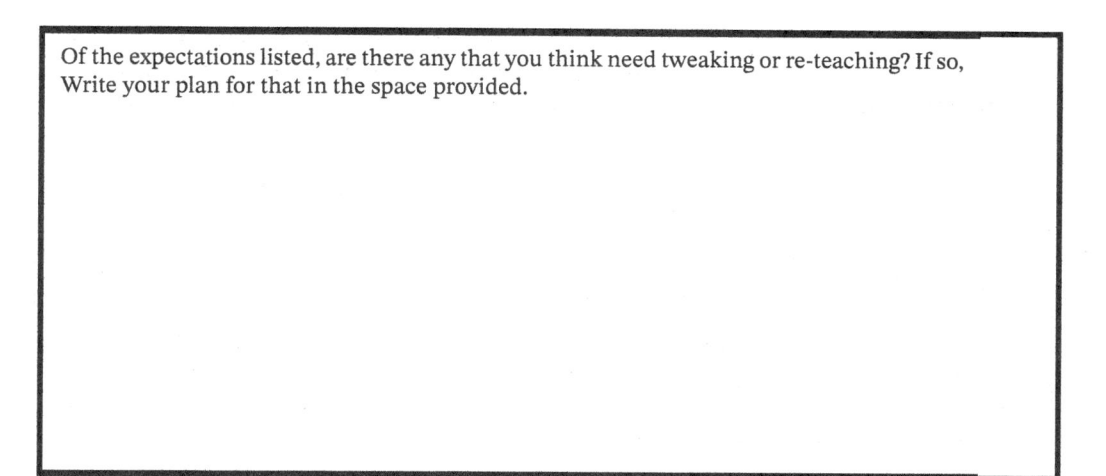

Of the expectations listed, are there any that you think need tweaking or re-teaching? If so, Write your plan for that in the space provided.

Road Mapping Routines for Independence

You're already living and breathing, but are you living and breathing classroom routines? Routines are where things really start coming together and turn your classroom into a well-oiled machine. Though every classroom will have its own set of routines and corresponding procedures, establishing and teaching them is critical to a year of thriving rather than simply surviving. Routines and procedures are all around us. The next time you go out shopping, see how many procedures you can spot.

What It Is

A routine is a general task or activity to be completed – one that is typically done on a consistent basis (daily or weekly). A procedure consists of the specific steps necessary to carry out said routine. These steps are a series of, you guessed it, behaviors! In behavior-land, this breakdown is called a *task analysis*. We are breaking down the overall routine into a series of smaller, teachable parts. A common trap we fall into is thinking that we are asking our students to do one simple thing, when we are asking them to carry out a sequenced order of separate behaviors, all of which require their own set of skills. It's often that we find ourselves saying "They know the routine!" or "They know what to do, they've done it before!" out of frustration when our students are not following a routine that has been laid out previously. Much like classroom expectations, we should not assume our students have the necessary knowledge of, or fluency in completing, common classroom routines. A lack of understanding of exactly what is expected of them can feel very overwhelming. If your student can communicate the steps of a routine in question, one can assume they do indeed have the knowledge part down. But, knowing something is not the same as being able to fluently engage in the series of cognitive and physical behaviors necessary to execute the known thing. Until we rely on muscle memory to carry out daily routines, we must rely heavily on strong executive skills to recall the series of steps (working memory), start the routine (initiation), continue through each step without giving up (persistence), ignore distractions (sustained attention), and more.

Routine:	Procedure:
A general task or activity to be completed, one that is typically done on a consistent basis (daily or weekly).	The specific steps necessary to engage in and complete the routine.

Why It's Effective

Having a well-mapped-out procedure for everyday routines will increase the chances students will succeed. A high percentage of problems in the classroom can be traced back to a routine or procedural issue. As students master each routine, their ability to seamlessly move from one activity to the next should increase, thus preventing disruptions. Having well-established routines also helps balance out the new activities each day brings; because they are already familiar and predictable, feelings of stress and overwhelm are diminished. Routines also assist in keeping the classroom organized and orderly, which in turn promotes safety and feelings of relaxation. Solid routines will also naturally create opportunities to provide students with positive feedback. A student independently carrying out a routine (if full independence is possible) should be a big deal, even if the routine seems trivial.

How to Do It

So, we know the school day is jam-packed with routines, but how do we help our students stick the landing on all of them? To paraphrase Ben Franklin, if we fail to prepare, we prepare to fail. It's too easy to forget many vital routines if we just wing it.

Steps to Implementing Routines:

1. Create a list of all routines.
2. Prioritize which ones you will teach first.
3. Give the routines a name.
4. Break down the routines into observable steps and write them down.

5. Create visuals of the routines to display.
6. Explicitly teach the routines.

To start, take out your schedule and brain dump a list of all the routines your students will need to execute from the moment they walk in (or even before) to the moment they exit. Maybe your list is long. This is a good thing – it means you are being thorough. It also means you will need to prioritize; there will be some routines your students will follow multiple times per day (e.g., transitioning within the room, using an attention signal, entering the classroom). These are going to be critical to teach day one to keep things running smoothly. If students struggle to transition or your attention signal isn't on point, it will be difficult to stay on track. Other routines will occur just once per day (e.g., passing in homework, completing the bell ringer, washing hands, etc.). These are still critical to teach early on as well. There will then be some routines that you will eventually need to teach, like how to fulfill a certain small group role or the routine of a fire drill, but they won't be a priority. Because there will be routines that are essential to teach day one and others that you can put on the backburner, consider creating a hierarchy of ones to teach within the first day, the first week, and the first month.

Once you have your list and have prioritized which routines to tackle first, pat yourself on the back, knowing you're doing a good thing for yourself and your students. Now it's time to break them down and create the corresponding procedures. Pick a routine to start with. Let's use the example of completing a journal entry as the bell ringer activity. First, give it a name. It can also be helpful to write down the duration of time you would estimate the routine should take to complete. Next, physically complete the routine yourself. Going through the steps of a procedure ensures you don't miss a step. It also helps you troubleshoot anything that might prevent your students from successfully completing the next step in the sequence. For example, you might realize that you want to include success criteria in the form of a checklist to ensure students completed all parts of the entry routine. As you walk to put the journal away, you also might realize that you forgot to create and label the designated spot where the journals should go. These two things could have had the potential to create major headaches down the road and you might have missed them had you not taken an extra moment to do a dry run. Write down each step or add any that you missed. Forms 3.4 and 3.5 within the appendix will assist you in breaking down routines and corresponding procedures.

We highly recommend creating a classroom routines binder for a few reasons. Once it's made, you can refer to it annually and won't have to reinvent the wheel. It can also be kept in a corner of the room for both students and staff to refer to and assist in self-monitoring. Referring a student to a visual of a procedure, rather than prompting them through it or getting on them for not following directions, will help you to fade out your prompts and limit power struggles. And this reason is our favorite: when students consistently struggle with a routine and you already have a visual breakdown of each step, you are in a much better position to identify what exactly is the root cause of the problem. It's often tempting to either (a) remove the activity that is occurring at the time of the problem (e.g., getting rid of journal entry as a bell ringer) or (b) hand out consequences (e.g., staying in from recess to complete the journal entry). Again, if we are looking for true, long-term positive behavior change, we need to get good at thinking about behavior and why it's occurring.

Imagine you were struggling to write a lesson plan (teacher routine) that was up to your administrator's standards and, as a consequence, your admin took away your planning time instead of sitting down with you and looking at the steps to try to figure out which part you were struggling with. An effective administrator would find where the breakdown was, remove any barriers to success, and make sure you had the skills to complete each step.

When a student or group of students struggles with a routine, refer to the procedure and figure out which step is the source of the breakdown and why. Let's go back to the journal entry example. Maybe the students do well with the first few steps. They get their journal as they enter, sit down, put the date at the top, read the prompt, write their entry, and complete their checklist. But you notice the step that requires them to put their journal in the bin on your desk is where disruptions are occurring. You observe and realize this is occurring because too many students are getting up at the same time. The area becomes congested, and some students start fooling around. Instead of doing an overhaul of the entire routine, you can just focus on how to make them more successful when it comes to that step. When you have each procedure written down you can also identify which skills are needed for each step. If a student is struggling on a certain step of a procedure, think about what skills the student needs to be able to complete the step and explicitly teach those. Remember, these often consist of executive skills. So, if a student is struggling on "write journal entry," you need to ensure they have the skills to plan, organize, initiate, etc.

Now that you have your procedures down, think about how you will display the procedures in a visual format. Remember, we are doing everything possible to increase the chances that students follow the procedure. We find teachers and students have great success when procedures are displayed on the board via PowerPoint slides, Canva, or even Classroomscreen. The slides can then be switched out as the activity or day progresses to display the next routine. Perhaps you display the procedure for getting attention during an independent activity. Maybe you display the procedure for the morning entry routine or how to create a heading on a paper during writing. There is no right or wrong procedure to display; but until your students are performing the routine as independently as possible and it's not causing challenges, we suggest pairing your routines with visuals.

List, check. Procedure breakdowns, check. Visuals, check. We've discussed the groundwork; now it's time to wrap our head around how to effectively teach your classroom routines. Do not – we repeat – do *not* try to teach your routines all in one day. Or two days. Or three days. If you prioritized, you should already know which routines will be critical to teach on day one. True, explicit teaching of a skill isn't something you can do in three minutes. So technically, it's physically impossible to teach all classroom routines in a matter of a day or two. Our students deserve (and so do you!) to have the time well spent truly helping them understand, buy in, and build the muscle memory for all the routines specific to your classroom. It's all about putting in the time now to save time in the long run. And if you're feeling the pressure to jump into the curriculum from other staff, gather your newfound knowledge of the importance of routines and respectfully advocate for you and your students. You can even highlight this section and "accidentally" leave this book open on the table in the teacher's lounge. Things won't change if things don't change – and change for your classroom or the classrooms you support starts with you.

Just like our schedules and expectations, explicitly teaching procedures will ensure students can carry out the exact steps to common daily activities with fluency. Teaching your routines in the context of a structured lesson will leave no room for error or unaccountability. As terribly tempting as it may be to simply *tell* your students how to move from point A to point B or *tell* them where to put the pencils, providing instruction, modeling, having them physically practice, and then providing them with feedback will help hold them accountable and drive home the importance of the routine. When you provide instructions, be sure to discuss the rationale. Why is this routine so important? How will following the procedure benefit them? Then model the routine. Physically show them what it looks like and sounds like to put the pencil back in the correct bucket or to complete the entry routine. During the modeling portion, have students check your moves against the visual of the procedure, making note of what steps you did well and which steps you would need to correct. Then, invite one student up to model. Again, have the students provide feedback on their classmate. Invite all students to then go through the motions of the routine, giving them positive and constructive feedback as they go. Don't allow the students to end the practice portion incorrectly, but rather ensure they end having performed the procedure correctly.

When it comes time for your class to carry out the routine in real time, pause. Use the visual and review the procedure as a class. Check for understanding before sending them off. As students complete the routine, actively supervise and provide positive feedback. If a step of the routine doesn't get followed, it is often more meaningful to immediately pause the routine and have students re-do the step or begin steps again. Allowing students to continue through the entire routine when they performed it incorrectly will often reinforce poor performance. We recommend using indirect questioning to ensure you are helping the students reflect on their behavior on their own. If a transition is going poorly, we might say, "Oops, pause. Refer to our procedure – which step didn't we complete correctly?" or "Using our 1-2-3 rating scale, please show me on your fingers how you think that transition went. . .A two? Okay, tell me why you rated it a two?" Alternatively, having students self-evaluate their performance after completing a routine appropriately will make for a great opportunity for positive feedback. But we know there are always those folks who say, "I'm not giving him positive feedback on a routine. It is just expected that he does it." And to that we ask, "Which would you rather: tell a student once every few days that you are proud of him for following the steps of the morning routine all on his own or deal with challenging behavior over the next nine months because you didn't feel like you should have to give someone positive feedback on something that is expected?" And to that one might counter, "Well, that's where consequences come in," and to that we kindly point out this is a teacher problem, not a student problem. This is where we need to check the ego at the door and change our own behavior to increase desirable student behavior. If we choose not to reinforce behavior that we just "expect," and we see an increase in challenging behavior because students aren't receiving the 4:1 ratio that is needed to establish a positive learning environment in which students are motivated to do well, that is on us. For your reference, an implementation checklist can be found in the appendix (see Form 3.4).

Activity: Pinpointing the Procedure

Scenario: Mrs. Beckett struggles to effectively wrap up the end of her classes. Her students often forget to write down their homework, or push in their chairs, and frequently leave materials and trash lying around. She is tired of using part of her planning period to tidy up.

In the space provided, develop a mock exit routine for Mrs. Beckett. List the procedures not only the students should follow, but Mrs. Beckett as well.

	Teacher	Students
1.		
2.		
3.		
4.		
5.		
6.		
7.		
8.		

Additional Considerations

Depending on the routine, think of ways to involve your students in the creation of the procedure. Remember, the more we do things *with* our students rather than *to* them, the more their motivation to cooperate and meet expectations will increase. This might look like having discussions around certain routines and building procedures together. This might look like taking students' pictures as they complete each step of the procedure and creating a visual using their photos. This might even look like asking a student if they're interested in making a poster of a certain procedure to hang up on display. Better yet, getting students involved in helping one another carry out the routine can have an even greater impact on the classroom community. Assigning "routine managers" or routine partners to double-check one another's performance against common routines can quite literally help the classroom run without you!

Activity: Reflecting on Your Needs

 Think about the routine (or routines) where your students struggle most and perhaps engage in challenging behavior. Give this routine a name and break it down into its individual steps. Some routines have mini-routines within them, so you may need to observe and decide whether students need an additional breakdown of these routines.

Routine:

1.
2.
3.
4.
5.
6.
7.
8.
9.
10.
11.
12.
13.
14.

CHAPTER 4

Leveling Up Your Instructional Practices

Preparing with Precorrection

Have you ever said or heard any of the following statements?

I hope I get a good report from art today.
I'm not going to keep telling them what's expected. They know.
We need to make good choices today (said once at morning meeting).
Nobody seemed to remember the hallway expectations, so we will have to practice them during your choice time.

While these statements are made as an attempt to remind students of expectations, they contain common mistakes and are largely ineffective in preventing challenging behavior. There are five common errors we make when attempting to set the stage for student success with precorrection.

1. **We frequently review expectations too far in advance:** If the challenging behavior typically occurs during the afternoon science center rotations, reminding students of expectations during the morning meeting is unlikely to have a positive impact on the behavior at 1:45 p.m. during science. Likewise, if we check in with our high schoolers prior to first period, reminding them of expectations for fourth period algebra likely won't result in much behavioral change.

2. **We provide vague or general reviews of expectations:** When we say things such as "do a good job," "get a good report," or "make good choices," we aren't providing the students with specific details of what behaviors they should engage in to be successful. In fact, we are requiring them to make a lot of inferences as to what is expected of them during that specific routine. As we've discussed already, many of our students struggle with executive skills, which can adversely impact them. We can't expect them to demonstrate strong metacognition skills to plan and prepare what needs to be done, self-monitor while doing what needs to be done, and evaluate their progress once done if they were never sure about what exactly needed to be done in the first place!

3. **We assume they remember all the expectations and fail to provide reviews:** Educators frequently fall deep into this assumption trap! As we already discussed, we have a lot of expectations, expected behaviors, routines, and procedures within our school day. Independent fluency with these does not occur overnight and meaningful reviews should be provided. In addition, within the school setting, there are often competing environmental stimuli that interfere with our attention and execution.

4. **We review expectations only after an incident has occurred:** While corrections sometimes need to occur, if we review the expectations only after a challenging behavior has occurred – well, a challenging behavior has already occurred. We are now being reactive rather than preventative. In addition, this review is now occurring too far in advance of the next occurrence of that challenging routine.

5. **We fail to scaffold:** We repeatedly tell our students what they need to do but neglect to fade these reviews over time to transfer the skill of thinking and planning their behavior over to them. In addition, we sometimes treat it as an all-or-nothing. We either tell them exactly what to do or don't tell them anything at all. Ideally, we want to scaffold and fade our reviews over time to allow for increased independence.

What It Is

Precorrection is a preventative strategy that focuses on the desirable behavior(s) the *student should engage in to be successful*. This is achieved by providing a meaningful review of the expected behaviors prior to a routine. This strategy can strategically be used to increase the likelihood of successful engagement in expected behaviors when used *immediately* before a challenging routine. A routine can be considered challenging when a student or group of students struggles to appropriately complete the procedure of the routine or engages in challenging behavior during it.

Precorrection differs from a correction in that corrections occur *after* a behavioral or skill error has been made. Corrections are reactive and often *focus on reminders of consequences, punishments, or discussions of what to do differently in the future*. While corrections have their place, these reviews are too far removed from the next occurrence of the challenging routine and typically unsuccessful in creating lasting behavior-change.

Precorrection:	Challenging Routine:
A meaningful review of the expected behaviors prior to a routine.	A routine within the day you can reliably predict a student will struggle to complete the procedure or will engage in challenging behavior.

Why It's Effective

Precorrection is effective in increasing desirable behaviors because it assists students with orienting toward expected behaviors or skills necessary to complete a given routine. When we provide meaningful, specific reviews prior to routines, we are effectively priming the students for success. Using precorrection also increases student confidence in their ability to successfully engage in the upcoming activity or routine. This increased confidence leads to feelings of competence, decreased anxiety, and increased motivation to follow expectations. They are therefore more successful, resulting in improved muscle memory for the expected behavior or skill over time.

How to Do It

For precorrection to be effective, expected behaviors, routines, and procedures need to have been identified, taught, and practiced. Precorrection can then be used as the meaningful review prior to challenging routines for an individual or all students. For your reference and planning, an Implementation Checklist can be found in the appendix (Form 4.1). This meaningful review can be provided in many ways.

Role play: Have students physically practice the skill.

"Students, when I say 'go,' please show me how to properly take cover if we have an earthquake."

Model/demonstration: Adult or peer(s) model the skill.

"Class, how do we show respect when someone says the answer we wanted to say? Yes, that's right, we use our hand signal for 'same'!"

Verbal: State the expectations aloud or have students state them.

"We are going to go into the room for whole group reading. Who can tell me one of the expected behaviors for transitioning to the carpet?"

Questions: Ask students to describe what the skill looks like/sounds like.

"Okay, squad, let's quickly discuss what meeting expectations during writing looks like and sounds like."

Quiz/discrimination: Describe or model the skill and ask for feedback.

"True or false? Is this the correct way to leave the classroom when the bell rings? (Teacher knocks the chair over when standing and then jumps to hit the top of the door frame when leaving the room.) You are all correct, that is not how we should

leave. What do I need to do differently? Yes, I need to push in my chair. What else? Correct, I need to keep my feet on the floor and my hands by my sides when I exit. Why does this matter? That's right."

Visuals: Reference or point to visuals or posters.

"Before we begin our independent work (points to poster), remember our criteria for listening to music. Only one earbud can be in, the volume should be low enough that others cannot hear it, and you need to remove the ear bud when the attention signal is given. Any questions?"

Indirect questioning: Stating challenge or difficulty that could occur and asking for feedback of what they could/should do.

"For this lesson we will be doing partner work. A hurdle that might come up is disagreeing with your partner. What are some things you can do to work though that as a team?"

Future pacing: Assisting students in visualizing themselves engaging in the skill or behavior.

"Before we transition into the hallway, I want you to close your eyes and visualize yourself in the hallway. Your hands are by your side, your voice is quiet, and you are walking behind the person in front of you. Can you see yourself doing this? What does it feel like to successfully get to recess on time?"

Additional Considerations

Our goal is to increase our students' competence in independently meeting expectations. However, this won't happen if we don't fade our supports over time. Precorrection can serve as a tool to assist our students in breaking down routines and helping them to engage in appropriate private behaviors – their internal thoughts – to assist them in accomplishing what they need to. Remember, competence increases motivation while weak skills decrease motivation.

We don't have to use precorrection all day long for every student and routine. Many students won't require this level of support, and the directives are unnecessary. Aim to differentiate as needed. Rather than providing precorrection in perpetuity, be strategic in when and why you use it. Target the routines one or more of your students struggle most with and then fade over time as success is achieved.

One way to successfully fade precorrection is to utilize verbal scaffolding to require the students to think and infer what problems they may face and what skills they should use – rather than giving them the answer. By providing these prompts we allow them to engage in some mental trial and error, learn to self-talk and problem-solve, and eventually internalize this process. The following are a few examples of how we can phrase our precorrection to turn the thinking over to them:

"Before we transition into the hallway, what can you tell yourself while you're walking to keep from touching the art on the wall?"

"At recess, you might get upset if you get tagged. How do you envision yourself staying cool in the situation? What are some positive outcomes that will occur if you stay cool? I'll go first. . ."

"Before we jump into our discussion, I want to hear a few people's plans for how they will be respectful when disagreeing with another's opinion."

Activity: Observe the Oversight

 Read through the following scenarios and see if you can observe the oversight made by the teacher when it comes to reviewing the expectations.

Scenario 1: *During morning meeting, Ms. Pearson sits her class down for a discussion about their behavior. She points out that she is disappointed in their choices during math centers in the afternoons and that she hopes they can have a better day. Later that day the timer for writing goes off. Ms. Pearson says, "Please put your writing folders away and transition to your first math center."*

Oversight: _____

Scenario 2: *Mr. Riviera greets his students at the door as they walk into his history class. His students are required to go directly to their desks and complete the bell ringer. He notices three students make a pit-stop at a peer's desk and start making jokes. Soon, the other students join in. Frustrated, Mr. Riviera walks over to the student's desk and tells the boys that they will be practicing the entry routine during their recess. The boys roll their eyes, and he tacks on detention for being disrespectful.*

Oversight: _____

Scenario 3: *Mr. Hansen finishes his lesson right before the fifth period bell rings. He hates sounding like a broken-record and believes his high schoolers should know what to do at this point in the year. He then watches as most of his students pack up, leave a mess on their desk, and walk out without writing down their homework. "They'll be sorry once they see their report card!" he laughs.*

Oversight: _____

(continued)

Activity: Observe the Oversight (*continued*)

Scenario 4: Mrs. Landry walks her second graders to recess. As soon as she gets to the recess doors, she pulls a small group of girls aside and says, "Let's remember to make safe choices on the playground, okay?" The girls reply "Yes, Mrs. Landry!" and run out the door.

Oversight: _____

Scenario 5: Before Ms. Forest walked her students back to class, she told them that they needed to stay quiet in the hallway because if they talked, they would lose their movie that afternoon.

Oversight: _____

Encouraging Cooperation with Instructional Choice

As an adult, before you even arrive at school, you likely make many choices. For example, you may choose what to wear, whether to eat breakfast, whether you are going to make or stop for coffee, which way to drive to work, and perhaps what music to listen to on your commute. Even within your school day, you have the freedom to make choices, big and small.

Now, consider your students and their opportunities for choices within their day. They may have few choices prior to arriving at school and even fewer once they arrive at school. For many, the classroom is a place of demands, structure, and routine – very much a one-size-fits-all setting.

While providing directions, expectations, structure, and routine are important, we can inadvertently set the stage for more challenging behavior when we don't provide opportunities for choice. We've already discussed that autonomy is one of our fundamental needs that increases motivation. When opportunities for autonomy are not provided within the classroom, our students are likely to perceive the environment as monotonous, controlling, or even coercive. This lack of autonomy then increases their motivation to look for it when and where they can as well as escape situations where it isn't provided. They may do this by engaging in challenging behaviors that interfere with their learning or the learning of others. However, we can proactively meet their need for autonomy by embedding instructional choice throughout the day.

What It Is

Instructional choice is a preventative strategy where we provide opportunities for students to independently make selections from two or more options. We can provide instructional choice in two ways, either across activities or within activities.

Why It's Effective

How things get done isn't always as important as the fact that it gets done.

The overall goal of instructional choice is to increase student cooperation, not to gain compliance. Instructional choice is very effective in increasing student motivation, and thereby their cooperation, to engage in expected tasks and activities because it provides students with a measure of input and control over their environment, thus promoting self-determination. When students have frequent and varied opportunities to make choices throughout their instructional day, satiation, which tanks motivation, decreases significantly. Additionally, our preferences change over time, so providing freedom rather than restriction in choices is a powerful motivator. Instructional choice is also an effective tool to differentiate instruction, tasks, and activities for individual learner needs at the class-wide level. For students who have or may have experienced adverse childhood experiences, consistently providing instructional choice can positively impact their quality of life. In fact, providing choice is arguably one of the best ways to minimize re-traumatization for students who have in the past felt powerless in certain traumatic situations. Finally, when we provide instructional choice, it makes times when choices are not available more tolerable for our students. Essentially, by consistently providing instructional choice, we can build momentum, which results in better management of frustration when choices aren't available or can't be provided.

How to Do It

Instructional choice can be provided across activities or within activities to increase the likelihood of student cooperation. When providing choice across activities, you are providing choices that allow the student to determine *when* they complete something. Students might be offered the choice of choosing the order in which they complete daily or weekly independent work tasks. They may also be provided a choice in completing something before or after lunch, or whether they would like to work on their reading or math intervention tasks first.

For those times when the activity itself isn't a choice, because it must be done during a specific time block or lesson, then we can opt to provide choice within the activity. When providing choice within activities, you are providing choices that allow the student to determine the following:

- *With whom* they work
- *Where* they work
- *What materials* they use
- *What or how* they do their work

For example, we may provide choices within how they complete their science research project – either a PowerPoint presentation or a written essay. If the purpose of the project is to research and learn about the life cycle of giant salamanders, then that's the task being assessed, not the essay writing. Likewise, if we are assessing their ability to write an essay, we may instead provide students the option to pick their topic as a way of increasing motivation. Within the school day, simply providing choices in where they work within the room (back table or desk) and with whom they work (alone or with a peer) can go a long way in increasing student motivation.

Across Activities	
When	
• Order of independent tasks?	
• Math or reading first?	
• Before or after lunch?	

Within Activities	
With Whom	**Where**
• Mrs. Wilson or Mr. Thompson?	• Bean bag or chair?
• Caleb or Peter?	• Sit or stand?
• By yourself or with a peer?	• Back table or desk?
Materials	**What/How**
• Marker or pencil?	• Choice of topic?
• Wax sticks or pipe cleaners?	• PowerPoint or essay?
• Speech to text or keyboard?	• Skip or run for their PE warm-ups?
• Chromebook or worksheet?	• Respond verbally or in writing?

To effectively implement instructional choice, it should be used as a *preventative strategy*, meaning choices should be provided to the student(s) *before* challenging behaviors occur. **Instructional choice should never be used as a form of coercion or worded in a way that provides students with a choice between a positive outcome and a negative outcome.** When we present choices in this way, we are not using instructional choice. We are instead attempting to set limits, though still not necessarily in a supportive and effective way. (We will discuss limit setting further in our chapter on effective responses to challenging behaviors.) Further, using instructional choice as a means of coercing or gaining control can result in harmful outcomes, especially for students who have histories of being given coercive choices such as being presented choices of nonpreferred, uncomfortable, or even abusive options and forced to choose one. For many students who have experienced abuse from adults, attempts to coerce or control them can be re-traumatizing (Kolu, 2024). Therefore, it is important to remember that instructional choice should be provided in a positive manner with the goal of increasing cooperation and not gaining compliance. The following are some examples and non-examples of instructional choice.

Examples:

"It's time to do our PE warm-ups. Would you rather run or skip?"

"Where would you prefer to do our reading conference? At your desk or the back table?"

"Class, please get started on your paragraph" (walks over to student). "Hey, would you like me to help you get started or do you want to try your topic sentence on your own?"

"I'm going to have everyone line up now. Would you like to line up with the group or hold the door for everyone?"

In these examples, instructional choice is being provided *before* the student engages in challenging behavior and in a way that is meant to gain their cooperation in engaging in the expected task or activity.

Non-Examples:

"You can do your work now or during recess. You choose."

"I can call your parents and tell them you aren't following directions, or you can start your writing."

"Clean up or no choice time."

"If you choose to do it now, you will be able to join in Fun Friday. If not, then you will miss it."

In these examples, *coercive limit setting* is being utilized in an attempt to stop a current challenging behavior. Remember, that instructional choice should be utilized prior to, not in response to, challenging behavior. Statements such as these are likely to increase challenging behaviors, harm your relationship with your students, and generally are ineffective in long-term behavior change. We will cover effective limit setting in Chapter 6.

Steps to Implementing Instructional Choice:

1. **Identify routines:** Prior to implementing instructional choice, it is helpful to first identify routines and activities in which you can provide choice to your students. You may choose to focus on routines that one or more of your students find challenging or you may choose to provide choice throughout the day to proactively meet your students' need for autonomy.

2. **Determine available choices:** Next, you will need to determine what choices you will provide to students. Remember to consider possible choices across or within activities with the goal to increase student motivation to engage.

3. **Determine presentation:** After determining what choices you will provide, you will need to decide how these will be presented to students in the moment. Will you provide choice verbally, with the use of a visual, or both?

4. **Pre-teach choices to students:** This may seem silly, but pre-teaching available choices highlights for students all the different choices they have within their day. This will save you time later, limits balking when instructions are given, and allows you to teach students how to make choices.

5. **Implement by providing choices:** After planning, provide choices to your students when and where you need to with the following format!

    a. Present choice.

    b. Allow time to select from choices provided.

    c. Provide positive feedback.

    d. Provide student with chosen selection.

An implementation checklist to assist you in planning and utilizing instructional choice can be found in the appendix (see Form 4.2).

Additional Considerations

Instructional choice can easily be utilized across all grade levels, with different student populations, in any setting, and with any activity. Simply adjust your language and the choices provided to meet the needs of your learners. Preschoolers, high schoolers, and everyone in between benefit from autonomy. Aim to provide it when and where you can in an age- and developmentally appropriate way.

For students who frequently engage in challenging behaviors, it can seem counterintuitive to provide choices, feeling almost as if by doing so we will lose all control over them. Remember, though, that it isn't about being in control or gaining compliance. It is about encouraging cooperation by increasing their motivation – which we now know occurs when students have avenues of autonomy. Our students who struggle the most, with or without behavioral disorders, often have choices and privileges taken away from them. This can easily snowball when we continue to limit their choices to "gain control" resulting in more challenging behaviors as they seek autonomy. If you are thinking of a particular student as you read this, consider instead one challenging routine in that you can provide choice to them to increase cooperation. Start and build from there. Ensure you pre-teach the choices, how to make a choice, and then honor their choices to build momentum and motivation.

When you begin implementing instructional choice, you may encounter students who don't make a choice when they are provided. If this occurs, you may need to investigate why (by asking them about it in private), utilizing visuals to assist in understanding/selecting a choice, providing additional prompts, or choosing for them and moving on. However, if you choose for them and then they indicate they want the other option – let them! It was a choice you provided, so let them, and move on. You've just gained their cooperation; don't lose it by picking a battle.

You may also find that you have students who try to negotiate another option when presented their choices. If this occurs, you can approach it in a couple of different ways. If it's an appropriate, easy option that doesn't interfere with the lesson or task, you can go with it. Or you can stick with your original choices and say something along the lines of "That's a great option; I'll consider that as an option for next time. These are your options right now, though." There's really no right or wrong, and, on a side note, teaching our students to appropriately negotiate is a valuable life skill. There are times you can negotiate, times when you can't, and correct ways and wrong ways to go about it. Don't be afraid to be flexible.

Activity: Choice or Coercion?

Read the following scenarios. First, determine whether the staff member is using instructional choice (check "yes" or "no"). If they are not, give some examples of how they could use instructional choice proactively to increase student success in meeting expectations or following routines.

Scenario 1: Mr. Clemens passes out his ninth graders' writing assignment. Caleb (a student who struggles with planning and initiation) throws his paper on the floor as soon as it lands on his desk. Mr. Clemens stops in his tracks, looks at Caleb and says, "You can either do it now or during detention – your choice."

- ☐ Yes
- ☐ No – Examples: _____
_____

Scenario 2: Mrs. Frost is about to transition her kindergarteners to recess. She walks over to Tommy before giving the class direction and says, "It's almost time to put on our outside gear. Would you like to put your cool red jacket on first or your boots that make you go fast?"

- ☐ Yes
- ☐ No – Examples: _____
_____

Scenario 3: Right before Ms. Taylor releases her sixth graders to silent read, she says, "You may read at your desks, under your desks, or on one of the carpet squares. Whatever makes you most comfortable and focused."

(continued)

Activity: Choice or Coercion? *(continued)*

☐ Yes
☐ No – Examples: _____
_____

Scenario 4: Mr. Smith passes out the four-page Spanish test and tells his class to get started. His students flip through the test and start to groan. "You better get moving or you will be late for lunch," he declares. _____

☐ Yes
☐ No – Examples: _____
_____

Increasing Opportunities to Respond

Think about a recent professional development training you attended. What are some things you did during the training in addition to watching and listening to the presenter? Were you checking your emails? Making a grocery list? Grading papers? Scrolling Facebook on your phone? Dreaming of summer?

It's difficult to engage others and sustain it over time when teaching a lesson. This is true whether the learners are preschoolers or adults. You can easily end up with an entire class that's disengaged. Or you can end up with one or two students actively raising their hands and engaging while the rest checkout. In addition, while many may "look" like they are attending because they are orienting toward instruction and they are quiet, they may not actually be paying attention or understanding what is being taught. Likewise, you might have students clearly engaging in off-task or even disruptive behavior. There are many reasons that students (adults and children alike) are disengaged during lessons. Think back for a second to our discussion of executive functioning skills. Strong skills assist us in engaging and putting aside that grocery list while weak skills make it more difficult for us to sustain attention, inhibit responses, shift between topics, and so on.

> *So why do we expect our students to be fully attentive 100% of the time if we as adults struggle with this?*

Whole-group instruction often wins out over other instructional formats because it is the most feasible delivery method. Imagine presenting a professional development training 1:1 to 500 participants! That's not efficient, so it doesn't happen. But what if we could maximize whole-group instruction to increase engagement with all our students, not just the ones volunteering or being called on? Well, we can by increasing opportunities for all students to respond with the use of active student response methods.

What It Is

Active student responding is an evidence-based strategy that increases class-wide engagement and allows for on-the-spot assessment of comprehension. It occurs when students make an *observable* response that you can see or hear to an instructional question or prompt. A wide variety of response methods can be utilized from gestures, verbal responses, written responses, and more to engage and assess in the moment. *The goal of active student responding is to generate multiple opportunities to respond during instruction by asking lots of questions to which all students can respond in some way.*

> **Active Student Responding:**
>
> Occurs when students make an observable response to an instructional question or prompt.

Why It's Effective

Active student responding is an incredibly effective tool for engaging *all* students during group instruction as it focuses on engaging in active responses rather than passive attending. Let's face it, time on-task or attending isn't always an accurate measure of engagement or learning because it is difficult to assess if individual students are comprehending the information. An observable response is a much easier measure of engagement, especially if the response can provide us feedback on their level of understanding. Further, active student responses allow for all students to participate simultaneously instead of just one at a time, thereby increasing student engagement with the content that builds their fluency and automaticity. Building skill fluency in any concept allows our students to tackle newer, more complex concepts over time. Plus, as students gain skill fluency, they feel more competent, which is one of our fundamental needs that increases our motivation!

When all students are engaging in active student responses, the teacher can continuously assess and adjust instruction based on student understanding/performance in real time rather than waiting until they are past the point of frustration. This provides us with an excellent idea of which students might need additional instruction or support outside of the lesson. As more opportunities to respond are provided for each student, positive feedback for each student also increases, boosting positive student-teacher interactions. The use of active student responding and high rates of opportunities to respond also decreases downtime due to the rapid instructional pacing. Finally, engaging students in active student responses is generally incompatible with simultaneously engaging in challenging behavior – and is one of the reasons it is such a great preventative instructional strategy. While some students may get creative and engage in both at the same time, it is significantly less likely as instruction is just more enjoyable when you are actively engaged and using varied response modalities.

When we utilize active student responding, we provide high rates of opportunities to respond for all students. This leads to increased engagement and decreased off-task behaviors. This then results in all students making more correct responses and results in increased learning.

How to Do It

To implement active student response methods, we first need to discriminate between active and passive responses. General examples of active responses include the following:

- Reading words aloud
- Saying an answer/chorally responding
- Marking/writing answers
- Discussing with a peer
- Holding up a card

These are all observable actions that we can see and/or hear that engage the students and give us feedback on their understanding.

Passive responses include the following:

- Hearing someone else speak
- Being quiet
- Watching a video orienting toward instruction

While we do want our students to orient toward us, listen, and stay quiet, these responses don't provide us with any feedback on actual student engagement or understanding of content.

Implementing active student responses involves five steps that flow easily together once you are familiar with the format.

Steps to Implementing Active Student Responses:

1. State question/prompt
2. Give wait time
3. Cue response
4. Scan to assess
5. Provide feedback

To assist you in understanding how this would look in real time within your classroom, here are some examples of different skills and ways that you can use active student responding within your instructional day. The sky's the limit, though, so be creative!

Skill: Math Facts
1. **Question/prompt:** "Class, what is 9×8?"
2. **Wait:** Pause while students write the answer on their individual whiteboard.

3. **Cue:** "Hold them up."
4. **Scan:** Assess who is accurate versus inaccurate.
5. **Feedback:** "You got it! 72. Here's the next one...."

Skill: Science Terms
1. **Question/prompt:** "Class, a frog is an _____?"
2. **Wait:** Pause while students clip a clothespin on the corresponding animal classification.
3. **Cue:** "Show me."
4. **Scan:** Assess who is accurate versus inaccurate.
5. **Feedback:** "Most of you are correct – it's an amphibian. For those who put mammal, mammals are warm blooded; a frog is cold blooded, making it an amphibian. Here's our next one. . .get ready. . .."

Skill: Reading Comprehension
1. **Question/prompt:** "Partner B, you're going to turn and tell partner A the main idea of that paragraph."
2. **Wait:** Pause while students think.
3. **Cue:** "Turn and talk."
4. **Scan:** Listen in to determine if students are accurately describing the main idea.
5. **Feedback:** "Yes, that was the main idea. Okay, class, next paragraph, hand on your head if you're ready to sustain attention. . .."

Skill: History Facts
1. **Question/prompt:** "True or false: The United States has 50 states."
2. **Wait:** Pause while students choose whether to stack a red or green cup on top.
3. **Cue:** "Show your cups."
4. **Scan:** Assess who is accurate versus inaccurate.
5. **Feedback:** "True, excellent. Some of you said it was false. The United States has 50 states – everyone, how many states? (Students respond, "50!") Great. Turn and tell your partner how many states the United States has using a full sentence."

Skill: Automotive Class
1. **Question/prompt:** "Now that we've written down the steps to bleeding brake lines on our index cards, go ahead and shuffle them. Okay, now organize the steps in order on your own."
2. **Wait:** Pause while students place index cards in order of steps.
3. **Cue:** "With your partner, turn and review each other's steps."
4. **Scan:** Assess who is accurate versus inaccurate.
5. **Feedback:** Visit partner pairs and provide corrective and positive feedback as needed on organizing the steps: "Good catch on remembering which line to bleed first."

Skill: Morning Meeting

1. **Question/prompt:** "Which day comes before Monday?"
2. **Wait:** Pause while students choose the corresponding day card.
3. **Cue:** "Show me."
4. **Scan:** Assess who is accurate versus inaccurate.
5. **Feedback:** "You got it! Sunday comes before Monday."
   - Which day comes *after* Thursday?
   - Which day starts with the letter *M*?
   - Which day comes two days after Tuesday?

When implementing active student response methods, ensure that you are maintaining a brisk pace of questions, cueing, and feedback. If you are prompting simple responses, such as choral responses, gestures, or response cards, aim for three to five active responses per minute. If you are prompting complex responses, such as written sentences or discussions, aim for approximately one response per minute. Keep the pace brisk and you are far more likely to maintain student engagement! An implementation checklist can be found in the appendix (see Form 4.3).

At this point, you may be beginning to ponder all the different ways you can utilize active student responses. Here's a list of potential ideas to start you out.

Response cards: Students hold up a preprinted card that corresponds to their answer such as:

- True/False
- Yes/No
- Agree/Disagree
- Multiple Choice
- Even/Odd
- Colors
- Symbols
- Story Elements

Gestures: Students use gestures and signals to respond:

- "Hold up one finger if you agree, hold up two if you disagree."
- "Hand on your head if you have the answer."
- "Thumbs up if the equation is true; thumbs down if it's false."

Movement: Students use full body movements to respond:

- "Stand up if the animal lives in the forest, sit down if the animal lives in the desert."
- "Turn in a circle if you think the answer is true, sit on the floor if you think it's false."

Choral response: All students respond verbally to the question in unison:

- "Repeat after me."
- "Row 1/Table 1/March Birthdays read number one."
- "I'm going to read this passage. When I get to a blank, call out the missing word."

Guided notes: Students fill an instructor-prepared handout with concepts, key facts, and other fill-in-the-blank responses:

- Videos
- Lectures
- Reading passages

Written response: Each student has a personal writing space to jot down their answers:

- Whiteboard
- Sticky notes
- Paper
- Boogie boards

Electronic response: Students respond on their individual electronic device:

- Kahoot
- Quizziz
- Mentimeter

Turn & talk: Students are given a cue to turn and talk/teach/tell their partner in response to a teacher question or prompt such as:

- Teacher: "Ready, set, TEACH." Students: "OKAY" (students teach their partner what was just taught to them).
- "Partner B, tell your partner three words that describe the main character."

Peer tutoring: Students are provided with the materials to quiz and practice concepts with one another. The "tutor" quizzes their partner by asking preprinted questions. When their partner responds, students give previously taught corrective and positive feedback before moving on to the next question.

Four corners: Students move to a certain corner or area of the room that corresponds to their response to the question or prompt. Students then discuss their answers as a small group before coming back together.

Write the room: Students move about the room writing responses to various questions and prompts posted.

Additional active student response methods are described in Form 4.4 in the appendix.

Additional Considerations

When it comes to implementing active student response methods, there's no need to break the bank creating beautiful response cards and begging to use the color printer and laminator. Just like we discussed regarding visuals, function matters more than aesthetics. Raid the supply closet (with the office administrators' permission of course) and utilize materials you already have at your disposal.

To increase student understanding of various active student response methods and decrease distractibility with any materials, be sure to pre-teach expectations. Be detailed and ensure that students understand the question, think, cue sequence.

Active student response methods are best implemented as a means of engaging and building fluency. Aim to utilize many of these when reviewing and building on previously taught content. However, active student responses can also be used to engage and gauge initial understanding prior to presenting new materials. To do so, adjust the format of your active student responses to turn and talks, think/pair/shares, or four corners, for example.

No matter what grade level you teach, aim to increase opportunities for all students to respond by using active student response methods. This strategy is incredibly easy to differentiate and use for all learners. Simply adjust the language and content as needed. In fact, we consistently utilize various active student response methods throughout all our workshops – both virtual and in-person.

Activity: Increasing Opportunities to Respond

 Read the following scenarios. Then, brainstorm some ways the teacher can increase opportunities for all students to respond through active student responding.

Scenario: Ms. Tomlinson notices her class is having a difficult time appropriately waiting their turn for the restroom in the hallway. How can she incorporate opportunities to respond to increase appropriate behavior?

Ideas for OTR: _____
_____

Scenario: Mr. Dayton notices his students' heads drifting down toward their desks during his mini-lesson on the periodic table. How can he incorporate opportunities to respond to increase the chances of his students staying awake and engaged?

Ideas for OTR: _____
_____

> ***Scenario:*** *Mrs. Langley is becoming frustrated that her first graders keep calling out and rolling around the carpet during morning meeting. How can she incorporate opportunities to respond to increase the chances of her students participating appropriately and staying in their space?*
>
> Ideas for OTR: _____
> _____

Getting Our Steps in with Active Supervision

As educators, our attention is constantly pulled and shifted due to competing stimuli and demands within our environment. Because of this, we might end up taking time once students are settled into independent work to sit at our desk, check our email, or finish prepping for another lesson. Or we might stop to talk with a co-worker in the hallway or during recess duty about an upcoming grade-level meeting or our weekend plans. While this all seems innocent enough, the problem is, when we shift our attention away from our students, we are more likely to end up in reactive mode – stepping in to respond to a challenging behavior rather than preventing one from occurring. This is especially more likely to occur during times of the day that are naturally less structured, such as recess, transitions in the hallway/passing time, and lunch. It's easy to think the students will be fine, because they know the expectations, when in reality these times of day are incredibly challenging for many students due to the wide variety of executive functioning and social-emotional skills required of them to be successful. Plus, as we learned regarding expectations, knowing and doing are two different things. The good news is, we have far more influence over the environment than we think, and if we change our behavior and implement active supervision, we can effectively prevent a wide variety of behaviors from leaving one's seat without permission, to running in the halls, fighting, tardiness, inappropriate conversations, and more!

What It Is

Active supervision is a procedure for continuously monitoring students through strategic movement, scanning, and intentional interactions. It is a proactive strategy that allows us to interact with students in a purposeful way to prevent challenging behaviors from occurring. Active supervision promotes safety and supports trauma-informed methods by ensuring staff are visible and engaged. This allows staff to notice subtle changes in behavior of students early on, intervene before the situation escalates, and as a result, student engagement, safety, and learning increases.

> ### Active Supervision:
>
> A preventative strategy that involves the continuous monitoring of students through strategic movement, scanning, and interactions.

Why It's Effective

One of the primary reasons that active supervision is so effective is that it focuses on prevention over responding. It is easy to get stuck in reactive mode, often feeling as if we are constantly putting out fires. Active supervision allows us to get ahead of this in a meaningful and manageable way. When we are stuck in a cycle of responding we run the risk of inadvertently reinforcing or strengthening the challenging behaviors. We also increase our negative interactions with students. By flipping our focus to prevention, we then create opportunities to increase positive interactions with students and strengthen desired behaviors.

Active supervision utilizes several evidence-based strategies such as precorrection, prompting, modeling, and reinforcement. Using these strategies systematically within active supervision increases its effectiveness because it supports staff in their awareness of *how* they are running their environment. It places emphasis on noticing subtle changes in behavior and prompting of desired behaviors before things get out of hand. Consistent implementation promotes following expectations, safety, productivity, and engagement, which equates to less time for students to engage in off-task behaviors.

When we move about the room, prompt appropriate behavior, and frequently interact with our students in positive ways, we are showing them that we are available and that we care. We care about helping them work through challenges, about their safety, and about promoting a happy, positive environment. We show them that we care enough to recognize desirable behaviors, when they are meeting expectations, and about helping them correct their behavior so that they can continue to be successful.

How to Do It

First, a little reminder – the physical presence of an adult within a setting does not meet criteria as active supervision if the adults are not engaging in the expected behaviors of the strategy.

To implement active supervision, we need to first determine which activities or settings would benefit most from this strategy. Start by thinking about activities during the day that most challenging behaviors occur. More than likely, this will include less structured times of the day such as transitions, recess, lunch, independent work, choice time, etc. Now, this doesn't mean that active supervision doesn't matter at other times of the day, but rather that there are certain activities that stand out as having a higher need for the use of active supervision. If necessary, review your classroom or building discipline data to look for patterns.

Next, we need to ensure that expectations and corresponding expected behaviors have been identified for each of the activities we've selected. For example:

Lunchroom

- Stay in your assigned seat
- Raise your hand, wait to throw away trash or be excused
- Use indoor voice

Passing Time

- Walk
- Go directly to your destination
- Stay to the right in the hallway

This is important because it clarifies what behaviors are expected for both staff and students, thus allowing staff to utilize precorrection and reinforcement.

Our next step is to determine appropriate staff placement by identifying hot spots, mapping out zones, and assigning expected staff behaviors. If you're targeting the lunchroom, for example, assign different areas of the room for each staff to supervise. If you are alone, map out a track that you will move through during the period to cover all areas and visit students who require support more often. If you're in the hallway, map out zones where staff should supervise. If it is just you, think about and define a specific space, such as your doorway to the bathroom. The playground is an important place to have assigned zones for staff to supervise. If we know students tend to struggle more on the basketball court than on the monkey bars, we want to ensure a staff member either is zoned there or is at least frequently passing through that area. Then, we implement active supervision.

Steps to Implementing Active Supervision:

1. Move
2. Scan
3. Interact

Move: Active supervision involves intentional movement through various zones and locations. We want to use our proximity as a tool, moving toward behaviors rather than using our voice from afar. We want to ensure that we frequently visit areas where we have more challenging behaviors. This allows us to intervene earlier and creates predictability for students as they know that staff will be checking in regularly.

Scan: While moving throughout our zones, we should be scanning and assessing our students. We want to watch for subtle changes in behavior as this is our best point of intervention and allows us to be proactive. Watch for changes in student body language and listen to their tone of voice and word choice. It is helpful to take the time to get to know your students so that you can easily observe when a shift has occurred.

Interact: While moving and scanning we want to also interact with our students in meaningful ways. This is our opportunity to provide precorrection for expected behaviors, acknowledge students for engaging in expected behaviors, offer assistance, and answer questions. In addition, this is also our opportunity to calmly and privately provide corrective feedback to students who may be engaging in challenging behaviors.

Let's look at examples of how to use active supervision to support students in meeting expectations.

Consider an elementary school recess where students have inconsistently followed expectations on how to safely dismount the swing. Perhaps a student was recently injured, and staff are now zoned to supervise this area. Simply placing an adult in this area will not result in students following expectations. If the adult does not scan the setting, fails to engage with the students or provide precorrection for expected behaviors, and does not provide acknowledgment of appropriate behavior, little is likely to change regarding safely dismounting the swings. This is true even if the staff member then lectures the student on their inappropriate behavior. It already happened at this point and will likely not have the desired outcome tomorrow at recess. However, if the adult moves through the area, interacting with students in a meaningful way, we will see better outcomes. Ideally, the staff member should greet and engage with students as they enter their zone. They should then pre-correct for the expected behaviors – "Omar, remember to come to a stop before getting off the swing" or "Aaliyah, can you show me how to safely dismount the swing?" Remember, precorrection can be provided in a variety of ways, including peer modeling. Finally, the staff member also needs to acknowledge when someone correctly dismounts the swing – "Yes, Omar! (Gestures for a high five.) Thanks for being safe when you got off the swing." Or, if they don't follow expectations, the staff member should provide corrective feedback and maybe a do-over if appropriate.

Active supervision is equally important (and effective) in preventing challenging behaviors at the secondary level. If passing periods, lunch, locker rooms, or even science labs are consistent routines that result in challenging behaviors, then active supervision should be utilized. To do so effectively, consider the zones that staff need to remain in or rotate through. Determine if staff should be standing in the hallway during passing time, rotating through the science classroom rather than at their desk, or stationed in a specific area of the lunchroom. Then, ensure that staff are scanning their zones and interacting with students before problem behaviors arise! At the secondary level it is just as necessary to use precorrection to increase expectation following as it is at the elementary level – don't fall victim to thinking this strategy does apply. One of the wonderful things about precorrection is that it is easy to differentiate by adjusting the language and delivery used. Finally, when it comes to providing corrections, it's important to do so privately whenever possible for this age group.

For your reference, an implementation checklist for active supervision is included within the appendix (see Form 4.5).

Additional Considerations

When training staff in the use of active supervision, ensure that all staff are trained. Don't leave out the librarian, custodian, lunch/recess monitors, speech pathologists – include all staff, even if itinerant. Everyone has a role in keeping students safe, happy, and engaged.

Be careful not to fall into the trap of thinking that to implement active supervision more staff are required. This isn't the case. Rather, we need to use the staff we have in an intentional way to move, scan, and interact with students with the goal of preventing challenging behaviors.

Remember that like the other strategies we've discussed, active supervision can effectively be used across various age, grade, and developmental levels. Simply differentiate the language used to fit student needs.

Activity: What's Missing?

 Read through the following scenarios. Determine what staff can do to more effectively implement active supervision to prevent challenging student behavior.

Scenario 1: *The staff at Carson Middle School dread lunch duty. Due to consistent challenging behaviors, the teachers often enforce a silent lunch. They feel bad that the students can't interact with their friends, but things are so problematic they feel they have no other choice. Ms. Whitlock is scheduled for lunch duty alone most days. She typically positions herself by the microphone since she so often uses it to get the students' attention when they don't follow directions. Mr. Hansley and Mr. Patterson often stand by the door to block the students from leaving. They typically chat and schedule their tee times for the weekend in between student redirects.*

Staff behaviors to increase: _____

Scenario 2: *Right down the road from Carson Middle School, the staff at Starview Elementary dread recess duty. Mrs. Cromwell, Mrs. Marley, and Mr. Keller are often stationed on the playground. They walk around to each area watching the students play, typically only interjecting to break up fights and respond to students who come up to them. They often circle back together to have smalltalk and catch up, only to be interrupted by another peer conflict with the frequent response, "Well, looks like it's time to go write my fourth office referral of the week! Catch you two later."*

(continued)

Activity: What's Missing? (*continued*)

Staff behaviors to increase: _____

Scenario 3: *Mr. Adler arranges his students' desks so they have a clear view of the board, as well as his desk. He usually sits at his desk while teaching so he can navigate his computer (he also has a knee injury that hurts if he stands for too long). If there is an issue, he talks to the student in front of the class or from across the room. The only times students see him get up is to write on the board or escort a student out of the classroom. He tells the principal, "These kids are in high school now – I'm not holding their hand anymore. If they want to make rude comments and interrupt lessons in front of everyone, they can deal with the consequences of getting called out for it."*

Staff behaviors to increase: _____

Packaging Up Your Lesson Delivery

In the past, have you spent a significant chunk of time making lesson plans and prepping materials only to have the lesson tank? It's frustrating and all too common because we are here to teach (it's literally in the job title!). Yet when our class is off-task or students aren't available for learning, we can't teach. Over time, this only adds to our stress, making us wonder why we should even bother with lesson planning.

These feelings of frustration then sometimes lead us to think *"**They** need to behave, so **we** can teach, then they can learn."*

This thinking places all responsibility on the students to change and engage with our lessons. Yes, they should have a role in their engagement in our class, but we share that responsibility with them. Think back to our discussion of the role of behavior and remember that their behavior is influenced by ours. This means, as leaders, there are behaviors we can engage in that will nurture student engagement. In this case, we can package and deliver our lessons in an effective, evidence-based way.

Then we can shift our thinking to: *"If **we** have effective instructional delivery, **they** will be more engaged, then they can learn."*

Students and teachers spend the bulk of their school day occupied in lessons across a variety of content categories. It would be inappropriate if we tried to change student behavior without examining how these lessons are being designed and delivered. When we shift our thinking and include the components of effective lesson delivery, rather than just focusing on how we are going to respond when they are off-task, we will naturally see engagement increase and off-task behaviors decrease. Students will then be in a better space to learn and make meaningful connections to the content. They will also be more motivated to persist as they will gain competency, one of our fundamental needs! *Please note that we fully recognize there are other impactful teaching methodologies out there and this is not intended to be used for all teaching opportunities or without adaptation.*

What It Is

Effective lesson design and delivery involves a three-part structure: opening, body, and closing. Each section includes several components to keep students engaged, maximize motivation, and pace instruction appropriately. See Form 4.6 in the appendix for an implementation guide.

Opening (quickly engage students)

1. Hook students with starter activity.
2. Identify the topic, skill, or concept.
3. Review learning targets.
4. Review lesson agenda.
5. Precorrection.

Body (maintain attention and active involvement)

1. Discuss the rationale.
2. Provide instruction.
3. Guided release (I do, we do, you do).
4. Discuss success criteria.
5. Provide ongoing feedback.
6. Check for understanding.

Closing (review, reflect, and prepare for transition)

1. Give advance notice of time left or time until the next activity.
2. Brief review of content.
3. Reflection (lesson itself, student behavior, teacher behavior).
4. Prepare for transition.

Why It's Effective

Designing and delivering lessons that include brain-based elements results in much more than just high rates of retention and improved academic achievement; mood, motivation, participation, resiliency, and executive skills are also positively impacted.

A predictable lesson format packed with nuanced daily content can put students' minds and bodies at ease while helping to orient and maintain their attention from beginning to end.

How to Do It

Opening   The goal of the opening of any lesson is to hook students and engage them as quickly as possible. We want to start off strong as the first few minutes are predictive of how the remainder of the lesson will go. Ideally, we want as little downtime as possible, so have your materials ready to go and sink that hook!

One way to hook our students is to begin with a *starter task* (aka entry tasks or bell ringers). These should be simple tasks that all students can be successful at. For some students this may be one of the only opportunities they have that day to feel successful. Starter tasks need to be brief, independent of prior knowledge, related to lesson content, and displayed for students to easily see.

Examples:

- "List as many _____ as you can."
- "Look at the pictures and write down...."
- "Turn and tell your partner about a time when...."
- "Draw what comes to mind when you hear the word _____."

Next, we want to provide a brief review of the *learning targets* (aka objectives or outcomes). Quickly state what the students will learn, understand, or be able to do by the end of the lesson. Doing this can seem mundane or pointless at times, so why does this really matter for our students? Imagine driving down the highway but no one told you where you were going? How would you feel? Providing learning targets and reviewing them with our students provides predictability, just like the starter task. Adapt these based on student age and developmental level to make them meaningful!

Examples:

- "Alright team, we are continuing paragraph writing today – here are our goals...."
- "By the end of this lesson we will be able to...."

Now we want to review the *lesson agenda* that outlines what they are going to do to meet their learning targets. We learned all about lesson agendas in the previous chapter's discussion of schedules and lesson agendas. As a reminder, lesson agendas reduce anxiety and create predictability – notice a theme? When a student's stress response is lower their window of tolerance is larger, making them more available and motivated to engage. In addition, lesson agendas are excellent tools for organizing and orienting toward what is completed and what remains of the lesson.

Examples:

- "Let's take a look at the order of events that are going to help us achieve our outcomes."
- "We have four more activities to do for reading. Let's see what they are."
- "We already knocked our starter activity out of the park, so let's check it off! Way to go."

Don't forget to use *precorrection* to review expectations before jumping into your lesson!

Examples:

- "I am going to go over our first step for long-division momentarily. Casey, can you please remind us what we do if we get confused along the way. . .."
- "Everyone, show me our hand signal to use when we have something to share. . .."

And just like that, you've completed the opening of your lesson. This should be brief while moving at an intentional pace. Remember, downtime is our enemy, so reduce it or eliminate it where you can to maximize student engagement.

Body The goal of the body is to maintain student attention and active involvement. While the only behavior we truly have control over is our own, we can engage in specific behaviors that increase the likelihood that students are successful. Most of our lesson instruction is going to occur here, within the body of the lesson. This is ideally where students will be productively engaged in the activities that will help them to meet their learning targets. This is also where explicit instruction comes into play.

When and where we can, we want to build *rationale* for why it is important to learn this information or master this skill. Doing this can significantly build motivation to participate and engage. Essentially, from the student's perspective we are answering the question, "Why should I care?" Show your students how this activity or lesson connects to the bigger picture – how this will help them now or in the future. Just like us adults in our professional development trainings, if we don't feel that the information being taught pertains to us, we check out and work on that grocery list instead.

Examples:

- "Dillon, you want to be a sports broadcaster. This information will be important for you to know because. . .."
- "How many of you are saving up for something? What are you saving up for? Let's talk about how this applies to. . .."

Next, provide your direct *instruction* of the content. Don't forget to include your active student response methods to maximize opportunities for all students to respond and engage. In addition, break instruction down and deliver in smaller chunks as needed.

Examples:

- "I'm going to read the definition of a democracy. Thumbs up if you are ready. (Read definition.) Okay, turn and teach your partner what a democracy is. Ready? Teach. (Students turn and teach.)
- "Choral response, repeat after me. A period (a period) goes at the end (goes at the end) of a sentence (of a sentence)."

Ideally, we should provide students with *success criteria* to assist them in determining if they have met the learning target. The success criteria provided will depend on the task, skill, and grade/developmental level of the students. In most situations, this should be provided visually and not just verbally as having a visual to reference will assist students in self-motivating. This also allows them to learn to self-evaluate and self-monitor. And. . .just like many components of the opening, this provides students with predictability because the expectations and what success looks like are clear. There's no need to guess which reduces anxiety as well.

Examples:

- Scoring rubrics
- Checklists
- Worked example

Good instruction also includes *modeling* and *opportunities to practice* the skill. Simply telling the students what to do without modeling and systematically turning responsibility over to them is less likely to be effective. Instead, we can follow the "I do, We do, You do" model.

I do: Teacher models and talks through task out loud.
We do: Teacher and students complete the task together.
You do: Students complete the task without the teacher.

This is where active supervision – moving, scanning, and interacting comes into play during our lessons. Throughout opportunities to practice the skill we want to ensure that we are providing *ongoing feedback* as well as frequent *checks for understanding*. We all learn from feedback, both positive and corrective. Ongoing feedback is essential in keeping students motivated to persist through less preferred or difficult tasks. Likewise, frequent checks for understanding can prevent challenging behaviors and maintain student motivation.

Feedback Examples:

- "Nate, I see you're going back into the chapter to look for the quote – nice strategy!"
- "Taliah, you're referencing your definition sheet. Great problem-solving."

Checks for Understanding Examples:

- "I noticed you're still on your first paragraph. What part is tripping you up?"
- "Okay, Lailah, after you carry the two, what is your next step?"

Closing   Just like the opening, the closing should be brief with the goal of reviewing, reflecting, and preparing for the transition to the next activity. This is our opportunity to refocus ourselves and our students so that we are primed and ready.

Preparing for the closing should involve *advanced notice*. Consider a countdown timer on the board or another form of a visual or audible timer. Many students struggle with stopping activities because they aren't sure how to find a stopping point if they aren't finished. We can always pre-teach these routines in addition to where to put materials when their work is finished or incomplete. We can also post a mini-closing lesson agenda on the board if that would be helpful. If our goal is to build competence, to increase motivation, then we can also use verbal scaffolding to assist our students in preparing for transitions.

Examples:

- "Peek at the timer. Think about how to best manage those last five minutes so you can meet the success criteria."
- "Who can remind us of what we can do if we aren't finished with our work?"

Prior to transitioning to the next activity, take a moment to *review* the lesson content. Take the time to model how to stop and think about the task we just completed, if there is anything left to do, and how to self-reflect and/or check their work against success criteria. This can be done in a variety of interactive ways.

Examples:

- "If the principal came in and asked you what you just learned about, what would you give as your elevator speech?"
- "Grab your sticky notes. Write one question for the next class to answer so they know what to be listening for."

Don't forget to pause and *reflect* on the lesson content, student behavior, and teacher behavior. After all, we created expectations at the start of the year for a reason, we precorrected for them immediately before the activity, we reinforced them during the lesson, and now we need to reflect on them at the closing. It's a nice, three-pronged cycle of reviewing beforehand, reinforcing during, and reflecting afterward. Reflect on student expectations by asking them how they did in meeting expectations, if there were specific things they struggled with, what might help them, and to reflect on the outcomes. Doing this helps to build our students' metacognition skills. Likewise, reflect on how you met your teacher expectations. Acknowledge what you could have done better or differently and ask for feedback from your students as well. This goes such a long way in terms of creating a positive classroom culture and making your classroom a place that students want to be!

Examples:

- "Which part of today's lesson gave you the most trouble? Let's problem-solve that."
- "What part of today's lesson did you like most? Least? Why?"
- "Show of fingers, self-reflect, and give yourself a rating. Why did you pick that?"
- "What could I do the same/differently next time to make the lesson easier to understand?"

Finally, prepare for the transition to the next activity by breaking down the routine and beginning the first step. Transitions involve four steps: stopping the current activity, cognitively shifting to the next, physically shifting to the next, and then initiating the next task or activity. We can increase the likelihood of a successful transition by clarifying and starting the next step.

Examples:

- "Okay, when the red light turns on, everyone, stand up."
- "Please turn your attention to the board for our end-of-class routine."

Activity: Lesson Leftovers

 Read through the following scenarios. Determine which missing lesson components might be contributing to the challenging routine.

Scenario 1: Mr. Benson is leading his English lesson and feels good. His students seemed interested in his semester's poetry unit. After discussing the rationale and providing his instruction, he sends his students off into pairs to complete their assignment. He sits at his desk and checks his emails. After roughly five minutes, he overhears some students talking about the upcoming high school dance. He scans the room and sees another group in the back of the room doodling on their papers. He goes to investigate. "What's going on?" he asks. "We don't know what to do. . .," they reply. Frustrated, Mr. Benson says, "Well, I gave the instructions already, so that shows me you must not have been paying attention." The boys look at one another confused. . ..

Missing component(s): _____

Scenario 2: Ms. Mackenzie is introducing long-division to her fifth graders. After modeling how to do two problems, she tells her students to finish the rest of the worksheet on their own as their exit assessment. She walks around the room quietly, watching as students work through the problems. As she approaches one student, she notices their paper on the ground. His head is down, covered by his arms. She kneels beside him and whispers, "Hey, what's going on?"

"I hate this," he says.

"I hear you. Long-division can feel complex. Can you tell me what part about it you hate?"

"I don't know if I'm doing it right! I was paying attention, I swear!"

"Okay, why don't you pick up your paper and we will work a few problems together."

Missing component(s): _____

Scenario 3: Mrs. Russo's third graders are finishing up their collaborative group activity at their desks. She gets their attention and asks each team captain to place their completed assignment in the finished basket. As the groups finish, she calls the tables one by one to get their lunches and line up. She can't wait for them to go to lunch, especially after this lesson. She feels like they just don't care about their learning like the kids in years past. The pandemic really has decreased their motivation to do just about anything these days. When talking to Ms. June in the teacher's lounge she says, "I'm over these learning targets – our students don't give a hoot about them." Ms. June rolls her eyes and nods.

Missing component(s): _____

Additional Considerations

Here are some additional tips for you to incorporate within your lessons to ensure that student engagement and motivation soars!

Verify the vibes: Check in regularly to ensure your students' prefrontal cortexes are in control. Regulated students are available for learning. We can teach our class to do a body scan where everyone pauses and checks in with their thoughts, feelings, heart rate, and stress. You may need to dim the lights and do a quick mindfulness activity or get them up and moving momentarily. But using body scans as a regular practice will help students become more aware of what their body is telling them so they can start advocating for themselves.

Sell it so they'll buy it: If we aren't enjoying the lesson, they won't, either. Our students will be more likely to cooperate and participate if you look like you're having a good time – since most students don't like to miss out on a good time. But if you have a flat affect, are droning on and on, and are just "teaching to teach," that's a bummer.

This doesn't mean you have to fake it, but try to fall in love with long-digit division somehow. Convince yourself that the periodic table is the best thing since sliced bread. Communicate your interest for the content and the desire to want your students to share that interest and get pumped when they are engaging with it. That will build behavioral momentum. It doesn't matter if it's the most boring topic in the world; find a way to teach with at least a hint of enthusiasm and passion.

Embody the power walk: When we walk with intention, we are moving about at a quick and intentional pace, doing a lot less talking. Use active supervision to move around the room. Your proximity will naturally keep more students in tune to the lesson. But if you are just standing at the front the whole time, we know the students in the back will start to entertain themselves. Research also shows that students are more attentive and engaged if instruction is delivered at a brisk rate. If we slow down too much, their bodies and thoughts will start to wander. And talk less. The more you talk, the less they will listen.

Incorporate active student responding as much as possible: The more opportunities we give all students to respond, the more engaged they likely will be.

Connect the content: We talked about this when we reviewed the opening of a lesson, but it's worth repeating. Focus on the *why* of the lesson or the skill. When you can connect it to students' lives, it's going to become more meaningful, and the motivation to persist through the lesson will increase. This can be a challenge, we know, especially with topics or content we don't really use in everyday life, so you may have to get creative, but really spend time when planning your lesson, thinking about different ways to relate it to their lives.

Live the lesson: How can you make the content come to life? Instead of just reading off a worksheet about the topic, can you pull up Google images? Can you bring in real objects or examples? Can you show a YouTube clip? Can you throw up some decorations that make it feel like they are living the scene? That extra bit of effort to make the content real can go a long way in keeping your students engaged (and we know this extra five minutes of prep can save you a lot of time that you would spend dealing with off-task behavior).

Beat the behaviors: No longer are we taking appropriate behavior for granted and getting on our class when they are off-task. We as educators know how terrible it can feel when nobody acknowledges our hard work. This means providing positive feedback and verbal scaffolding regarding behavior while your students are on task! When things are going well is the time you want to intervene. This is a secret not many know, but now you do! Acknowledge cooperation and participation early in the lesson to build that behavioral momentum and increase motivation. Smile, wink, give nods and high-fives, provide verbal praise, and generally draw positive attention to their participation and cooperation by interspersing lessons with class-wide chants or phrases. Even if it's just "Wow, everyone's bodies are facing the speaker – that's showing respect." Or "I see everyone following along as we review the agenda – nice job keeping yourself on track." Or even "Holy cow, it's only one minute into our lesson, and everyone is participating. You're on a roll." If things usually fall apart at minute 10, pause and reflect at minute 9 or 8. Beat the behaviors.

CHAPTER 5

Reinforcing Desirable Behaviors

Rewards and Incentives and Bribery, Oh My!

What comes to mind when you hear the terms *reinforcement* or *consequence*?

There are many misconceptions surrounding these terms and what we think should or should not happen after behaviors – both desirable and challenging. Much of what we believe about this has to do with our past experiences, culture, and well. . .social media. So, let's provide some clarification.

Consequence:	Reinforcement:
An event or stimulus occurring immediately after a behavior that **increases or decreases** the behavior over time.	An event of stimulus occurring immediately after a behavior that **increases** the behavior over time.

The term *consequence* is commonly used to refer to an intended punishment. However, when we are considering behaviors, a more accurate description of consequences is *outcomes*. Put simply, what was the outcome that happened in the environment concurrent or immediately after a behavior? That outcome was the consequence. *A consequence may punish (decrease) a behavior, but consequences may also reinforce (increase) a behavior.*

Reinforcement is always occurring within our environment, regardless of whether we are aware of it, believe in it, or acknowledge it. It is both a naturally occurring and contrived phenomenon. Simply put, if a behavior helps us to get more of what we want or away from what we don't want, then the consequence (outcome) reinforced our behavior. Here's where this concept gets tricky for us, though. We often make assumptions that certain outcomes are punishers and others are reinforcers, especially when it comes to our students. We assume that because we scolded the student or took away their recess that we've provided a consequence that is a punishment. However, if the behavior doesn't decrease over time, our consequence may actually be serving as reinforcement. You may now be wondering, what student would like to be scolded or miss recess, but if that consequence helps them meet a need (for connection with an adult or escape from social situations at recess), then we just might see the behavior continue to occur. And another consideration to ponder is if we continue to observe our students engaging in challenging behaviors despite the consequences occurring – they may not have the skills to engage in the desirable behaviors when and where they need to.

Common Statements and Misunderstandings Regarding Reinforcement

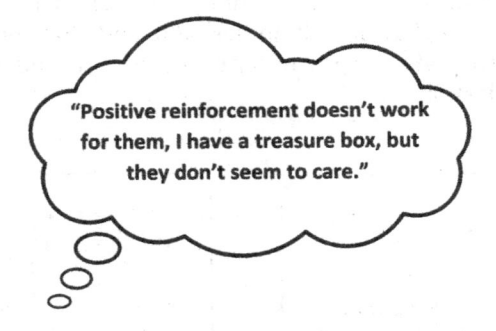

Reinforcement isn't something that works or doesn't work, nor is it a specific object – it's an effect. A reinforcer isn't always tangible, either. What may be occurring in a situation such as this is that the incentive or reward is simply just that – an incentive or reward. *Rewards don't necessarily increase behavior.* One can receive a reward for doing something, and it might in fact be something they like, but it may not be a reinforcer, meaning it won't increase a desirable behavior. I like chocolate, but I'm not about to spend three hours lesson planning for a bar of chocolate. Another thing that may be happening in this situation is that the sources of motivation for engaging in challenging behaviors may outweigh any sources of motivation to engage in alternative behaviors. For example, if in the moment a student just wants to get away from a difficult math test, they often aren't thinking about a trip to the treasure box days from now – they want out now. Avoiding feelings of continued frustration, failure, and delaying the poor grade that results in physical abuse waiting for them at home may be more important than whatever is in that box. Another reason may be that the class or student lacks some skills necessary to meet whatever expectations you are trying to reinforce with the treasure box. If I say, "Everyone needs to have good behavior during recess for the next two days to earn a trip to the box," well, that right there is the equation for failure. Assuming students will have fully mastered every skill needed to stay calm, cool, and collected during the numerous high-stakes situations that we know occur during unstructured times is a bit misguided.

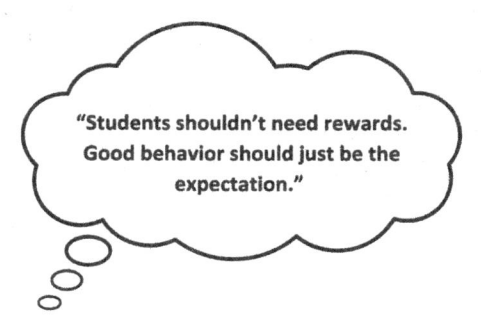

Ah, this is a common one, but lots of things are inaccurate about this statement. Tomorrow, as you go through the day, think about everything you do and why you do it. You open the fridge to get access to food – reward. You answer your phone to get access to your friend – reward. You take out the trash to avoid a stinky garage – reward. In this case, all these rewards are reinforcers because they increase the likelihood that you do them again. What is usually meant by this is that we shouldn't have to use "contrived" or excessive amounts of "unnatural, adult-imposed things" to encourage appropriate behavior. Expecting "good behavior" to occur without it getting reinforced in some way isn't scientifically possible. Effective educators embed reinforcement all day long; they just don't realize it. But, when we are unsure of how to embed it or how to help kids contact more natural forms of reinforcement, we end up having to rely more on contrived things such as treasure boxes, stickers, free homework passes, etc.

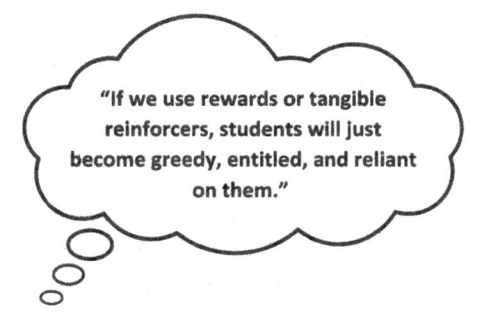

Valid! Keep in mind that reinforcers come in a wide variety of forms. We do things to not only access certain physical "toys," but people, interactions, activities, pleasant feelings, and sensations as well. Relying solely on "toy-like" items to serve as motivation to do things is not real life. Tangible rewards can also be ineffective when they are being used to reinforce the wrong skills. We typically want to focus on using them to reinforce skills that help our students learn and grow new skills and navigate situations that challenge them in one way or another. In addition, tangible rewards become a problem when there is too heavy of a focus on them. We end up taking away focus from other natural sources of motivation that students may not even realize exist. For example, it's common that schools use PBIS points. It's also common for the focus to shift more toward the points and rewards. It becomes "I'm going to engage in appropriate behavior so I can get a cool keychain" instead of "I'm going to engage in appropriate behavior, even though it feels hard, because it brings me closer to graduating and I want to graduate." When using contrived reinforcers, it's important to pair these things with more natural sources of reinforcement and fade them out eventually.

When folks say this, what they usually mean is, "They aren't motivated to do the thing I want them to do by the singular thing I want them to do it for." They are in fact very motivated! Maybe they aren't motivated to earn breaks, but they *are* motivated to get kicked out of history class because they can't handle the embarrassment of not knowing the right answer (competence is missing). Maybe they are very motivated by doing well in this class, but the uncomfortable feelings associated with that embarrassment become pitted against the immediate and momentary relief of leaving class.

Maybe you have a student who isn't motivated to go to class and earn time to play basketball with staff, but they are motivated to avoid class because they were never given the opportunity to make their own choices (autonomy is missing). Might these students be motivated to do well in school deep down? Yes, but the immediate relief of uncomfortable feelings becomes more enticing than tolerating a class, day after day, in which they have no sense of control. Maybe they aren't motivated to earn free time for working quietly, but rather they are motivated to gain interaction from their teacher (by throwing paper across the room) because their parents are never home (relatedness is missing). Once you identify the varying sources of motivation behind challenging behavior, you can start to investigate the reason it exists.

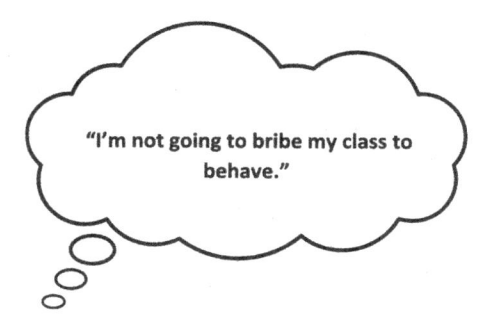

Good! We don't want you to because bribery is ineffective long-term. Bribery usually works only temporarily. We accidentally use it out of desperation to get an undesirable behavior that is already occurring to stop. For example, "If you stop blurting and remember to raise your hands for the remainder of English, we can have five extra minutes of free period" or "Okay, if you just get down off the table and do your work, I'll give you some time to draw at the end of class." The confusing part is that students often stop engaging in the challenging behavior in the moment but often *increase* it over time – oops! We then reinforce our own behavior as staff because we ended up doing something that got the behavior to stop. We promised something and the behavior went away. Magic! I'm going to do that again! However, bribery contrasts positive reinforcement in that it promises the reward *before* seeing a desirable behavior in hopes that it will occur, and if often promised during the challenging behavior.

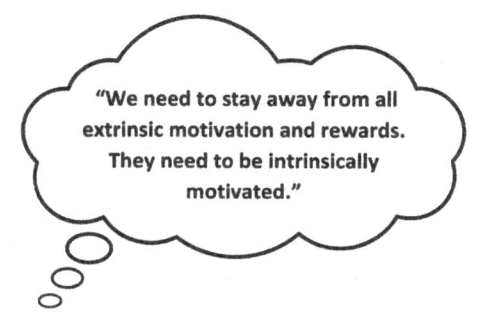

This is such a common misunderstanding that spreads like wildfire. Do not die on this hill. We *all* access forms of extrinsic motivation and external sources of reinforcement all day long. Nobody gets gas, pays taxes, goes grocery shopping, takes care of bills, goes the speed limits, cleans before guests arrive, etc., just because it brings us internal joy. . .that's not real life. Trying to get a student to do anything we ask of them simply because it should make them feel innately good or satisfying isn't appropriate. Maintaining peer friendships, getting good grades so one can go on to college and get a job, posting on social media to gain followers, making teachers-pay-teachers products to bring in extra income, and completing page 46 in the math book because the teacher gives them a pat on the back and a smile, are all very appropriate and extrinsic forms of motivation and reinforcement. A balance of both extrinsic and intrinsic motivation is what the real world brings to the table, a world that we need to prepare our students for.

Improving Feedback with Behavior-Specific Praise

You've likely heard the phrase "Catch them being good." You are also likely sick of hearing it by now. But what does "good" even mean? "Good" is subjective. What good behavior looks like to one educator might be different for another educator. And we often hold students to such high standards that anything less than what we deem "good" is "bad." If nobody is clear on what "good" looks like and sounds like, behavior-specific praise won't be effective. It's also often based on what *we* say "good behavior" is – but what about our students? If we want them to engage in behaviors that we can provide positive feedback on, they need to agree to some extent that those behaviors are indeed helping them in some way. And this is why establishing classroom expectations with students is so important. One of the most effective ways to catch students being "good" is to use behavior-specific praise.

> ### Behavior-Specific Praise:
>
> A statement that clearly points out the desirable behavior or skill that has been performed.

We all experience and learn from feedback in many forms both in and outside of school. We receive feedback from colleagues, mentors, family, friends, and community members. Positive feedback is incredibly impactful in shaping behaviors. When we receive feedback from workshop participants regarding our instructional delivery, the verbiage we used, or the way we explained a concept (all behaviors) that was particularly helpful to a participant or group, we tend to engage in those same behaviors again in future workshops.

Consider for a moment. . .Where do you experience positive feedback outside of school? How does that impact your future behaviors?

What It Is

Behavior-specific praise (BSP) is a statement that clearly points out the desirable behavior or skill that has been performed. It's one type of interaction we engage in with our students. Our ability to interact with students is undoubtedly one of the biggest reasons educators struggle with certain classes or students. Interactions can quickly become coercive, so mastering interaction strategies is essential to ensuring a calm, positive classroom environment.

The purpose of BSP is to increase the future occurrence of the specific behavior we are calling attention to. An example of this could be "Class, you rocked the hallway expectations just now by staying quiet and keeping your hands by your side." If we just said, "Class, you rocked the hallway expectations" (general praise), the awareness wouldn't be brought to the exact behaviors that resulted in them rocking the hallway expectations. Even when we assume that students know what they're doing well, they often don't. Let's say a student is working on a math assignment and I came over and said, "Good job!" They aren't going to know the specific thing I am giving them feedback on that they should do again the next time math rolls around. Are they doing a good job persisting through a challenging question? Are they doing a good job staying quiet during the math assignment? Are they doing a good job skipping the difficult problems and trying the easy ones first? For behavior-specific praise to be most effective, we need to explicitly state what the student is doing and tie that into the feedback.

There is certainly a time and place for general praise such as "Nice job," "Way to go," and "Good job" as a means of providing encouragement and continued motivation, but it doesn't point out the specifics of what they did, so it's not as effective in increasing specific desirable behaviors.

There is also a time and a place for behavioral reflections, which are common statements in which the teacher describes or refers to the everyday activities in which a student engages. These statements are not contingent on engagement in specific desirable behaviors. This type of statement demonstrates to the student that the staff member is interested in what the student is doing. We can use behavior reflections to build rapport and to establish a positive supportive classroom environment. We might smile and say, "I notice you're outlining your paper before you start writing." Note that the teacher is simply describing what the student is doing, rather than providing positive feedback. Reflections are often better suited for students who find praise uncomfortable. Behavior-specific praise, general praise, and behavior reflections all have their roles within the classroom, but BSP takes the cake when it comes to increasing desirable behavior and preventing challenging behaviors at large.

It is crucial to be aware of how and when we connect with our students. Connecting with them throughout the day (no matter what behaviors they are displaying) is just as important as when they display specific target behaviors. This noncontingent attention and connection is especially important for our students who have experienced trauma or have had aversive experiences with adults (family members and school staff included) who were more punitive or inconsistent in their interactions.

Nonexamples:

- "Hey, great work."
- "Thank you for being safe today."

- "I noticed you are adding to your story. Can't wait to read it."
- "Your behavior is unacceptable. Go to the Think Spot." (Not positive feedback!)

Examples:

- "I hear you; your body feels hot and tight. Nice job naming that sensation. What would help you feel more focused?"
- "I saw you using your checklist. That seemed to help you stay on track. What do you think?"
- "Everyone, please pause. Rate yourself one through three on how that transition went. Yes – I agree it was a three! What did you do that made it a three?"

Additional examples of behavior-specific praise can be found in the appendix (Form 5.1).

Why It's Effective

Specific positive feedback is one of the most valuable, life-changing tools we have. For most of us, praise functions as a reinforcer, meaning it increases the likelihood that the desirable behavior occurs again in the future. When we don't receive specific positive feedback, or, if the only feedback we receive is corrective, then we are required to make inferences about what it is we should be doing. This increases the likelihood we will make errors and do the "wrong" thing more often, which in turn can quickly lead to increased feelings of anxiety and self-doubt.

When students repeatedly fail, situations, settings, and people can quickly become aversive, especially in the classroom. In addition, if we fail to deliver positive feedback to our students but dole out corrections regularly, we can easily become someone who signals that "life isn't so great when you're in my presence." All of this can decrease the motivation to try and increase the motivation to escape or avoid those situations or people that evoke those feelings. Unfortunately, students who seem to lack motivation in the classroom are frequently labeled as "noncompliant," "defiant," and "oppositional." However, these descriptions only describe how their behavior is experienced by us, the adults. These labels don't tell us why the student is showing a lack of motivation. We've already learned that missing or weak executive skills and inconsistent implementation of universal supports (visuals, expectations, routines, instructional strategies) can impact student motivation. Likewise, insufficient specific positive feedback can also adversely impact student motivation, behavior, and harm the adult-student relationship.

Behavior-specific praise provides us with evidence of progress toward our goals and values. We can't always see small progress, so proof of success is beneficial to build self-efficacy (one's belief in one's ability to succeed). This in turn increases motivation to persist through difficult or boring tasks and situations. Behavior-specific praise also helps to develop metacognition and self-awareness. We are often poor observers of our own behavior and how our behavior (both desirable and challenging) results in certain outcomes. Behavior-specific praise assists us in understanding these outcomes and connecting to more naturally occurring forms of reinforcement (as opposed to contrived outcomes like a sticker or trip to the treasure box). Understanding how our actions help us to get more of what we want/need then increases our motivation to use the behavior or skill again in the future.

How to Do It

Steps to Implementing Behavior-Specific Praise:

1. Determine target behavior(s).
2. Observe for target behavior(s).
3. Gain attention of class or individual.
4. Deliver statement of praise.

Prior to implementing behavior-specific praise, we first need to identify the specific skills or behaviors that would benefit your students if they engaged in them more often. As we discussed in previous chapters, it can be helpful to consider the challenging routines for the student or students and what skills or behaviors would help them to navigate that routine successfully. It's also important to note that when considering target behaviors to increase, we should consider and select behaviors that will be meaningful to the students, not just benefit us. Ideally, behaviors to increase should assist the student in increasing independence and their ability to navigate stressors and/or meet their needs.

Note, the goal of behavior-specific praise is to use it intentionally to increase specific behaviors that students either aren't using or using enough. So, we don't need to acknowledge *all* the "good" behavior or focus on the things they are already frequently doing well. That would be very difficult, exhausting, and meaningless.

Here are some examples of skills and corresponding behaviors (the procedure of the routine) that would assist students in navigating challenging routines more efficiently:

Skill: *Requesting assistance*
Corresponding behaviors: *Raise hand, wait quietly for staff to respond, continue task while waiting.*

Skill: *Flexibility*
Corresponding behaviors: *Say, "No big deal, put my work in the "Parkinglot" bin, and start the next task.*

Skill: *Organization*
Corresponding behaviors: *Put papers in blue folder, put binder in backpack, put pencils in pencil box.*

In these examples, the corresponding behaviors the student needs to engage in to appropriately navigate the challenging routine may vary based on the age, developmental level, or grade level/subject. Adjustment of these is one way to differentiate across learners.

After determining which behaviors will be targeted to increase, consider if explicit teaching of these behaviors is needed. Often, students truly don't know how to engage in a skill or aren't fluent in engaging in the skill or its corresponding behaviors. This is true even for students in middle and high school – remember, executive skills are often hidden, and we each develop them at different rates. So, ask yourself, "Do the students already have the skills in their repertoire or might there be skills that haven't fully developed?"

You probably already know by the eye rolls and under-the-breath snide comments that positive feedback is not always a welcome interaction for some students. In fact, praise is aversive for some students and can potentially lead to re-traumatization. There are many reasons why this might be. Some students, particularly those who have a history of abuse, or unsafe and unpredictable interactions with adults in their life, may be very wary of it. It may be a signal or pre-condition that bad things are about to happen. For people who have experienced abuse, the history of hearing praise might not have been pleasant or predictable (Kolu, 2017). For others, it can trigger anxiety because they think they now have a bar to reach in the future. Others may have self-esteem issues or engage in negative self-talk. Social anxiety and depression are among other reasons why a student may not openly welcome behavior-specific praise. So, before jumping into using behavior-specific praise, we highly recommend conducting a student preference survey (see Form 5.2 in the appendix) on how they want to receive positive feedback (this can also be done for corrective feedback as well). To do this, discuss or present a visual format of options and have students choose which ones they are most comfortable with (e.g., praise in front of the class, written note, thumbs up or head nod, private conversation after class, in an email, statement of observation, etc.).

Once you have determined which behaviors would benefit from increasing and you are aware of how particular students prefer their positive feedback, start observing the behaviors. When you see them engage in the behavior or skill, deliver the feedback.

Here are some more examples of what this might sound like:

- "You kept your cool when Emmet made that comment. What were you telling yourself that helped you do that?"
- "I saw you really persisting through that tricky math problem. I thought you were stuck for a moment! What did you do to get unstuck?"
- "Way to go, Class. I noticed you referring to the agenda as you worked with your partners."
- "You stuck with that role I assigned you even though you wanted a different one. That was flexible of you."

To assist you in implementing behavior-specific praise, an implementation checklist can be found in the appendix (see Form 5.3).

Activity: Reflecting on Your Needs

 Consider routines in your day that your students struggle to meet expectations or engage in challenging behaviors. Jot down some of the behaviors/ skills you would like to target with behavior-specific praise. Then, come up with a handful of corresponding BSP statements you can utilize following their occurrence.

Desirable Behavior	Behavior-Specific Praise Statement
Example: Transitioning safely and quietly from the group table back to their individual desks	*Class, what a great transition. Let's pause and discuss what made that so smooth (discusses specific behaviors). What were the positive outcomes because of following our transition procedure?*

Additional Considerations

In the beginning, deliver behavior-specific praise as soon as opportunity allows after the student(s) engage in the targeted behavior. We will help students increase self-awareness and self-monitoring if an immediate connection is made. When you use behavior-specific praise, bring attention to the conditions under which the positive feedback is being utilized and start helping them to recognize these situations are more challenging for them.

Examples:

- "Evie, when you joined the game of tag, the rules were already established. You showed flexibility by playing by those rules this time, and they kept playing with you instead of walking away."
- "I said, "No, not right now," and I noticed you stayed calm and said, "Okay," instead of cursing – great response inhibition. How did that feel? That skill is really going to help you when you start your job next year."
- "Class, you rocked the hallway expectations transitioning to recess by staying quiet and keeping your hands by your side. It allowed us to get out to recess immediately, so you had more time for football."

It's also important to bring attention to the natural outcomes of the desirable behavior they just engaged in. A big reason why students (and adults alike) don't modify their behavior over time is because we aren't good at observing our own behavior and the effect it has on the environment. We often don't have the skill to stop and notice how what we just said or did is either moving us further away or closer to our goals or the things that matter to us. We need to help students in making the connection between their behavior and the natural outcomes – the natural sources of reinforcement. This is not, "Johnny, you asked for help appropriately so you earn a point or a trip to the treasure chest!" that's not the naturally occurring outcome. What happens when the treasure chest or PBIS points aren't there anymore? Instead, we need to assist them in connecting to and understanding the bigger, more natural sources of reinforcement in life that they actually value – like having friends, connections, autonomy, and in this example, gaining help and assistance. Guiding students to discover connections between their actions and how that helps them to do the things they want to do, or achieve their goals, is the ultimate reinforcement.

When delivering behavior-specific praise, be sincere and authentic. Students know when you aren't and that can seriously harm rapport and quickly decrease the effectiveness of behavior-specific praise. You can still be factual and to-the-point while showing enthusiasm.

Examples:

Insincere: "Oh my gosh! You are just so amazing, Johnny, I wish more students were like you. The way you just asked for that pen instead of grabbing it was stellar!"

Sincere: "Hey, I appreciate you asking first this time. It makes me feel like I can trust you with my things. You can borrow my pen."

Vary the delivery of your praise. No one likes to hear "Good job," "Good job," "Good job" all day long. . . .

Examples:

- Woah. . .amazing.
- Fantastic.
- Class, give yourself a silent celebration.

- Yes! Nice walking feet!
- You just stopped me in my tracks. Do you know why?

Give the harder skills the bigger party. This is called differential reinforcement. This doesn't have to be an actual party, but it is something to keep in mind, especially for the students who are gaining a massive following for challenging behavior – flip the script and give them a huge celebration when they engage in the desirable behaviors instead. Know your students, but simply put, using differential reinforcement in this case means you vary the way you present the feedback. So, if a skill or behavior has been easy for a student to learn and they just needed a little boost in motivation, then you can just keep it simple, but if this is a behavior or skill that is more complex and they have been really struggling to engage in it or they are now doing it and it's keeping themselves and others safe when before things were unsafe, that's a reason to give a higher-quality celebration.

Examples:

Easy skill, small party: "Nice work referring to the word wall this time, Ainsley."

Difficult skill, big party: "Dude! You totally just kept emotional control by walking away when he laughed at you. What do you say we go call your dad and let him know?"

Aim for that 4:1 ratio. We should interact with students four times more often when they are behaving appropriately than when they are behaving inappropriately. Interactions with students are considered positive or negative based on whether the feedback given to the student is positive or corrective. Behavior-specific praise can be one, or more, of those four interactions.

Differentiate the frequency of feedback based on need. Just like we differentiate instruction, we should be differentiating our feedback – this not about being equal but rather equitable. The ratio is what we are trying to nail. For example, one student might benefit from four positives to one constructive feedback statement, whereas another might benefit from sixteen positives and four constructive feedback statements over the same amount of time. So, everyone is getting what they need, and we are being equitable without making students who get less positive feedback and interactions feel like they are getting the short end of the stick.

Praise effort and approximations. Not every behavior or skill can be mastered overnight. It takes time, persistence, and practice to generalize skills – so we can use them when and where we need them. Think back to our discussion of efficiency and skill in Chapter 2. Sometimes we use behaviors to meet our needs because we have the muscle memory and learning history for using them. They become quick and efficient for us, especially if we are also missing skills. We cannot expect our students to become proficient in every new skill at the snap of our fingers. So, we need to consider the effort they are putting in and praise their progress as they go. Over time, we can continue to praise closer and closer approximations to the desired behavior, making the path to the end goal clear but in a systematic and achievable way. This helps in another way as well. Students who can't visualize or get a good read on how close they are to their goal are more likely to lose motivation. Praising effort and approximations helps them to recognize their progress and maintain their motivation.

Further, we often inadvertently teach kids to have an all-or-nothing mindset by not celebrating small wins on the way to the championship. We need to motivate them to persist and keep a growth mindset. We can do this by praising the student's *effort* to engage in a behavior or complete a task rather than praising the outcome or their ability. When you are praising a student for being smart or getting an A on their reading test, we aren't going to see any specific behaviors increase. We want to praise those discrete, smaller behaviors that have to do with their effort – the outcome will be the overall goal they meet. They may earn a good grade (they may not), but did they persist, did they ask for help, did they use a specific strategy to help themselves? Those are the skills and behaviors they may need to engage in to reach their goal outcome, and those are the things we want to praise.

Example: "Let's check your tally sheet – only ten blurts today, so five less than yesterday. Way to go. We are on the right track!"

Non-example: "You blurted ten times during this lesson. You just earned yourself a letter home to your parents."

Example: "We met four out of our six entry routine steps. Getting better! Which two steps do we need to shift our focus to tomorrow?"

Non-example: "Class, you still haven't shown me you can transition, so it looks like we will practice during recess."

Pairing behavior-specific praise with graphic feedback can also increase motivation to engage in certain behaviors again. While we are praising progress and approximations, we can level that up by providing our students a visual representation of their great progress. Remember, *competency (feeling like you have the skills to do something) is a fundamental and natural reinforcer.* We track things all the time to keep us motivated – calories, steps, reps at the gym, water intake, books we've read, etc. This graphic feedback could be in their personal binder or a giant graph up on the bulletin board for the whole class. When you see yourself making progress, that alone is motivation to keep persisting. Seeing your progress is the reinforcer – not a sticker or a trip to the school store.

Teaching students how to solicit positive feedback is another fantastic way of increasing desirable behaviors. We've already learned that we use behaviors to meet our needs. Sometimes a student's need for connection isn't being met effectively or they lack the skills to do so in appropriate ways, so they resort to other behaviors that get that need met more consistently and predictably (i.e., efficiently).

One reason students seek connection is to obtain positive feedback and encouragement. Since they don't always have the skills in their repertoire to solicit specific positive feedback in an appropriate way, we must teach it. Along the same lines, you can teach students how to provide positive praise to each other. For some, peer attention is more valuable (reinforcing) than adult attention. If you have students who are highly motivated to gain peer attention, teaching them to request it and others to provide it is a great way to embed and meet that need in a proactive way.

Use reflexive questioning to transfer thinking and further build metacognition. This might be done by using an indirect prompt to query and elicit student feedback.

Examples:
- "How did that feel?"
- "How did you do that?"
- "Did you follow your plan? Use your strategy?"

- "How did your plan/strategy work out for you?"
- "What were the outcomes of what you just did?"
- "What did you notice that happened as a result of that?"

And lastly, work toward fading behavior-specific praise over time. You can't sustain praising your students every single time they engage in a desired behavior immediately after it happens. That's exhausting and not real life. We also don't want our kids to require an immediate schedule of reinforcement to function because that's not going to be helpful in a job, in their household, or in the community. We want to move toward a natural schedule of reinforcement where reinforcement is delayed or occurs intermittently. Over time, as students begin to demonstrate expected behaviors more often, we can then begin to fade our statements of specific praise. We can begin to delay them and perhaps provide them at the end of the lesson or during the end-of-day check-in. On top of that, we can also teach students to self-praise so they are less reliant on praise from others and can access the positive feelings associated with accomplishment no matter where they are! The following are three ways that you can systematically fade your delivery of behavior specific praise:

Fade the rate: In the beginning when learning or engaging in a new skill or a behavior, we want to reinforce it every single time it occurs. After momentum is gained, you can then fade to providing feedback every other time. Eventually when behaviors and skills are being performed consistently you can praise intermittently.

Fade the immediacy: When the behavior or skill is initially targeted, provide praise immediately upon engagement in the behavior. You might then move to every 15 minutes and eventually provide praise at the end of the period if the behavior occurred.

Fade the specificity: At first you might say, "You looked at him, asked first, and waited for this response. That was very respectful of you." As the student increases their engagement in the targeted behavior, you might then move to saying, "Nice job with classroom expectation number four."

Finally, remember that phrase "Catch them being good!" we discussed at the beginning of this section? We challenge you to now *catch them putting in the effort to engage in behaviors that will help them become more independent and live a meaningful life.* Focusing on behaviors that matter to the student, that help them be more successful and praising the effort and progress they make – that should be the focus! That's the powerful stuff that increases motivation, persistence, and ultimately results in student success!

Embedding Reinforcement into the Classroom

"It's time!" (said in the voice of UFC's Bruce Buffer). Ideally the excitement has been building and you are just itching to know how to harness the power of motivation and reinforcement without relying on the use of rewards with the hope of gaining momentary compliance.

> **Contrived Reinforcement:**
>
> Rewards or incentives provided contingent upon engagement in targeted behaviors with the goal of increasing the behavior.

> **Natural Reinforcement:**
>
> Outcomes that occur naturally within the environment that pay-off use of a targeted behavior (i.e., the behavior worked to meet a need).

But first, we must clarify some additional misconceptions in this area. For starters, it's not our job to decide what is motivating to someone else. There may be things that our students are very motivated by that we can embed and use within the classroom context in a natural fashion, but sometimes we cannot. However, to the best of our ability, we want to meet our students where they currently are. Some students struggle so intensely that utilizing contrived reinforcers may be one of the only ways to help them increase necessary skills and reach a place of relaxation.

In fact, many adults, neurodivergent included, contrive reinforcement systems to self-motivate. For example, initially allowing oneself a treat after going to the gym until the positive effects (changes in health and body) begin to accumulate and serve as the natural reinforcement now motivating continued trips to the gym. Those who excel at minimizing challenging behavior recognize there is a time and a place for leaning on less natural sources of motivation initially, especially when students are learning new skills. They enable us to bridge the gap and help students encounter reinforcement long before they might be able to meet more natural forms of it, thus preventing them from giving up and motivating them to continue to use emerging skills. When such skills are close to being mastered, contrived reinforcers can then be faded as the student is now encountering natural sources of motivation and reinforcement that they weren't able to access prior.

Over the course of our careers, we have observed the use of contrived reinforcers to drastically change the trajectory of students' lives and allow them to successfully transition into less restrictive environments. When used effectively, they have immediately reduced challenging behavior while quickly reinforcing alternative skills that the student was previously struggling to learn, leading to more confident, independent, happy learners who no longer needed behavior intervention plans. If it has been deemed that students will benefit from contrived forms of reinforcement, just know the goal should always be to fade to more naturally occurring forms of reinforcement at more natural rates (delivery) over time. In reality, no one will forever follow a student around with tokens, points, or tangible items to reinforce every desirable behavior.

Contrived reinforcers, which are often rewards of some kind, become a problem in schools when they become the focus of behavior-change. Overreliance on these sources of reinforcement easily overshadows the natural reinforcement opportunities we can and should embed within the classroom. Then, we end up getting ourselves into a pickle by thinking:

> *"The more restrictions I put in place and the more things they have to earn, the more control I will have over them. I will make them earn the ability to make choices, to interact with friends, to gain my attention, and obtain support with academics, by only helping them when they are behaving. Yes, this should do the trick!"*

However, this line of thinking backfires. Why? Because when we reduce a student's ability to access their basic and fundamental needs (sources of reinforcement) contingent upon what we deem desirable behavior, we end up creating long-term states of deprivation, thus *fueling* their motivation to get those needs met in the easiest, fastest, most reliable way possible – enter challenging behavior.

Let's use the common example: *"You can have dessert if you eat your vegetables."*

Now, this usually goes one of two ways. Either the child immediately gobbles up the vegetables and races for the Tupperware of brownies, or he starts to argue. In both instances we have unknowingly shifted the focus of the dinner to be about earning a contrived reinforcer (dessert). What happens when you run out of dessert items? Are you going to race to the store mid-meal to get more just to ensure there's ice cream? That's not sustainable. Instead, how can we keep the focus on the vegetables and make the vegetables more appealing in and of themselves? In essence, how can we embed reinforcement into the behavior of eating vegetables and increase motivation to eat them?

Well, we can discuss all the positive health outcomes of eating vegetables, we can add cheese to them, we can chop them finely and mix them with the rice, we can opt for a different kind of vegetable, or we can alternate bites with a favorite stuffed animal. The focus on earning desert becomes more about compliance, rather than supporting underlying needs and identifying proactive ways to increase cooperation. We don't realize it, but introducing rewards and incentives with strings attached to the conditions under which students must earn them can actually *increase* feelings of stress and anxiety around what they have to do. This then often results in escape/avoidance behaviors. Of course, this is not always the case, but it is a potential side effect of poorly implemented reinforcement systems.

So, how does this whole vegetable-desert scenario apply to the classroom? Ideally, we should be infusing reinforcement into the classroom in naturally occurring ways and moving our focus away from the long-term reliance on contrived rewards or reinforcers. Instead of, "What tangible reward can I use to get my students to come to class and do their work?" the question becomes, "How can I make my classroom, my lessons, and my interactions more naturally reinforcing?" This will assist in minimizing coercion and keeping the focus on supporting student motivation in ways that sustain desirable behaviors over time, even when no one is looking.

And this brings us back to the fundamental reinforcers that we spoke about at the start of this book. If students are in a state of deprivation when it comes to their basic needs, opportunity for choice (autonomy), skill level and feelings of confidence (competence), and feelings of connection (relatedness), challenging behaviors will skyrocket. When these needs are met proactively, desirable behaviors should be maintained. But don't let this seemingly overwhelming task of trying to meet all these individualized needs fool you into thinking this is unattainable – remember, we aren't targeting individual students with universal supports, rather the entire class at once. You can then determine how you want to individualize if the need arises. The most efficient way we have found to tackle embedding reinforcement into the classroom is to grab four sheets of paper and label each of them. Each piece of paper will then become an area to brain-dump ideas of how to meet that need within your setting.

The Basics	Autonomy	Competence	Relatedness
In what ways can I embed opportunities to get basic needs met? (e.g., food, water, sleep, safety, comfort, regulation)	In what ways can I embed opportunities for meaningful choice, independence, and involvement in decision-making free from feelings of coercion?	In what ways can I embed opportunities for students to feel knowledgeable, skilled, and assured that they can effectively navigate their environment and reach their goals?	In what ways can I embed opportunities to experience secure attachments? How can I help students feel respected and supported, even during their toughest moments?

Here are some ideas to help get you started.

The Basics

- Actively listen when students are talking to you.
- Use priming before upcoming and new activities, settings, or situations.
- Keep the room clean and organized.
- Provide advanced notice of changes, activities, visitors, etc.
- Conduct regular body scans and wellness checks.
- Teach regulation skills, including the use of a regulation space/binder/box.
- Keep yourself regulated, especially during the times it's the most difficult.
- Create a safety box for personal belongings (phones, tablets, special items).
- Celebrate when students act in alignment with their values.
- Build movement opportunities into lessons (e.g., active student responding techniques) or schedule in movement breaks between lessons based on the type of movement students need to regulate.

Autonomy

- Involve students in creating classroom expectations.
- Ensure expected behaviors taught are flexible and give students a variety of ways to get their needs met while still meeting the expectation.
- Have students create classroom décor and displays (bulletin boards, name tags, etc.).
- Provide instructional choice often (pay attention to how students respond).

- Frequently ask students for feedback and make changes that honor that feedback as appropriate.
- Limit and fade unnecessary prompts.
- Provide opportunity for creativity.
- Teach and model decision-making and problem-solving.

Competence

- Precorrect challenging routines (discuss barriers to success and behaviors needed to overcome these barriers and contact what's valuable to them).
- Use shaping to achieve success by meeting them where they are and providing positive feedback on small approximations toward the overall skill, behavior, or goal.
- Track progress visually.
- Narrate your thought process.
- Model growth mindset language.
- Provide frequent checks for understanding.
- Provide worked models or success criteria during lessons.
- Celebrate effort and small achievements.
- Explicitly teach skills necessary for routines and situations that prove more challenging.

Relatedness

- Create demand-free opportunities to join your students in engaging in things they prefer.
- Act in ways that show students things are better with you than without you.
- Smile.
- Greet students at the door as they enter and bid them farewell as they exit.
- Come up with individual handshakes.
- Get comfortable with apologizing.
- Ask questions that show you are interested in students' lives outside of school.
- Teach students to celebrate one another (shout-out sticky notes, end-of-day honors, silent celebrations, etc.).
- Conduct team-building activities.
- Develop class-wide goals.
- Use manners (say, "Please" and "Thank you").
- Come up with a class name/team names.
- Bring attention to things students have in common with one another, as well as what they have in common with staff.
- Validate and empathize, even when you don't agree.
- Allow them to express themselves and voice opinion without judgment.
- Back off when they are showing you they cannot handle something, then re-assess and move forward collaboratively.

CHAPTER 6

Responding to Challenging Behaviors

While we've spent most of this book discussing preventative strategies, challenging behaviors may still occur from time to time. Students may engage in behaviors that are distracting, disruptive, and, at times, even dangerous. As we move through this chapter, we will provide a reframe on typical educator responses to challenging behaviors as well as challenge you to reflect on your current or past practices. We will then outline a core universal response that can assist you in responding effectively should the unforeseen occur.

> **Challenging Behavior:**
>
> Distracting, disruptive, or dangerous behavior that interferes with the student's learning or the learning of others.

Breaking Tradition

Over the years, we've observed patterns in how educators tend to respond to challenging student behavior. We like to use the analogy of camps to describe the patterns that occur. As you read the descriptions of the camps in this chapter, don't fear if you currently attend or have previously attended one of the less desirable camps. We've visited some of these camps over the course of our careers too but with experience and mentorship have found the camp that serves students and educators best.

Camp catchall: At this camp, educators are trying all the things all the time! Educators here are trying to be supportive yet have no clear plan or roadmap of how to do so. As a result, they end up being very inconsistent and ineffective in their responses to challenging behaviors.

Camp emotion: Educators in this camp tend to be emotional in their responses to challenging student behavior. They tend to utilize traditional punitive punishment procedures and will continue to use these procedures even when student behavior does not improve over time.

Camp support: This camp is the happiest to attend for both students and educators! Here, educators utilize consistent interventions, which are responsive, restorative, and investigative. These educators plan responses to challenging behaviors, pre-teach these to their students, and follow through with planned responses. They avoid emotional reactions, engage in practices that support students during crises, and investigate past student behavior with the goal of understanding and preventing future challenges.

Ideally, we all want to be part of Camp Support as it is the most effective and, well, supportive place to be. To get there, though, we need to first break some traditions.

If you remember, we defined consequences in the previous chapter as the *outcome* that occurs immediately after a behavior that either increases or decreases the behavior over time. Consequences may punish or reinforce a behavior. We also discussed that consequences and punishment aren't necessarily the same thing, though the terms tend to be used interchangeably. However, within the school setting, traditional consequences for challenging behaviors tend to be provided with the intention of punishing the student. Sometimes we can get stuck in the mindset that all we need to do to motivate students not to engage in challenging behaviors again is to provide a "consequence." However, this results in the implementation of consequences that are misapplied, overused, and unresponsive to student needs.

Misapplied

Traditional responses to challenging behaviors are often misapplied. This means that our strategy might be effective in stopping the behavior in the moment, but over time it might reinforce the behavior and contribute to it occurring more often or at a higher intensity. This is more likely to result if we don't make any other changes within the environment, consider student needs, or teach alternative skills.

Examples:

Jorge has a strong need to connect with adults and has gone all morning without sustained quality interactions with an adult. He now begins engaging in disruptive behavior, such as roaming the room and knocking items off desks and shelves. We might respond to Jorge's behavior by saying "Why don't you go take a walk with Ms. P" or "Maybe you and Mr. T should go shoot some hoops to help you regulate." While prompting a break or change in activity is a common response, it carries some flaws. Specifically, if Jorge takes the walk with Ms. P or shoots hoops with Mr. T. and the disruptive behavior stops, then it stopped because we met the need by way of the problem behavior. In short, the problem behavior resulted in meeting the need (connection with an adult) and we are likely to see it continue to occur over time. This is especially true if we don't consider how we can meet the need preventatively or make other adjustments to the environment in the future.

Sarah is easily overwhelmed by writing tasks, specifically those that require writing by hand for a sustained time. When she engages in disruptive behavior during these tasks, her teacher consistently sends her to the buddy room (without her task) where she sits and listens to an ELA lesson. The disruptive behavior stops when the expectation to complete the task is removed. Over time, we are likely to see this disruptive behavior occur or even increase when there are other tasks she finds difficult and wants to escape.

Many of our "traditional" consequences in a school setting are ineffective because they don't consider that behavior is functional. Remember, it meets a need and serves a purpose – to assist in getting what we want or need and away from what we don't want or find aversive. All too often, well-meaning educators might think or say: "I'll just ignore him! Or I won't let him escape! Then I won't reinforce the behavior!"

This is called *extinction* – where we attempt to withhold the reinforcement (attention, access to tangibles, escape, sensory) and make the behavior ineffective in meeting the student's needs. *This is not what we should be doing as it isn't safe or realistic within the school setting.* There are many, us included, who also argue that extinction procedures, especially when used in isolation, are not ethical. When this approach is utilized, you are more likely to see an increase in the intensity of behaviors used to meet the students' needs – the behaviors will get worse.

So, what should you do? We've just explained how our well-intended responses may be reinforcing the behaviors but that we shouldn't withhold reinforcement for the behaviors – make your minds up, Amanda and Danielle!

It's okay to reinforce the behavior. Often, that is preferable. What we need to do is consider the consequences (outcomes) that might be reinforcing the behaviors and adjust our proactive strategies accordingly. *We are only misapplying our responses if we continue to put all our energy into responding to challenging behaviors, don't consider and implement preventative strategies, and don't reflect on whether the consequences are misapplied.*

Overused

Another reason that traditional consequences aren't effective in reducing challenging behaviors is that they are overused. Many school settings provide consequences for all the things and fail to include preventative strategies to increase student success. If our students are constantly losing privileges or recess minutes, being sent from the room, having their parents called, or given detentions, why should they care about school anymore? They aren't successful and often end up in a cycle of thinking "This is just what happens in this classroom. I always get into trouble."

To set our students up for success, we need to be aware of the balance of prevention strategies to consequence strategies in place. Ideally, 80% of our practices should focus on supporting and preventing challenging behaviors. Everything we've talked about thus far in this book has been focused on ensuring that you know and understand what strategies to have in place and why they should be in place. We need the right preventative strategies to gain the best outcomes for our students.

Unresponsive

Traditional consequences are often unresponsive to individual student communication needs, potential trauma histories, missing skills, and so much more! When we raise our voice, threaten to call home, get into their personal space, or move their name down on the public stoplight, we are reacting in an unresponsive way. Losing recess minutes doesn't help a student to learn missing executive functioning skills. Providing reprimands and using your proximity to intimidate a student doesn't help a student who has experienced trauma feel safe and supported. Writing their name on the board doesn't help a student to maintain their dignity. Forcing compliance on a student who is dysregulated doesn't help them to regulate and return to using their thinking brain. Ignoring or turning your back on a student doesn't help a student who has been neglected or had inconsistent adults in their life. And an out-of-school suspension doesn't help the student who wants out of school because everything is so aversive! None of these "consequences" helps or improves behavior, yet they occur every day in educational settings.

There seems to be a mindset that if we don't apply a "consequence," nothing has been done to address the behavior. However, we need to be thinking further than this and consider if the consequence is helping the student with what they need help with. Ross Greene, author of *Lost at School*, posits that "Kids do well if they can" (2014, p. 10), and we agree! You can't punish missing skills into a student. When we hold to the mindset that students are choosing to engage in challenging behaviors, we assume that they have all the skills they need. Just think back for a moment on our earlier discussion in Chapter 2 about executive functioning skills. We as adults have varying strengths and weaknesses in executive functioning skills, so it stands to reason that many of our students do as well. So, be cautious of applying a consequence just because, as it likely isn't helping the students with what they actually need help with. Instead, consider what skills we might need to teach, and again, what preventative strategies need to be beefed up to increase their success.

There are of course times when we can't continue to teach while a student is engaging in challenging behavior within our room. There are times when a student is dysregulated and going to recess is not a good idea. But, when we misapply and overuse consequences or we use them in a way that is unresponsive to student needs, well, that is when our applied consequences become *punitive*. When this happens, student frustration is likely to increase. They were upset before, but now they feel targeted, unsupported, and as if they can't possibly be successful – so they quit trying. Now, we've likely increased their motivation to go against the classroom or school expectations, and can you blame them? When we get stuck in the mindset that they will eventually "learn their lesson" and "not do it again," we continue to increase the harshness of our consequences when behavior doesn't change. As a result, we push the student further and further from the classroom community, tanking their motivation and harming all rapport.

Common Motivations for Ineffective Responses

Even though there are decades of research with supporting evidence of the ineffectiveness of traditional consequences on improving student behavior, our educational systems continue to respond in traditional, punitive, and unproductive ways. Let's discuss some of the factors that motivate us to continue to respond in these ways.

We want the behavior to stop.

Our students struggle with this same skill, which is called *delayed discounting*, where we delay a larger later (potential) reward for a smaller sooner (more assured) reward. In the heat of the moment, we aren't usually thinking about the long-term benefits of responding in a more thoughtful way. We have an urgent need (the behavior to stop in this moment), so we do whatever we think will make it happen. Unfortunately, this usually doesn't help us in the long run.

It feels personal.

Usually, things feel personal when we have a deeper issue going on. Certain beliefs, values, past traumas, experiences, and just the daily stressors of life can make those moments feel more personal to us. Usually, though, students aren't aware or consciously thinking of these things, but this can also help us pinpoint certain skills they might be missing that we can then teach.

They need to know their behavior is not okay.

How many students can spew out, verbatim, what they should have done instead? Or what the classroom expectations are that they violated? Yep. . .most. The issue is that they are missing skills, they haven't generalized the skills, and/or the behavior is meeting their need. Regardless, this means we must figure out what that need is and teach/reinforce an alternative way to meet it.

We want to make an example out of them.

If we must use a student's tough moments to teach our other students what happens when you violate an expectation, we aren't doing a good enough job teaching those expectations. We shouldn't be commanding a student to go to the office or the think spot just to show our other students what happens when you keep interrupting a lesson.

We want to show that we are the ones in control.

Losing control of our emotions and behaviors is quite the opposite of being in control. We can't control a student's behavior, only influence it. What have we controlled if we react in a way that ruins any rapport built? What have we controlled if they don't want to come to our class anymore? What have we controlled if they now avoid asking for help when they are struggling because they don't trust us to support them?

We want to show the other students we will protect their learning.

Losing your cool when lessons are interrupted doesn't scream "I'm a protector." The best way to protect our class's learning time is to problem-solve why that student is having difficulty and make changes so they are more likely to be successful in the future. The result? Less interruptions and more learning opportunities which is *true* protection of learning in the long-term!

We need a break.

Very fair! We all engage in behaviors to get away from things that are aversive. Sometimes we get stuck in this cycle where we engage in behaviors to escape students with challenging behavior because we are often met with problem behavior, but it's up to us to break this dynamic, not the student. We reinforce our own faulty thinking when we react ("See? They are so disrespectful" said to a student who is simply reacting to our own unhelpful behaviors). If we then send the student out of the classroom, that reinforces our behavior because we temporarily escaped the "problem" and feelings of frustration. However, because of this, we are more likely to react that way in the future. The best break will be given when you learn to effectively de-escalate and help get students back on track more quickly, or, better yet, keep them engaged so you don't need a break from them in the first place!

We think alternatives will take too much time, take too much effort, or won't be effective.

We hear that! Learning a new skill does feel tiring and time-consuming, and the last thing we need is to feel like we have more on our already full plate. But take a moment to calculate all the minutes you spend dealing with students who are disengaged. Calculate the time spent on redirects. On calls home. On incident reports. On team meetings. You will likely continue to spend more time on punitive, ineffective consequences to challenging behavior, than if you commit to making a change. The investment comes when you put in the time *now* to save more time *later*.

The parents just need to be inconvenienced.

Parents have their own sources of motivation and underdeveloped skills – just like us and our students. Making their life more difficult is not likely to result in long-term positive behavior change. In addition, they have very little impact in the moment on their student's specific behavior every Wednesday at 1 p.m. during art.

We want to hold them "accountable."

Good news! You can still have boundaries and be well-liked by your students. The bad news? You can't hold someone accountable who doesn't have the skills to consistently meet the current expectations. But more good news – the way we respond will help to hold them accountable more than any other traditional type of consequence. Making sure we are responding in a way that repairs harm done, while collaboratively identifying the skill they need to learn to independently navigate stressors and avoid violating school expectations will help them to become independent members of society.

We don't know what else to do.

Nobody does, until they do. Remember, behavior can be changed. Current skills can be strengthened, and new skills can be learned!

Ultimately, we can respond in a way to challenging student behavior that attempts to meet their needs as well as our own.

The Mirror: Taking a Long, Hard Look

Consider what happens when firefighters arrive on the scene. Do they start yelling "Who started this?" or "Why didn't you remember to unplug your space heater?" No, they immediately work to put out the fire. They save the investigation for later when safety has been ensured. Likewise, if there is a medical emergency, does the doctor come into the room blaming the patient for eating too much processed food? No, they stabilize them and provide them the care that they need. Just like firefighters and medical personnel, we need to take an approach to managing challenging student behavior that is supportive, maintains safety, and avoids confrontation.

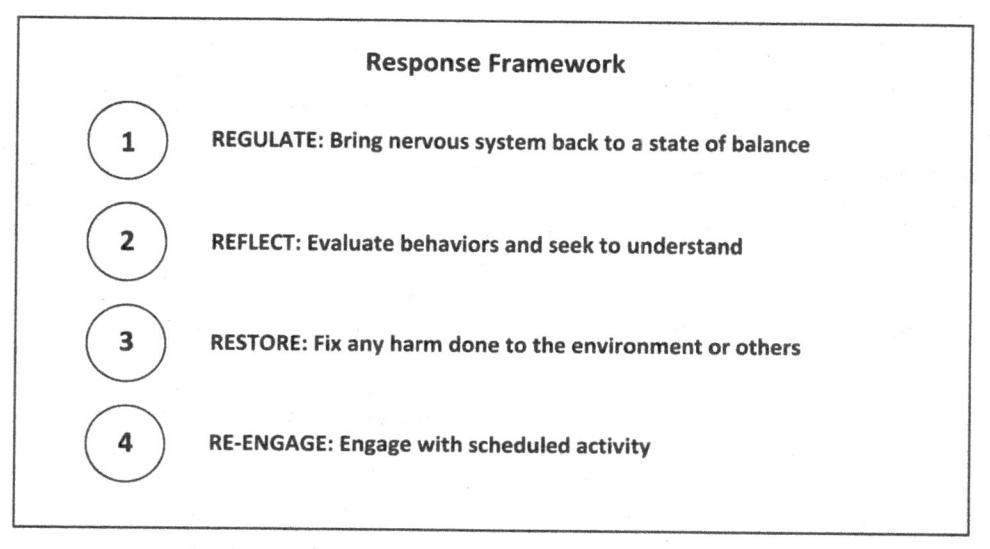

Our plan, or framework for effectively addressing challenging student behavior, should involve regulating, reflecting, restoring, and re-engaging – for both the student and ourselves. We will talk about each of these in detail later in this chapter. For now, we need to first discuss the importance of maintaining our own rational behavior when students are engaging in distracting, disruptive, or dangerous behaviors.

For every student behavior, there is a corresponding staff behavior. We can think of this as a chain that links and influences our future behaviors. A challenging student behavior occurs, and we say or do something in response. We might redirect them verbally to their seat, we might say something like "That's not appropriate," we might ask "How can I help?" or we might just ignore it and continue teaching. This influences what the student says or does next.

What we do or say has the power to either escalate or de-escalate the challenging behavior both in the moment and over time. The more we are aware of our own behavior and its influence on student behavior, the more likely we are to respond in a way that supports and de-escalates challenging behavior quickly and effectively. To assist you in effectively regulating yourself, we've included a reflection form in the appendix (see Form 6.1).

Responding Rather than Reacting

When faced with challenging student behavior we, as the adults, can either react or respond. There are clear differences between the two, and we want to choose responses over reactions. Let's dive into the differences between the two.

Reactions are determined in the moment without thought or planning. These tend to be in the heat of the moment decisions and focus heavily on applying consequences for challenging behavior. As they aren't pre-planned, reactions are usually unpredictable and inconsistent. For example, if you've never taught your students what will happen if they become dysregulated or misbehave and you keep reacting differently – sometimes raising your voice, sometimes taking away privileges, sometimes threatening to call home – the classroom quickly becomes a place that doesn't feel safe and supportive. Reactions are emotional in nature often manifesting in the form of raising our voices, getting into the space of students, and even behaving irrationally as our amygdala takes over our functioning. We might even humiliate or embarrass students by failing to consider student perspective, skillset, or unique needs at that moment. When we react, we tend to focus entirely on the challenging behavior, engaging in "No," "Stop," "Don't" instructions, which requires our students then to infer what behavior needs to be engaged in (think back to our discussion of expectations/expected behaviors in Chapter 4). Finally, reactions are harmful and increase challenging behaviors in the moment as they escalate the situation.

When we react, we are essentially handing our student a pair of boxing gloves and letting them know that we are prepared to fight and win. This tells our students that it is time for them to prioritize their safety. Many of our "difficult" kids continue to be "difficult" because we as adults allow our emotions to take over our actions and engage in inflexible behaviors, often doubling down on gaining their compliance. This added layer makes things worse for the student. If the spelling worksheet was already challenging for them, it's now worse because the adult is making the situation worse. Does it really matter in that moment if they complete the spelling worksheet? Chances are at this point they're too dysregulated to do so – their thinking brain is no longer in control – and neither is the adult's when they are reacting!

Think instead about all the skills you as the adult could be modeling and teaching surrounding challenges for your students. Those are more important than a spelling worksheet! And, if we are going to hold Johnny to such high expectations, shouldn't we do the same for ourselves? Yes! We absolutely should, which is why it is imperative that we respond, not react, to challenging student behavior.

Responses are predetermined, planned, consistent, and predictable outcomes! Outcomes become predictable when we have taught them ahead of time and when we experience them each time we engage in the behavior. Because things are predictable and predetermined, there's no harm if we follow through – this will help build trust. They won't hate you in the long-run if you follow through on something you heavily pre-taught – they will hate you if you become emotional, make empty threats, and come up with consequences in the moment. Also, when these responses are predictable, consistent, and pre-determined, we can get back to teaching a whole lot faster because the student already knows the plan, and therefore, they are likely to be less emotional and disruptive. Responses are also nonemotional. This is just simply what occurs after the profanity, derogatory names, or destruction of the writing assignment. We aren't flying off the handle, because we now have a procedure in place, a routine if you will, that we go through after something like this happens.

Responses place the emphasis of focus on engaging in appropriate behaviors, or replacement behaviors for the challenging behaviors. Most educators are in the teaching business because they care about students and want to help them. Therefore, we can (and should) use this incident as an opportunity to investigate with the student what skills they might be struggling with, what their motivation was for engaging in the challenging behavior, and what we can teach and reinforce instead. By doing so, we are now considering their perspectives and needs and ultimately identifying preventative strategies we can put into place.

Reactions often send a *big* message for our students who have experienced traumatic events or inconsistent caregivers. We are now acting in ways that reinforce their thinking or beliefs about staff – we are essentially proving them right! "These people are unpredictable, unsafe, and don't care about my needs!" But by *responding* you build trust and safety in that moment, providing new evidence to them that a calm, supportive, and consistent adult does exist in their life – that's you!

Activity: Reaction or Response?

 Read the following scenarios and determine whether the staff behavior is more characteristic of a reaction or a response:

Statement	Reaction	Response
"This hallway behavior is unacceptable. I don't know how many times I have to tell you. If it continues you will lose part of your recess time."		
"Class, we didn't meet the hallway expectations just then. When this happens, we know the outcome is that we reflect on why it was difficult, and we go back and try it again."		
"I understand you still don't want to do math. We will conference after class to problem-solve. I'm here when you are ready."		

(continued)

Activity: Reaction or Response? *(continued)*

"Oh, you still are refusing to do math? You know what that means – you get to miss part of your recess and chat with me after class."

(Hands on hips) "Do I have to call your mom? I don't think she would be too happy with what you just said."

"I have tried to problem-solve with you, but you seem to be still upset. I'm going to circle back in about 5 minutes to check on you."

"If you stop, you can earn an extra point."

(Raised voice) "You are this close to earning yourself a detention."

"You're not in trouble, I just want to talk."

"I'll give you some time and space."

(Yelling) "Knock it off!"

(Kneeling down next to the desk) "I care about helping you make the right choice that gets you closer to your goals."

"Go to the office right now before I have someone come escort you."

(Raised brows) "It looks like you're choosing to make a bad choice. That's unfortunate. . ."

(Relaxed posture) "I hear you that this doesn't feel fair, but I need to enforce the expectations to keep everyone feeling safe."

(Walking quickly towards the student) "What did you just say to me?!"

(Whispering) "What would be most helpful right now? Working through this with me after class or taking a moment to cool off first and trying it in a moment?"

Checking Our Communication

A response at its core is about effective communication. You can't problem-solve with a student if you can't effectively communicate with them, nor can you establish trust or help them learn new skills. You also can't assist them in regulating when the need arises if you can't communicate in a way that meets their needs. Think back to our discussion of the brain (Chapter 2); when our prefrontal cortex is in control, we are rational, able to think before we act, and are available for learning. When our limbic system is engaged because we perceive a physical, emotional, or psychological threat, our emotional brain takes charge, and we are no longer rational or available for learning. When an individual's emotional brain is taking over, it's like losing bars of service on our cell phone. Communication, both expressive and receptive, becomes far more difficult. They aren't understanding everything being said, you might struggle to understand them, and everyone can easily become frustrated. This is where our communication skills matter most and have the greatest impact on de-escalating a situation.

We have three core communication types to be aware of and use effectively during challenging student behavior: verbal, paraverbal, and nonverbal. Verbal refers to the actual words that you use to communicate your message. Paraverbal refers to your tone of voice, your cadence, and your volume when speaking. And nonverbal refers to your body language, proximity, eye contact, and use of touch.

	Reaction-Based Behaviors	Response-Based Behaviors
Nonverbal	• Tense or posturing • Furrowed brows or frowning • Cornering or getting into space • Hovering • Facing head-on • Crossed arms • Pointing or shaking finger/fist • Glaring, staring, rolling eyes, side eye, or "teacher look" • Physical touch w/out consent • Quick movements	• Relaxed posture • Relaxed affect • Giving physical space • Getting to eye level (if appropriate) • Facing same direction or parallel • Hands clasped or relaxed by side • Non-threatening eye contact or averted gaze • Avoiding touch or w/consent • Slow, confident movements • Remembering to breathe
Paraverbal	• Raised voice or yelling • Threatening tone • Fast and uneven rate	• Low or normal volume • Kind, yet confident tone • Slow and steady
Verbal	• In public • "Wishy-washy" • Lectures or long explanations • Rapid-fire directions • Threats or ultimatums • Bribes • Judgmental • Sarcasm • Disparaging or dismissive remarks • Interrupting • No/stop/don't statements	• In private • Clear and brief • Allowing time to process • Labeling what's happening • Validation • Empathy • Encouragement • Answering information-seeking questions • Positive limit setting

By engaging in solid communication in the form of response-based behaviors, we will naturally model (mirror) what we want the student to do with their body. This prompts the child to engage in regulatory behavior and supports their brain in forming new connections. We are also modeling how we want our students to respond to their world. So, model for them how it's possible to stay calm in the face of a stressor, communicate with respect, and treat someone with dignity even if you disagree with what they are doing. Be what you want to see! You want quiet? Lower your voice and be quiet. You want kind? Be kind no matter the circumstance.

Finally, in the words of Dr. Greg Hanley (2024), a well-known and respected behavior analyst, ". . .prioritize safety, rapport, and the televisibility of what we do above all else." Essentially, if your interactions with a student were broadcast for all the world to see, would you be proud of how you responded? Would the world be? If it doesn't feel good, then you probably shouldn't be doing it. Aim for responding to needs rather than reacting to behavior and you'll be off to a good start!

Activity: Reflecting on Your Needs

 After reading the previous information, reflect on how you typically react or respond when your students engage in challenging behaviors.

What things do you say? (Verbal communication.)

-
-
-
-
-
-

How is it said? (Paraverbal communication.)

-
-
-
-
-

What do you do? (Nonverbal communication.)

-
-
-

-
-
-

Which behaviors are you committed to working on? List them here.

_____

_____

Regulating: The Art of Defusing

Before we break down a plan for effective responses to challenging behaviors, please know that we understand what it is like to experience challenging behaviors in the classroom. We know what it is like to have lessons interrupted, to be called every name in the book, to have classrooms destroyed, and be physically injured by students. While *we* have spent a significant portion of our careers working with students with the *most* challenging behaviors, these situations can and do occur within any educational setting. The key to limiting this likelihood, as we've repeatedly stated throughout this book, is to ensure we are effectively implementing preventative strategies. Universal supports, when implemented with fidelity, drastically reduce challenging behaviors by creating supportive, predictable, and safe environments where students' needs are preventatively met.

The framework we outline is effective for intervening to de-escalate challenging student behavior. Please keep in mind that this is intended to be a universal approach, meant to positively impact all students. Because we don't know your specific situation, we cannot provide specific insights. Therefore, you will need to adapt this approach to your classroom or individual students. Also, keep in mind that for students who repeatedly engage in dangerous challenging behaviors, you may need to involve other professionals in developing an individualized plan to increase appropriate replacement behaviors.

Why It's Effective

When a student's emotional brain begins to take control of their thoughts and actions, how and when we intervene has the power to either support and de-escalate or prolong and escalate the situation. Clearly, as we've discussed, we want to focus on utilizing effective responses early on to assist the student in regulating and returning to learning. When we do so, we are interacting in a way that is nonconfrontational. This creates a sense of safety, assists us in maintaining rapport with the student, and avoids the potential for re-traumatization. In addition, this framework of responses allows us to model for our students appropriate ways to respond to stressors in our environment.

This framework is easily adapted to respond to challenging student behavior – whether it be distracting, disruptive, or dangerous. This can be as simple as a quick redirect or a much lengthier process. The framework isn't rigid and allows for flexibility and differentiation. For example, consider being a passenger on a plane enroute to your favorite destination. If a storm were to hit, would you prefer the pilot who decides to rigidly hold the course despite the risk of harm and anxiety that may create? Or would you prefer the pilot who alters course to reduce anxiety and ensure a safe arrival? We'd prefer the pilot who would adjust based on new wind speed, loss of visibility, and risk of dangerous turbulence. We'd prefer the pilot who would make minor adjustments or completely divert the flight based on that flight's needs – not stick to a one-size-fits-all, rigid approach.

Developing Your Response Framework

Identifying and Leveling Behaviors

As we want to engage in planned and pre-taught responses rather than in-the-moment emotional reactions to challenging behaviors, we suggest you take the time to develop a response continuum as shown here that fits your classroom needs. Consider the common challenging behaviors that typically occur within your classroom for an individual or group of students, individualizing as needed. This template can be found in the appendix (see Form 6.2).

Mild Behaviors (Distracting)	Immediate Response (Regulating)	Follow-Up Response (Reflecting & Restoring)
Moderate Behaviors (Disruptive)	**Immediate Response**	**Follow-Up Response**
High-Magnitude Behaviors (Dangerous)	**Immediate Response**	**Follow-Up Response**

Start by considering behaviors that occur in your classroom that could be categorized as mild (distracting), moderate (disruptive), and high magnitude (dangerous). For clarity, let's take some time to define these levels of behaviors.

Mild behaviors: These behaviors tend to be distracting within the learning environment but do not interrupt the flow of your instruction. They may signal to you that a student is not engaged in the lesson or that something is amiss with a student, such as their emotional brain is taking control.

Examples of mild behaviors could include squirming in their seat, rocking, calling out an answer, tapping a pencil, leaving their seat to gather materials, or whispering to a peer. Now, without context, we may look at this list and think calling out is more than distracting. And yes, calling out during state testing could be disruptive. Or calling out 17 times in a 2-minute period could be more than distracting. But generally, when we are referring to mild behaviors, these do not significantly interrupt our teaching.

Mild behaviors can also include behaviors we might consider as demonstrating anxiety or frustration, such as putting their head down, crossing their arms, furrowing their brow, pushing their paper onto the floor, or refusing to work. Sometimes these mild behaviors are subtle, easy to miss, and even easier to misinterpret. These behaviors can appear to be deliberate, causing us to think "They're just refusing!" But these behaviors are important to notice and respond to effectively! Often, these subtle behaviors are precursors for moderate or high-magnitude behaviors. How we respond at the mild level very much influences the escalation cycle.

A note of caution here: more times than we can count, we have observed teaching staff excessively redirecting students for distracting behaviors that *are not* interfering with the student's ability to focus or complete their task or for their peers to do so. Take, for example, a student who quietly rocks in their seat during whole-group instruction. He engages in opportunities to respond and is responding accurately, indicating he is engaged and understanding the lesson. His peers are also appropriately responding. It would be inappropriate to repeatedly interrupt the lesson to correct his rocking behavior simply because we, the adult, find it annoying. That's a teacher problem, not a student problem. Adults and students alike will engage in self-stimulatory behaviors that feel good. So, we caution you to ensure that you spend your energy on behaviors that are signaling that something is wrong or are interrupting your instruction.

Moderate behaviors: These behaviors do not present risk of harm to the student or to others, but they do disrupt our ability to continue instruction. They may signal to you that the student's prefrontal cortex is no longer fully functioning and that higher-magnitude behaviors may occur.

Behaviors we might observe at this level include statements of refusal ("I'm not doing this" or "This is stupid"), challenging statements ("No" or "I don't care"), crying, repeatedly calling out during instruction, roaming the room, cursing, screaming, or knocking items over. Students engaging in moderate behaviors may seem more emotional than the situation calls for and may express that in a way that involves more overt (externalizing) behaviors.

Behaviors may also be considered moderate if you've already provided your immediate response at the mild level and the student continues to engage in them. For example, if a student was calling out and you responded with your pre-taught reminder of expectations and he continues to call out, then the behavior may now be considered moderate as it is becoming increasingly more difficult to provide instruction while it continues to occur.

High-magnitude behaviors: These behaviors are dangerous or pose an imminent risk of harm to themselves or others. They signal to you that the student is no longer rational and that their emotional brain is currently in control. At this point you must stop instruction and shift to maintain safety.

Behaviors we might observe at this level include physical aggression directed at themselves or others, property destruction, or elopement from the building. Another note of caution: it is important not to assume all acts of physical aggression, property destruction, or elopement are high magnitude. We can easily provide a response that is disproportionate to the situation and harm our rapport with the student. For example, there is a big difference in knocking over a chair versus picking it up, aiming, and throwing it at another person. There is also a big difference between a 5-year-old doing this versus a 14-year-old. Each situation will be dynamic, and this is another reason you should have planned, but flexible responses already identified.

Identifying Immediate and Follow-Up Responses

After identifying your mild, moderate, and high-magnitude behaviors, we suggest then identifying your immediate in-the-moment responses and any additional follow-up responses for each level. As a reminder, note there is no way to prepare for every situation that arises, and in many cases, pivoting from the original plan may be most appropriate. Your ability to effectively navigate these situations will come with experience and continued learning.

Immediate (in-the-moment) responses should focus on *de-escalation and regulation.* The goal is to ensure that the student returns to calm with their prefrontal cortex in control. At each level, we provide prompts, redirects, and supports that can de-escalate the behavior. We want these to be *appropriate and proportionate* to the student and situation. For example, if a student is attempting to hit me, I'm not going to give them a hug in that moment. I will, however, provide support through my words and actions, with clear directions, and by maintaining safety. Likewise, if a student is tapping their pencil, I'm not sending them to the office and lecturing them. My immediate response should be *pre-determined and pre-taught.* This is imperative as it creates predictability and safety for students and ensures we will not react emotionally. Further, because these responses are pre-determined and pre-taught, it makes providing those responses (outcomes) quicker and easier in the moment.

Follow-up responses should involve *investigation and restoration*, if needed. These should be supportive rather than punitive. Remember, we already learned that consequences often end up becoming punitive when they are misapplied, overused, and unresponsive to student needs. To avoid this, spend time reflecting and investigating why the student engaged in the behavior so that we can work collaboratively to prevent it in the future. Additionally, we should identify what the student, and/or others need to do to restore any harm that was done. *We will cover the follow-up responses of reflecting and restoring in more detail later in this chapter.*

Suggested Immediate Response Framework

Let's talk through what this could look like in real life. In this section, we will walk you through various effective responses at the mild, moderate, and high-magnitude behavior levels. Note, these recommendations incorporate best practices in verbal de-escalation and our combined years of experience supporting students in crisis. Additionally, these recommendations will assist you in intervening early and are likely to prevent further escalation.

When a student or group of students engages in challenging behavior, one of the most effective first steps we can take is to pause. Yes, you read that correctly. Unless a student is in imminent danger, we want you to pause.

Benefits of pausing:

1. *Self-regulation:* It gives *you* a chance to self-regulate. It takes only one wrong action or statement to destroy rapport and all the amazing prevention efforts you have put in place. So, in that pause, you're going to remind yourself "I can do this, they are just having a hard time meeting expectations, I can figure out why, here we go."

2. *Student regulation:* It provides the disruptor a moment to chill out. Some students are accustomed to adults providing a rapid-fire reaction and immediately engaging in that back-and-forth power struggle. When we pause, we are less likely to engage in this struggle and our pause shows the student that we aren't going to do so.

3. *Modeling:* It is a skill you can model for your students. When they are stressed, you want them to stop and think about what to do next and potential outcomes of their actions. This is a way to model that.

4. *Avoids a prompt-dependency situation:* If we insert a little time delay, it gives the student a moment to figure things out for themselves, engage in those executive skills, and work through the issue on their own. This will only occur if you have been teaching and practicing those skills with them but resist the urge to fix everything all the time for them.

So, take the pause and take care of yourself first so that you can take care of others more effectively. And yes, you may be thinking "Yeah, yeah, I get it, but what do I do when they yell or refuse?" The first thing you should do is to ensure that *you* are regulating. You need to take that pause to engage in behaviors that physically create space between the student behavior (trigger) and your response. The steps we are discussing – regulating, reflecting, restoring, and re-engaging apply to us as much as they do to our students!

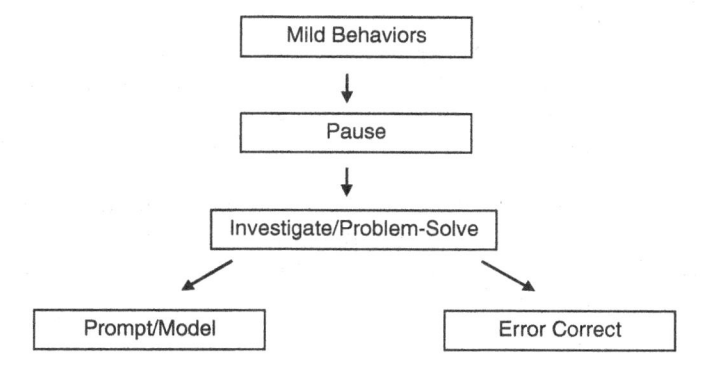

Mild behaviors: When an issue arises within the classroom, you may or may not immediately know what is at play. If you don't know why they put their head down or why they left their seat, pause, assess what behavior level is being demonstrated, and then investigate and problem-solve. From here you can then prompt alternative behavior, and/or error correct. Let's go through each of these in detail.

Investigate and Problem-Solve

You've paused enough to notice that in this situation your student is demonstrating mild behaviors. Perhaps they are showing subtle signs of frustration such as furrowing their eyebrows, scowling, putting their head down, looking away, or rocking and you now know that something is amiss. This is our best point of intervention! If we wait to intervene until higher magnitude behaviors occur, until they are more dysregulated, we are less likely to intervene as effectively. But here, at the earliest stages, there is a lot we can do.

Our first step should be to check in with the student. Maybe they put their head down and are off-task, or maybe they don't have the skills to complete the task or navigate a stressor, but you don't realize it. If you were to say, "You can do it now or during recess" and jump right to limit setting, that just might add stress to the situation and escalate them! We need to start with a more supportive and investigative response because keeping them in from recess won't fix the problem if they don't have the skills to complete the task. Being supportive will also help them to feel heard, and it increases the chances they will tell you what's wrong. From there you can problem-solve solutions and negotiate expectations.

Being supportive includes listening with empathy to our students. We don't have to agree with what they are feeling or why they are upset, but we do need to school our verbal, paraverbal, and nonverbal language to convey empathy. This means we behave in a way that is nonjudgmental and, in that moment, we provide them our undivided attention. We are listening to understand so that we can problem-solve a solution with them. Remember, our goal is to de-escalate and to help them regulate so that they can return to their routine and learning.

> *Aim to check in, acknowledge the* why, *and then meet the need – this is a great rule of thumb. Show empathy and recognize the student's problem and communicate concern.*

In Chapter 2, we identify efficiency and skill as the two primary factors that influence whether an individual uses a desirable or challenging behavior in any given situation. The students who engage in problem behaviors most are usually missing some type of skill as it relates to that specific trigger – be it social, communication, executive function, or academic. This creates a need, likely to gain assistance or to get away from the challenging task or situation altogether, and we see the behavior they use to meet that need. It's hard to navigate a situation when you don't have the skills to do it. In other cases, a student may have the necessary skills but is motivated to use the challenging behavior to meet a need because it is more efficient than the desirable behavior.

Prompt, Model, and Honor

For some situations, simply reminding the student of the expected behavior may be all that is needed. This can be accomplished with a gentle prompt to engage in the expected behavior, and if they do, you can follow up with reinforcement. For example, "Remember we are working independently, not with our friends. Is there something I can help you with? No? Okay – please get back to work." (Student obliges.) "Thank you for re-focusing."

At this level, we can offer choices or remind the student of available choices within or across the activity. Be sure to honor the choice they make. Humor can be very effective for some students, and not at all for others. It's important to know your students before using humor to interrupt and redirect. We can also use our proximity as a prompt, sometimes without much else as a way of encouraging desired behaviors. Think back to our discussion of active supervision and the role of proximity when scanning, prompting, and reinforcing behaviors. This doesn't mean you are threatening in your proximity and posture – you're just closer.

Other useful strategies we can utilize at this level include prompting with a pre-taught signal. This could be a way for the student to communicate a need to you, such as they need time or space, or help. Other times, a signal could be used as a reminder to engage in an expected behavior. For example, if Kyle frequently calls out during whole group instruction, rather than verbally reminding him to raise his hand, I could make eye contact and lift my hand in a gesture to prompt the expected behavior, or I could point to a visual reminder in the room to raise his hand. Either way, I'm helping Kyle to meet an expected behavior during whole group instruction and continuing to provide instruction.

Error Correct

We can utilize error correction as a method of nonconfrontationally correcting the behavior of a single student or a group of students. When correcting a behavior, we need to avoid saying things like "Don't run, stop, don't do that, no." Just like when we develop our expectations, we want to avoid the no, stop, don'ts! When we phrase our corrections this way, we are requiring the student, who may already be beginning to lose rationality, to make an inference to determine what they should do. Instead, remove that barrier and clearly state what they need to do.

When we correct an academic error, we provide feedback, prompt the correction to be made, check for understanding, reinforce the skill, and re-teach as needed. We should correct behavioral errors with a similar format. Specifically, we should remind the student of the expectation, prompt them to engage in it (or re-do), and provide low-level reinforcement. For example, "The expectation is that we walk. Please go back and walk." (Student does so.) "That's much better. Thank you."

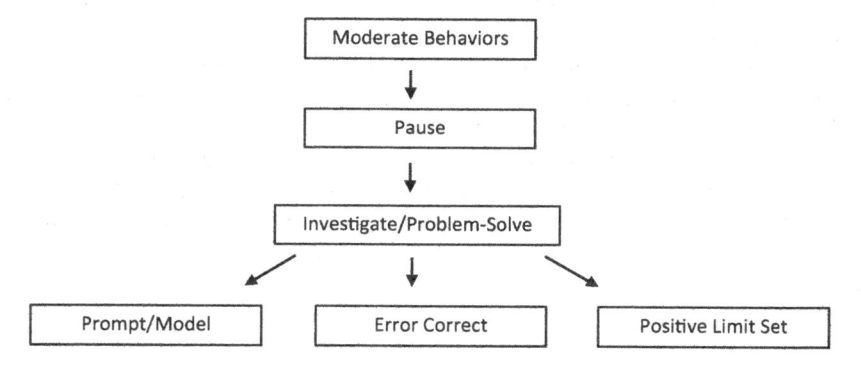

Moderate behaviors: When a student or group of students engage in disruptive behaviors that impede your ability to continue teaching, we should initially follow the same response plan of pausing before investigating and problem-solving. If needed, we can then prompt or model expected behaviors, replacement behaviors, or previously taught strategies, exactly as we would at the mild level. Where this differs is that we may not be able to use a pre-taught signal while continuing to teach. We likely will need to check in privately with the student at this level, as their behavior is telling us that they are slightly more dysregulated. Again, our goal is to assist them in regulating, so our response needs to still be supportive. If appropriate, we can utilize error correction procedures at the individual or group level. At the moderate level, we also have the option of using positive limit setting.

Positive Limit Setting

There are times where we do need to clearly set limits. However, there are effective ways of doing so that increase the likelihood of the student changing their behavior. Conversely, there are ineffective ways that are likely to increase the intensity of student behavior and harm your rapport with the student. Setting a limit is not the same as giving an ultimatum or a threat and should not be coercive. Rather, focus on the positive outcomes. How and when we use limit setting has the potential to de-escalate an escalating situation or to make things far worse.

Examples of ultimatums or threats:

- "If you don't stop, I will have the principal come down here."
- "You can either do your work now or do it during recess."
- "Keep it up and I will call your mom."

Examples of positive limit setting:

- "When you put your phone away, then you can join the basketball game."
- "When you lower your voice, then I can help you."
- "You're interrupting. When you take a seat, I can help you with your work."

Limit setting is not about winning the power struggle. In fact, if you approach it in this way, you've already lost. Before using limit setting, consider if the student has the skills (academic, executive functioning) to do what you are asking them to do. If they don't, let it go. Prompt them instead to do something else. Is the limit you are setting valid and reasonable? Or is it arbitrary? Is holding this limit worth damaging your relationship with your student? Is it worth the battle? More than likely, it is not. So, drop the rope. It's okay to drop the demand and come back to it later. It's also okay to drop the demand and not come back to it later – to do things differently next time! We'd much rather let the student sit at his desk and skip that spelling worksheet than risk harm to himself or to others. Consider it this way: the student behavior is giving us valuable information about what is hard for them! We can use this to inform what we do differently and how we support them in the future.

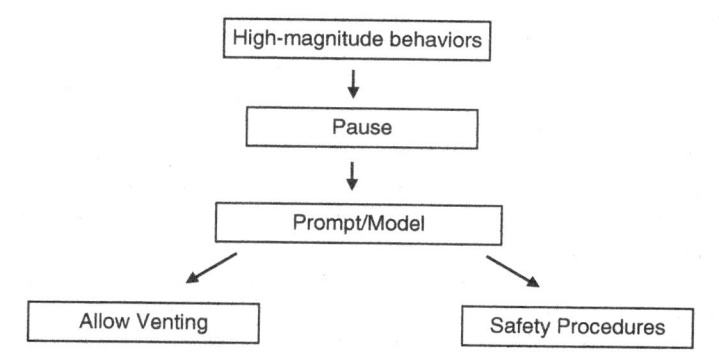

High-magnitude behaviors: These behaviors pose a risk of harm to the student or others and can be the most challenging for staff to effectively respond to. Our immediate response to these behaviors is to, again, pause long enough to ensure that we are regulating and ready to follow our response plan. We do not want to emotionally react! Responding rather than reacting can be the most challenging at this level, especially when behaviors are particularly dangerous.

As you look at the previous flow chart, you may think that we should jump straight to safety procedures, rather than prompting or modeling. However, our prompting and modeling at this level is going to focus on maintaining safety and working toward emotional regulation. When possible, we are going to prompt previously taught coping strategies or movement to a safer location. For example, "Let's move to the cool down area," "Breathe with me (points to nose)," or pointing to the figure 8 breathing visual while taking a deep breath.

When high-magnitude behaviors occur, the student's emotional brain is in control. This means their ability to process language and communicate their needs is significantly diminished. Therefore, our staff response is to limit our talking. We will provide only necessary instructions, and we will use short, clear, directive statements, such as "Walk with me" or "I need you to sit." We will allow time and space for the student to process and follow prompts. *We are* not *teaching them anything at this time. They are not available for learning, and trying to teach, reason, or problem-solve with them will only increase frustration – for all involved.*

If the student is unable to follow prompts or modeling and is expending their emotional energy verbally and/or physically, allow venting and follow your building safety procedures. This may include calling for support (from administration, the school psychologist, school counselor, behavioral support staff, or other predetermined staff).

When a student engages in high-magnitude behaviors, we need to consider maintaining their safety, the safety of other students, and staff safety. We also need to attempt to maintain their dignity. This could include removing peers from the room or prompting the student in crisis to leave with us. Note, room clears are far less disruptive to students when the procedure for engaging in them is taught and practiced, and materials are ready and accessible. Likewise, if the procedure for leaving to access a safe space in the building is taught, practiced, and then prompted early in the escalation cycle, a student in crisis is far more likely to engage in that procedure.

Often, while venting, students will make provocative statements. These may be hard for staff not to respond to, but it's important that we don't get into a back-and-forth with a student who isn't rational. Rather than arguing, "You don't mean that" or "That's not kind," offer periodic statements of support such as "I hear you" or "I understand." When a student is at their peak, less is more in terms of speaking. We can validate what they are feeling without agreeing with what they are saying. But trying to argue with a student that they don't really hate their mother or that they can't possibly follow through with that threat does no good in that moment. Staying quiet and not getting sucked into the student's irrational state can be challenging. In our experience, this is a skill that staff need to learn and practice over time, as their need to "do something" often fuels their verbal barrage.

Sometimes, students will occasionally throw out an information-seeking question among all the other verbal and physical behaviors. When that happens, go ahead and answer that question. Just keep your answer short, simple, and clear.[1]

We should always rely on effective verbal, paraverbal, and nonverbal communication when responding to high-magnitude behaviors. In addition, we can also make environmental adjustments that assist us in maintaining safety and de-escalating such as removing items from the environment, changing environments, or switching out with other staff who have a better relationship with the student.

Additional Considerations

The goal is de-escalation and emotional safety. Not winning. It's not about gaining compliance, holding the demand, or bending them to your will.

Did you happen to notice in the previous descriptions of effective responses to challenging behaviors that we didn't focus on obtaining student compliance? None of the examples says something to the effect of "You will listen to me" or "You will do as you're told." Compliance isn't everything and if we engage in a power struggle, we are then making a huge withdrawal from the relationship bank. It's better to opt out, offer a different choice, or meet them in the middle to maintain your relationship and their dignity. Then, come back around outside of that moment to problem-solve what should be in place preventatively to keep this from occurring again in the future.

In addition, when we go straight to holding demands, we are more likely to see defiance – cursing, laughing, smirking, sarcasm. Students don't necessarily do this because it's worked to get them kicked out of the room or something similar. Oftentimes it's the only thing their brain can think of doing in the moment because they don't have any other solid skills in their repertoire to get their need met. They might be nervous, confused, embarrassed, or just uncomfortable and this is how they are expressing it.

---

[1]*When a student is engaging in high-magnitude behaviors, we* must *follow our state and district procedures in regard to safety interventions. If you are not aware of your district and state policy on specific safety procedures such as physical restraints and/or seclusion, we strongly encourage you to seek out that information. We are further obligated to follow regulations as well as the boundaries of our own training and qualifications. In addition, the use of restraints and/or seclusion carry a high risk of physical and psychological trauma. These procedures should be utilized as an absolute last resort and* never *for the purpose of compliance or punishment.*

We should also be cautious about using limit setting before investigating and problem-solving. This can easily burn bridges and harm rapport with the student. There's a reason they are engaging in challenging behavior, and especially at the mild level, we need to investigate and problem-solve. If we skip this and go straight to limit setting, we miss out on the opportunity to figure out what is really going on and that information is incredibly valuable in preventing the student from engaging in the behavior again in the future.

Regarding problem-solving, ensure that you aren't just engaging in surface-level problem-solving. For example, "What's wrong? Oh, it's boring. Well, boring things are part of life." If we dismiss their concerns, worries, or stressors, we are missing out on opportunities to identify the *why* behind tasks, activities, and the sometimes less-fun things in life. We also miss out on chances to work on perseverance and frustration tolerance – both important life skills.

Don't be afraid to celebrate the small wins, especially when students self-correct. If they engage in a challenging behavior, regardless of level, and then reflect and immediately correct their behavior, celebrate that!

Finally, when it comes to immediate responses to challenging behaviors, we should have a clear delineation between what is teacher (classroom) managed and what is office managed. Your school handbook may already outline this, but when things are overwhelming, it can be easy to escape the frustration by sending the student to the office. We, just like our students, engage in behaviors that help us to get away from the things that we find aversive. Sometimes, what is aversive and overwhelming is student behavior. We want to avoid this, though, as it can quickly become a harmful cycle. *Usually*, the more we can manage in the classroom, the better the outcomes. It's important that your students know that they can trust you to help them during their toughest moments. Of course, there will be times when you simply cannot continue, and you need assistance. But the more you work with your students during and after a situation, the better relationship you will have with them. Ideally, if you need assistance from another staff, have that person help the student deescalate. Then re-enter the picture when they are calm and it's time to problem solve.

Reflecting: Problem-Solving and Planning for the Future

Sometimes, certain behaviors for certain students warrant a follow-up response of some kind. Often, this includes losing minutes from recess, losing points, receiving timeouts, calls home, detention, or additional work. However, as we've discussed, these follow-up consequences are often overused and unresponsive. A loss of points in the classroom system has nothing to do with eloping from the classroom and losing recess minutes has nothing to do with cursing during math. These consequences are very unlikely to create behavior change when and where we need it to occur, because they are unresponsive and aren't related to the challenging routine where the behavior occurs. Ideally, we want the follow-up response to be as natural as possible and as closely related to the incident as possible.

Let's think about this another way. If your students continue to fail their math test or struggle to meet their fluency benchmark, would you use those same consequences? We hope not! Clearly, there is an academic skill deficit influencing their performance. Yet, when it comes to behavior, we often fail to consider skill deficits! Most traditional responses to challenging behavior don't take into account the high skill level a student must have to modify their behavior under *future* circumstances.

What It Is

Reflection as a follow-up response is a *meaningful process*, meant to investigate why a behavior occurred and develop a plan to provide scaffolded support to prevent the problem and help the student navigate challenges more effectively. To truly achieve this, reflection needs to be done in a way that allows for discussion and collaboration between the adult and student. What happens all too often, though, is the student is given a "think sheet" and sent to another location away from others to independently complete it.

Here's our beef with this follow-up response. Traditional think sheets require a lot of skills! Skills kids don't often have. The idea behind reflection forms or think sheets is that if students are told to reflect on their behavior while in what is essentially a timeout, then they'll learn from their consequence and won't repeat the behavior again in the future. Instead, this ends up being another annoying thing they have to do to return to class. So, they quickly write down what they know we want to hear. Then, in the future, when the challenging routine occurs again, they engage in the same behavior because they haven't learned or practiced any new skills to help them through that routine. And so, the same kids get these sheets over and over again – and now we are using a consequence that is unresponsive. We wouldn't continue to give think sheets to students who were getting subtraction problems wrong. We would figure out where they are struggling, teach them the needed skills, give them feedback, and potentially change our instruction as well. One final issue with the think sheets is that they focus entirely on student behavior. It's all about what they did, what they will do differently, and how they made others feel. That's a lot of responsibility on one child or adolescent, especially since they likely lack the skills necessary to navigate that situation effectively. How do we hold someone accountable for something they don't have the skills for?

Reflection as a follow-up response is not necessary for every student or situation but can be highly effective in preventing future problems if done well. However, the process can easily go sideways if we fail to use effective communication skills and come across as angry, judgmental, or punitive. Ideally, we want our presence and interactions to signal joy to our students. Or at least, we want to signal that things aren't about to get worse for them. Therefore, investigate and problem-solve with the student without drilling or probing them in a way that makes them feel as if they are in trouble or that you are trying to teach them a lesson.

Why It's Effective

Reflection as a follow-up response helps all parties involved to sequence the events that led up to their specific actions, to share perspectives, and to build connections between the outcomes that occurred because of their behaviors. When we engage in reflection as a collaborative process, we can reestablish our relationship and connection with the student. This shows them through words and actions that they are an important team member within the classroom. Reflection provides students (and staff) the opportunity to practice evaluating past needs and actions to create effective future plans. From a planning perspective, reflection provides insight into what preventative strategies may be effective, what skills might need to be taught, and how best to respond in the future.

How to Do It

When reflecting on an incident with a student/group of students, seek to understand the following – both for the student(s) and for us:

- **Stage-setters:** What set the stage for the student behavior? For my behavior?
- **Thoughts:** What was the student thinking or saying to himself? What was I thinking to myself?
- **Emotions:** What was the student feeling at that time? What was I feeling at that time?
- **Skill-level:** What skills might be underdeveloped or missing that need building? For the student? For myself?
- **Harm done:** Was anything or anyone affected by the student's actions? By my actions?

We can't read our students' minds and we shouldn't assume to know what they were thinking during the challenging routine that the behavior occurred. In fact, we caution you not to make assumptions about why they did what they did. Assumptions can quickly lead us in the wrong direction and toward misapplied, overused, and unresponsive consequences. Instead, ask questions to gather the previous information and use that to form a plan.

Plans should ideally include the following:

Prevention strategies: Determine what *staff will do differently to adjust* the environment, their instruction, or their interactions to reduce the likelihood the challenging behavior will occur.

Teaching strategies: Determine what skills to teach that will assist the student in being more successful in navigating the challenging routine. Remember this could include executive functioning skills, academic skills, social skills, etc. If the student truly has the skill needed (think efficiency versus skill, from Chapter 2), then consider environmental adjustments as preventative strategies that will support using the skill when and where they need to.

Reinforcement strategies: Determine how use of the skill or desirable behavior will be reinforced. Will you honor the skill or behavior, deliver behavior-specific praise, deliver a contrived reinforcer? Will use of the skill or behavior assist the student in meeting fundamental needs, thereby increasing motivation?

Response strategies: Determine what actions the student will engage in should the challenging routine occur. What will staff do to support the student should the challenging routine occur?

The following scripts give examples of how you could begin the process of reflection with your class or a group of students:

"Lunch seemed to be a challenging routine today. I want to discuss what worked, and what didn't work, so we know what changes we need to make as a class team to be more successful tomorrow."

"Class, please pause. Show me with your thumb how this transition is going? (Students put thumbs down). Since we aren't meeting the expectations for this routine, we are going to go back for a redo."

"Class, please sit back down (wait for class to sit). I notice that we aren't meeting expectation #4. Can someone please tell me what is making this routine particularly difficult so we can problem-solve?"

The following scripts give examples of how you could begin the process of reflection with an individual student:

"Let's rewind to when things were going well. When you came into class you were smiling. Were things going well for you then? Yes? Cool! Then what happened?"

"Correct me if I'm wrong, okay? I have this feeling that you actually do want to complete your work and do well in school, but I'm wondering if _____ is why you don't want to today? Am I onto something?"

"Did you get what you wanted or needed? Did the result make things better or worse for you short-term? Long-term, did your behavior move you closer to or further away from your goals/values?"

We've included two separate templates in the appendix (Forms 6.3 and 6.4) to assist you in effectively reflecting on both student and staff behavior.

Additional Considerations

Whom should we reflect with: The reflection process is not appropriate for all students, so it's up to you to determine which students it's beneficial for. Ideally, the student should be able to engage in the process, either verbally or with the use of AAC or visuals. For students with a disability, this process should be differentiated to support meaningful engagement. For others, it's not appropriate to debrief, and it's more important to engage in restoration and return them to their schedule. If reflection did not occur or was significantly modified, be sure to take the time outside of that moment to focus on teaching missing skills.

When should we engage in reflection: If the incident that occurred was minor, the reflection can happen as part of the immediate response. This would be a simple and brief reflection, likely tied with the prompt to engage in expected behaviors. For other mild or moderate behaviors, you might want to prioritize re-engaging the student in the task or routine. You can then engage in the reflection process after class or at a natural transition point.

If a student was very dysregulated, wait to engage in reflection until they are emotionally available, meaning they have de-escalated, and their thinking brain has returned to command. For some, immediately moving to reflection may re-escalate them. Often, it is best to allow some time to pass. This could be 20–30 minutes for some, this could be the end of the day, or next day for others. Flexibility is good; just ensure that you are engaging in the reflection process to understand and plan. Finally, reflection sessions, restoration, and re-engagement can happen in the order that is best for the student, staff, and situation.

Restoring: Fixing Harm Done

What It Is

Sometimes there is damage after a storm. When challenging behaviors occur the student themselves, their peers, the adults, and the physical environment can all be impacted to varying extents. The process of restoration assists those involved in the incident, student, staff, and peers alike, in taking actionable steps to repair any harm or damage that has occurred – emotionally, physically, or environmentally.

Why It Is Effective

Prioritizing restoration is effective for many reasons in maintaining a supportive classroom community. By engaging in the process, we assist students in reconnecting to the environment. Those who were affected by the incident have the chance to be appropriately acknowledged. This allows us to build connections between actions and their corresponding impact, thereby increasing student motivation to engage in behaviors that better align with their values and goals in the future. The process also allows our students to practice vital life skills such as repairing relationships, resolving conflict, acknowledging their actions, building resiliency, etc.

How to Do It

A reasonable follow-up response to challenging behavior can include repairing harm. This can start with a conversation with the student or group of students, leading them through a discussion of the incident. Specifically, we want to encourage and support them in reflecting on who or what specifically was harmed. We need to model and support active listening and effective communication skills during this process. When a group is impacted, it can be helpful to establish group behavioral norms before beginning – ensuring that we, as the adult, also follow those norms. Then, through this discussion we need to determine *with student input* what restoration needs to occur. Further, when engaging in the process, we want to reinforce participation by all involved. For most of us, talking about our thoughts, feelings, and past behaviors can make us very uncomfortable. This is why it is so important to praise and reinforce honesty, accurate reflections, listening, perspective taking, collaboration, and accepting responsibility.

The following are examples of potential restoration activities:

Verbal or written apology

Conference (individual, small group, whole group)

Restitution (cleaning, fixing, repairing)

Behavior contract

School-based community service

Catch peers being good assistance

PowerPoint presentation*

Book report/study*

Research project*

Mentor younger students

Make a school video*

Lessons with assessments*

*For this to be appropriate as restoration, we want the project to relate to the missing skill or situation. The goal is learning and making things right, not assigning an arbitrary punitive task as punishment.

Re-engaging: Getting Everyone Back on Track

What It Is

Re-engaging our students is important not only so that they can return to learning but also so that we can reset and move forward. The reentry of a student after a challenging behavior is a critical time. Either this transition will support students as they successfully rejoin their class and normal activities, or it can retrigger challenging behaviors. There are two ways reentry might occur – before a restorative conversation or after the restorative conversation.

When the student is ready to return to the environment and routine, our words, attitude, and actions as adults can create two very different conditions.

We can use this time to create aversive conditions that increase stress and anxiety, decrease motivation to be in class, and neglect underdeveloped skills.

Or

We can provide positive learning conditions that increase feelings of safety, increase motivation to be in class, and focus on skills that can be taught and reinforced.

Clearly, we should strive to create the second condition as it promotes a supportive and positive environment likely to prevent challenging behaviors in the future. After all, just saying "Clean up your mess" isn't going to stop another mess from occurring. Further, we can't expect students to navigate their stressors if we can't do the same. We can't expect them to model empathy if we can't or don't. And we can't expect students to take emotional responsibility or learn from their mistakes if we are unwilling to apologize or do something different.

Why It Is Effective

When we transition a student back to class and normal activities in a meaningful and intentional way, they are far more likely to be successful in reintegrating into their routine. Intentional transition fosters continued learning, re-establishes rapport, and builds their confidence as well.

How to Do It

The goal of re-entry is to welcome the student back, assist them in successfully rejoining their routine, and return to implementing all the proactive supports we have in place. We understand that welcoming back a student who has just engaged in high-magnitude behaviors can be challenging. Sometimes we have some big feelings of our own about that. But "Welcome back" isn't synonymous with "I've already forgiven you for your actions." However, as the adults, we need to engage in planned responses, not emotional reactions. So, ensure that you welcome the student back in a way that is kind, supportive, and sincere – even if you are still a little miffed about their actions. Sarcasm, insincerity, and snark are all harmful to your relationship, both in the moment and in moving forward. Nothing re-escalates a student like an adult who clearly doesn't want them in their presence.

Our general steps to transition a student back to their schedule and routine are as follows:

1. Ensure readiness.
2. Clarify expectations.
3. Provide precorrection.
4. Welcome them back.

5. Provide proximity.
6. Reinforce behavioral improvements.
7. Prevent.

Ensure readiness: Prior to re-entry, we first want to ensure that the student is ready to do so. This is more than just asking them "Hey, are you ready to go back to class?" They know they should be in class and sometimes they would rather be there than with the counselor, principal, or wherever they are. But just because they say they are ready doesn't mean they are.

If the student engaged in high-magnitude behaviors that required removal from the classroom, we need to ensure some time has passed before returning to class. We also need to ensure that they are engaging in rational behavior, can follow instructions, and their body physically appears at baseline. In most cases of high-magnitude behaviors, we will also engage in our reflection before returning them to their schedule or routine. If we are intentionally choosing to do that later, be sure to let the student know.

Clarify expectations: If the student was physically out of the room, ensure that you clarify the expectations for their return. If needed, check with the classroom teacher, or if you're the teacher and someone is returning a student to your room, provide a check-in. What should the student be doing? Where should they be? How soon can you or someone else help catch them up in the lesson or activity? Don't just plop them in their seat and expect them to be successful.

If the student perhaps was engaging in disruptive behaviors and spent some time regulating in another location within the room, we still want to clarify expectations for them when they return to their routine.

Provide precorrection: If the challenge should occur again, what should the student do? How should they advocate for their needs? Navigate the stressor?

Welcome them back: Whether they are returning to the classroom or returning to their schedule and routine within the classroom, ensure that you sincerely welcome them back.

Provide proximity: If another staff has returned them to your classroom after regulating and reflecting, ask that they remain in proximity for a few minutes to ensure successful re-entry. If the student is returning to routine from within the room, ensure that you are using active supervision, specifically proximity to ensure successful re-entry.

Reinforce behavioral improvements: While scanning and remaining in proximity, ensure that you provide praise and reinforcement of desirable behaviors to build momentum and success!

Prevent: Return to implementing all your great prevention strategies (visual supports, precorrection, instructional choice, etc.).

CHAPTER 7

Putting It All Together

Common Classroom Challenges

You made it. Our exploration of all the ins and outs of the core universal supports that make up tier 1 of the Multi-Tiered System of Supports (MTSS) framework is near an end. We want you to take a moment to give yourself a pat on the back. Taking time out of your hectic schedule to read this book speaks volumes about the type of educator you are. You could have easily used this time to tackle that never-ending life list of to-dos, but instead, you chose to give yourself the gift of continued education. Knowledge is power. And when we know better, we can do better. But will you? It's a question we urge you to continue to circle back to. Either way, teaching is hard work. Continuing with traditional, ineffective practices and the challenging behaviors that come with them is hard. Working each day to improve your practices by implementing the strategies outlined in this book is hard. It is our assumption that the type of educator you want to be deep down aligns to the latter. If this is the case, improved outcomes for both you and your students are on the horizon.

But we would be remiss if we let our journey through these universal supports stop here. We've taken a deep dive into the most effective strategies to minimize challenging behavior in the classroom. We've discussed what these strategies are, why they are effective, how to implement them, and additional considerations for each. But what now? We can all agree that it's essential to understand each support in isolation. But, as soon as we walk back into our classroom, reality hits. And suddenly what we thought would be a simple transition back to their seats or a quiet moment of independent work turns into a three-ring circus.

We've also learned that behavior is circumstantial. It's also complex – that's part of the beauty of being human! There are frequently many variables contributing to the challenging routines you have identified in your specific classroom. This means that *often*, simply using one strategy alone won't result in substantial behavior change. Remember, this does *not* mean the strategy you are implementing isn't effective! Nor does it mean we should be tossing it in the garbage. What it means is that due to the nature of life not happening in a bubble, lots of different things influence student behavior (and ours) at once. Using a variety of different strategies to target as many of these variables as possible will help us cover our bases and prevent most challenging behavior. Consider some of your own challenges you face outside of work. Perhaps it's losing that last sneaky 10 pounds before summer. Maybe it's trying to navigate a relationship with a loved one. Or possibly you are struggling to get a good night's rest each evening. Overcoming all these challenges likely won't take one strategy alone – but rather, a culmination of different things you will do together that will result in that change you are so desperately hoping for.

At the start of this book, we discussed the pitfall of picking and choosing certain strategies while neglecting others. While it does still hold true that universal supports apply to all students, all the time, there is still a time and a place for each strategy within the context of the various activities, routines, and situations that occur across the school day. Thus, real-life application – being able to conceptualize what it looks like and sounds like to pull all these strategies together to address common problems and scenarios – is key.

In the following activities, you will find common classroom scenarios that you might observe or experience in your classroom. As you read through each, try your best to slow down and really consider everything that's going on within the environment before jumping to problem-solving. Start training your brain to consider all universal supports *first*, rather than trying to come up with intensive, individualized tier 3 solutions to what are often tier 1 problems.

Questions to Ask Yourself:
- What are the expectations for this activity, routine, or situation and in what ways have they been communicated or conveyed?
- What skills does this activity, routine, or situation require the student(s) to have?
- How is instruction being delivered?
- How is the physical environment arranged?
- To what extent are visual aids being utilized?
- What seems to be the level of rapport between teacher and student(s)?
- What might be going on for the student(s) that staff aren't aware of?
- Which fundamental needs might the student(s) be attempting to meet?

After reading through each scenario, consider and select the universal supports that would be most appropriate to focus on utilizing given the information provided. Then, challenge yourself to describe in detail how you would implement each selected support, including how they might look within the classroom as well as what you might say. This is your chance to really begin to apply the information you've learned throughout this book and work toward building your confidence within your own classroom. Therefore, we kindly suggest that you take the time to engage in these practice activities!

After each activity, you'll then have the opportunity to travel back in time to see each scenario play out differently when universal supports are implemented to address the specific needs of the scenario. While each situation is dynamic, the recommendations suggested for each scenario do align with the content within this book, our knowledge of universal supports, and our experiences. However, while this is what we would do given the scenario, know that each situation is unique, and you will still need to consider the nuances of your classroom and student needs to individualize the supports.

Transitions and Tribulations

Applied Practice: Transitions and Tribulations

Take 1:

It was a snowy Tuesday morning, and Mr. Thompson's "passionate" sixth graders' eyes were glued to the window as gigantic snowflakes piled up in mounds as high as their knees. He caught himself longingly staring out the window just the same, secretly hoping the superintendent would cancel school tomorrow. But alas, there was an entire literacy block ahead of them, and the clock was ticking.

Mr. Thompson returned his gaze to his sea of kids. "Okay, okay, come back to Earth. Our chapter books won't read themselves." The 23 pairs of eyes slowly averted from the window. "Alright, I want you to go back to your tables and get out your books. Mark for evidence within the text as you go – I will be coming around and looking for at least two marked-up sticky notes each. Casey, Tory, Alma, I'll see you at the back table." He stood up and made a waving motion with his hands as if to say, "Off you go". . . and go they did.

What seemed like one-third of Mr. Thompson's students made a beeline to the window to zero in on the snow as it picked up the pace, accumulating inch after inch. The other third took the long way back to their desks, making pit stops along the way. Mason and Nadir shoulder-checked one another as they raced between the chairs, knocking over a stack of binders as they went. Casey and Tory let out a loud groan as they dragged their feet to the back table. Mr. Thompson had had it.

This type of transition was typical, but he was a firm believer that his students knew the expectations, that he shouldn't have to waste his breath reviewing and rewarding them to do something that was simply expected, and that whatever consequence they had coming to them for not following the expectations is what they deserved.

He looked outside and looked back at his class – his eyes lit up. "You've just earned yourself 10 minutes off of recess for that transition." A reading book went careening across the floor and landed at Mr. Thompson's feet. It was Nadir's. "What are you going to do? Physically hold me against my will?" Nadir roared. Mr. Thompson could feel his heart start to race. "No, but I know someone who can." He turned and picked up the phone next to his desk. "Hi, Mr. Jackson. I have a student who is choosing to be defiant and engage in unsafe behavior. . .yes. . .room 302. . .thank you." He hung up the phone. "You can take your issue up with Mr. Jackson; he is on his way." The other students hurried to their seats and grabbed their books.

Mr. Thompson sat down with his small group. Nadir kicked the filing cabinet, sat down at his desk, put his hood up, and buried his head in his arms. "Take your hoodie off, you know the rules," Mr. Thompson bellowed across the room." Nadir didn't budge. And just as quickly as the snow piled up, so did Mr. Thompson's consequences.

(continued)

Applied Practice: Transitions and Tribulations *(continued)*

Physical Space

_____

_____

Expectations

_____

_____

_____

Routines

_____

_____

_____

Schedules

_____

_____

_____

Instructional Practices

_____

_____

_____

Reinforcement of Desirable Behavior

_____

_____

_____

Responses to Challenging Behavior

_____

_____

_____

Take 2:

It was a snowy Tuesday morning, and Mr. Thompson's "passionate" sixth graders' eyes were glued to the window as gigantic snowflakes piled up in mounds as high as their knees. He caught himself longingly staring out the window just the same, secretly hoping the superintendent would cancel school tomorrow. But alas, there was an entire literacy block ahead of them and the clock was ticking.

Mr. Thompson returned his gaze to his sea of kids. Literacy block wasn't much of a fan favorite, but any opportunity to connect to his students "eased the blow" of it so to speak. "My challenge to you is to build a snowman that is taller than me when you get outside this afternoon." His students quickly brought their attention back to him. "Challenge accepted," Nadir said as he grinned at Mason. Mr. Thompson smiled and tipped his pretend hat in his direction.

Nadir was one of his students whom many teachers deemed "difficult to connect with," but Mr. Thompson didn't operate like many of the other teachers. "Alright, Class, before we transition back to our desks, let's take a beat. Rate that lesson if you would, please." The students held up the number of fingers that corresponded to their rating.

After the students provided their feedback, Mr. Thompson asked them to once again give a rating, only this time, it was for their behavior. "What do you think?" Mr. Thompson inquired. "I think we mostly met expectations," Allison shared. "We kind of struggled with being responsible during partner-talk." Mr. Thompson wasn't one to give the types of consequences other teachers gave – what he found the most effective was to have his students work the problem and come up with their own solutions. They were quite good at it when given the chance.

Mr. Thompson and his class mapped out the issue on the board and brainstormed a handful of solutions. He then transferred this over to a space in the upper corner of his board to review before tomorrow's lesson. Mr. Thompson also took the time at the end of each lesson to solicit a review on his own teacher behavior. He found that taking the 30 seconds to do this saved him countless hours in the long run because of the powerful connection to students it built.

"Anyone willing to provide me with some personal feedback with regard to our expectations?" Mr. Thompson asked. Mason raised his hand. "M-dawg. Whatcha got for me?" Mr. Thompson pointed at Mason. "You were respectful when you gave your signal to return our attention instead of calling us out in front of everyone," Mason said. Nate raised his hand. "Yes." Mr. Thompson looked his way. "I didn't like the joke you made earlier." Mr. Thompson's students were very open with him. He didn't try to punish their opinions or responses, but rather sought to understand them. Perhaps this was one of the reasons why Nadir and Mason didn't give him much trouble compared to their other teachers. "Thank you for that feedback, Nadir. My apologies. I'm making a mental note to tone down my sarcasm," he said. Nadir nodded in approval.

"Alright team, we are about to make the transition back to our seats. Please look up at the board at our agenda for this next task," he said as he turned toward the board. He reviewed the upcoming assignment. "Please, mark for evidence within the text as you go – I will be coming around and looking for at least two marked-up sticky notes each," he read. "How many sticky notes?" he asked as he put his hand to his ear. "Two!" the class replied all together. If you forget what to do, please refer to our agenda on the board. If you are still unsure of what to do, ask your assigned literacy buddy." Mr. Thompson took a breath and smiled. "Following transition expectations means that you are walking straight to your assigned areas. Casey, Tory, Alma, please go to the back table."

(continued)

Applied Practice: Transitions and Tribulations *(continued)*

The rest of the class waited in position as the three transitioned first. "That was perfect. Nadir, all the way to Reina, go ahead." The small group moved swiftly to their desks. "Alright, the rest of you may go back to your desks," Mr. Thompson said as he got up and walked with the remaining students to ensure they moved in the desired direction. He let the students know he appreciated their swift shift. He made eye contact with Nadir and gave him a thumbs up. "Who would have ever believed. . .," Mr. Thompson thought to himself, ". . .that Nadir Bukhari would be one of my favorites." He chuckled to himself and made his way over to his small group and got back to work.

Circle Time Circus

Applied Practice: Circle Time Circus

Take 1:

Ms. Buxton looked down at her shoes. It was one of those days when she regretted not opting for sneakers. "Amateur move," she thought to herself as she stood waiting for the classroom timer to go off.

She looked at the schedule. Circle Time was up next. The bell chimed, and she walked to the carpet, watching as the aides, Ms. Campbell and Ms. Meyers, bribed the students in any way they could just to end their current activity. "No. . .stop. . .go to the carpet," Ms. Campbell said as she blocked a student from entering the leisure area. They finally corralled the students toward the Circle Time area.

Circle Time was a notoriously difficult time for her group. Disengagement and disruption were common, but she wanted her students to learn to tolerate listening to instruction for longer periods of time. The students and her aides made their way to the front of the room – save for Jeramiah – he knew the drill and bolted toward the door. Ms. Campbell quickly followed. "Great. . .down a staff member," Ms. Buxton said to herself. "If only the school would hire more staff. . .."

She turned to the board and pulled up a YouTube video of the story, The Very Busy Spider. Within 60 seconds Kailani started crawling around, picking at the carpet. "No, Kailani. Go back to your space." Kailani paid no mind. As the busy spider spun her web, Ms. Buxton's students spun out of control. Max stood up and bolted toward the sensory area. Ms. Buxton got up and blocked him. "Where's Max's AAC?" she asked Ms. Campbell, who was still at the classroom door holding the gate while Jeramiah attempted to pole-vault over it. "I don't know, maybe his backpack?" she replied. Back on the carpet Ms. Meyers sat with Sam and Andreanna. Andreanna's eyes stayed glued to the screen as Sam twirled in circles, flapping his hands. "Stop, Sam. Turn around and look. See? The spider is making a web," Ms. Meyers said as she positioned herself behind him.

Ms. Buxton motioned to Ms. Meyers to end the video. Ms. Meyers sprung up and happily shut the computer. "What are we doing next?" she mouthed to Ms. Buxton. Ms. Buxton didn't notice. She was too busy staring at the clock counting down the minutes until Choice Time.

Physical Space

_____

Expectations

_____

Routines

_____

Schedules

_____

Instructional Practices

_____

Reinforcement of Desirable Behavior

_____

Responses to Challenging Behavior

_____

_____

(continued)

Applied Practice: Circle Time Circus *(continued)*

Take 2:

Ms. Buxton looked down at a student as she waited for the classroom timer to go off. She looked at the schedule. Circle Time was up next. She got down on his level. "Theo, it's time to put your drawing in your parking lot." Theo looked up at her and put his paper on his blue mat. Ms. Buxton grinned, "Way to go, buddy!" she gave him a big high-five.

She scheduled times to practice transitioning from preferred activities each day so he could build his muscle memory, and what progress he was making! She showed him a picture card of a schedule and watched as he went to the bulletin board. He grabbed the next card on his schedule, walked to the carpet area, and placed his card on the Velcro landing pad. "Find your red circle, Theo," Ms. Buxton said. Theo scanned the carpet and sat down on his dot. "That's the red circle – nice job!" She gave his arms a little squeeze and his eyes lit up.

The other students and her aides made their way to the front of the room. She noticed Jeramiah glancing at the door. "A perfect time to work on 'Come here'," she thought (another skill she was working on with this student). "Jeramiah!" she said in an excited tone. He looked toward her. "Come here!" she put out her arms and smiled her biggest smile. Jeramiah looked back at the door and then back at Ms. Buxton – he ran over to her. She embraced him in a side hug. "Good listening, Jeramiah – you came here!" He melted into her side.

After the students were seated, she rolled over her giant easel. She reviewed the Circle Time activity agenda with the group. Once she was finished, she pointed to the first activity. "It's time for The Very Busy Spider," she said as Ms. Meyers handed each student a strip of paper with removable animals. Ms. Buxton kept her clipboard next to her with a list of skills each student was working on that she could target during Circle Time.

She knew downtime was the enemy, so she relied heavily on creating multiple opportunities for active engagement. She turned the book toward Max and showed him the page. "Max, what is it?" Ms. Buxton asked as she pointed to the horse. Max flipped through the pages on his AAC, located the horse, and tapped the screen. "Horse," said the synthesized voice. "Yes! That's a horse."

She quickly turned to Sam. "Sam, find the horse." Sam pointed to the brown, four-legged animal on the page. "Neigh, neigh. There he is," she said with enthusiasm. His vocalizations echoed across the room, and he started to flap his hands and bounce up and down. Seeing him happy and engaged made her day.

She continued, building in a healthy dose of imitation, matching, receptive and expressive labeling, intraverbal, and turn-taking opportunities. She did the same with the remainder of the Circle Time activities, adding lots of movement, songs, and interactive activities to work on an entire host of skills. There was a method to her madness, and that method was increasing her students' skills at a rapid pace. They were on the path to one heck of a great year.

Writing Retaliation

Applied Practice: Writing Retaliation

Take 1:

  Ms. Ellis stood at the back of the room, reheating her coffee in the microwave for the second time that day. Her tenth graders filed in with minimal enthusiasm; the feeling was mutual. Four more years of teaching English until she could retire. She was counting down the days, but mostly because of the class sitting right in front of her. There were a handful of students whom she described to the other teachers as "Lazy, disrespectful, unmotivated, and out to drive me into an early retirement."

  "Alright, have a seat," she barked. She shuffled her way to the front of the room. She turned to write on the board. "Today we are starting to write our expository pieces." Brent mumbled something under his breath. Ms. Ellis paused mid-sentence and glanced down at the floor, trying to figure out if she was hearing things. She continued writing. "Yesterday you should have completed your outline, and if you didn't finish it in class, you should have finished it for homework." Brent hadn't attended school yesterday, so his outline wasn't even started. Ms. Ellis continued, "Those of you who haven't had me review it yet, come back to my desk and I'll look it over. Everyone else, you may get started writing."

  She walked back to her desk as the class got their folders out. She opened her email to start working through her 14 unread messages. Just as she clicked to open the first message, she heard Brent mumble again, only louder this time. She took her hand off the mouse, wheeled away from the computer, looked in his direction, and took the bait. "Want to repeat that for the class, Mr. Williams?" "Yeah," he replied as he gave a nod. "This class sucks, and everyone knows it." Ms. Ellis stood up and wrote his name on the board next to her desk. "Maybe if you bothered showing up, it wouldn't suck as much. Enjoy detention," she retorted.

  He smirked. He would much rather spend after school in detention than go home and take a gamble on whether his dad would be sober or belligerent. "I'll enjoy it a lot more than writing pointless f***ing essays in your dumb-a** class," he countered. "GET OUT," Ms. Ellis yelled as she pointed to the door. Brent threw his bag over his shoulder, walked past his peers, and let the classroom door slam behind him.

  The rest of the students looked around, but no one seemed phased this time, save for Ms. Ellis. Her hands shook as she turned back to her email. She could have a letter of resignation drafted up and sent to her principal by the end of the period. She looked at the clock and then at her students. They were back at work, including the small few who typically tag-teamed with Brent. At least this time they let him have the spotlight. She looked back at the computer. . .challenge accepted.

(continued)

Applied Practice: Writing Retaliation (*continued*)

Physical Space
_____

_____

Expectations
_____

_____

Routines
_____

_____

Schedules
_____

_____

Instructional Practices
_____

_____

Reinforcement of Desirable Behavior
_____

_____

Responses to Challenging Behavior
_____

_____

Take 2:

Ms. Ellis stood at the classroom door as her coffee reheated in the microwave at the back of the room. She tracked her students as they made their way down the packed hallway during passing period. She greeted each of them with a warm smile and asked them how they were doing.

Aiysha, one of her students who had an extremely long route via the city bus, was moving ever so slowly. "You're doing great, Aiysha. You just keep showing up. I'm here for you." Aiysha thanked her and made her way into the classroom.

Brent trickled in behind her. Ms. Ellis faced him and put her hands on his shoulders. "I'm happy you're here," she said. "Is there anything you'd like to talk about before we start class?" She tried her best to gauge the "Brent weather." "I'm good," Brent said. Something told her he wasn't "good," but she didn't push him. They both turned and walked into the room.

"Alright everyone, it's great to see you all. Did anyone catch the Cavaliers game last night?" At least 40% of her class suddenly came to life. After a gripping discussion of the tournament, she started in with the day's lesson. Ms. Ellis turned to write on the board. "Today we are starting to write our expository pieces." Brent mumbled something under his breath. Ms. Ellis paused midsentence and glanced down at the floor. She caught the words, "class" and "sucks," but she couldn't make out the rest. She made a mental note and continued writing. "Yesterday you should have completed your outline, and if you didn't finish it in class, you should have finished it for homework." Brent hadn't attended school yesterday, so his outline wasn't even started. Ms. Ellis continued, "Those of you who haven't had me review it yet, come back to my desk and I'll look it over. Everyone else, you may get started writing."

She walked back toward her desk as the class got their folders out. She looked over at her computer screen as it sat with her email open – 14 unread messages. As tempting as it was to sit down and check those off her never-ending to-do list, she knew her time would be better spent preventing what had the likelihood to turn into a crisis. She grabbed a pad of sticky notes and a pen and wrote, "Come see me when you feel ready. MTW, a Bulls hat!? I thought we were cool!" Ms. Ellis knew detention wouldn't address what was truly going on for Brent, and he was starting to open up to her more and more as the weeks went on.

She started to make her way up and down the aisles, checking in on students as they worked. She subtly placed the sticky note on Brent's desk as she did her drive-by. After she had made her rounds, she started back to her desk. She continued to listen and scan as her students wrote. Brent hadn't moved. After a few minutes she moved about the room once more, strategically walking up and down the rows, keeping tabs on Brent. She looked over and his eyes met hers. She raised her brows and tilted her head as if to say, "Are you ready?" Sure enough, Brent stood up and made his way to the back of the room.

He fell into the green, deep-seated upholstered chair she had next to her desk. The armchair was used for a wide variety of purposes: some days all 23 students sat in it to have their work checked; other days only one or two students sat in it to have their wellness checked. Ms. Ellis made it known among her high schoolers that "The Chair" was a safe space. She made one last loop to ensure the class was on a roll before joining Brent.

(continued)

Applied Practice: Writing Retaliation (*continued*)

She lowered her voice and turned away from the class. "Would you like to go first, or shall I?" she started in. "You," Brent said. Ms. Ellis continued, "I think I overheard you mentioning that this class sucks. . .but. . .and please correct me if I'm wrong. . .I'm curious if something else is going on and that this isn't about my class as whole." Brent started fidgeting with his sneaker strap. "I don't have my outline done," he said. "I'm aware," she whispered.

He was a bright student, but heck, she also felt overwhelmed when she was behind on work; she could empathize. "I'm not sure how you're feeling, but I know when I'm behind on things I feel overwhelmed, and sometimes it can feel challenging to get started and try and catch up. . .is that perhaps how you are feeling?" Brent kept his eyes glued to his sneakers and nodded. "I see. . .well. . .I know you don't give a darn about my credentials," she joked "but. . .I in fact am highly qualified in helping you knock out this outline! What do you say?" The corner of Brent's mouth turned up slightly. "Okay," he replied. "I'm sorry I made that rude comment, Ms. E. I do like this class. . .it's actually one of the only classes I do like."

"Thank you for the apology, Brent." I have an idea. Would you like to hang on to this pad of sticky notes? If you are ever feeling overwhelmed again (or for any other reason), you can drop me a line on the sticky note and leave it at the top of your desk. When I do my walk-arounds, I will grab it, write you back, and stick it back on your desk as I walk back around. Does this seem like something that might work? I'm open to suggestions that allow me to continue leading the class and you to feel like you are getting what you need." Brent liked the idea. "Great, let's try that and check in with each other on how it's going each week."

Ms. Ellis then closed her eyes briefly and leaned in. "I know you felt overwhelmed about not having your outline done, but something inside is telling me that there is something else going on that is making getting your work done feel insurmountable." She opened her eyes. "Yeah. . .there is. Can we talk about it after class when everyone leaves?" Brent asked. "Absolutely," Ms. Ellis replied. Brent's body relaxed. "Now, let's get this outline done and help you move the ball down the field. I'm going to make sure you graduate if it's the last thing I do before I retire. And I'm trying to move to the beach sooner rather than later, so let's get going!" He laughed, grabbed his pencil, and they got to work.

Direct Instruction Disaster

Applied Practice: Direct Instruction Disaster

Take 1:

Ms. Hogan sat in her rocking chair by the board as her third graders cleaned up their desks after snack. It felt good to sit for once. Her eyes felt heavy and fluttered dangerously as her chair glided back and forth. She would have forfeited half her paycheck in that instant to be able to shut her eyes and drift off in solitude for a mere 10 minutes.

Her students started trickling over to the carpet. She did a quick headcount to make sure all students were accounted for. Once the last student sat down, she started. "Okay, boys and girls, we are continuing our grammar unit. Today we are going to learn about irregular plural nouns." She leaned and extended her arm to point to a list of words on the board. "These are different from our regular plural nouns – they don't follow the same rule. We can't just add an -s or -es at the end. . .."

Ms. Hogan continued her instruction for another five minutes, and it ended up being the longest five minutes of her life. As she talked on, students one by one started turning their attention to anywhere but the board. "Gabriel, turn around, I'm tired of asking you," she said as she felt her stomach churn. Moments later, she paused, yet again. "Kai and Isla, if you turn and speak to one another again I'm going to send a letter home." Kai's eyes got wide. "In fact, you know what? Kai, move over here." Ms. Hogan pointed to an empty space next to her rocking chair. She suddenly stood up. "Let's see who has been listening so far."

Her disdainful tone was obvious as she scanned the room. Her eyes landed on Camille. She had been blurting out off-topic comments and she was over it. "Camille, which one of these is the plural spelling of 'leaf'?" Camille looked at the options on the board. "The first one!" she shouted. "That's not correct, and it is my guess that you don't know the answer because you haven't been paying attention this whole time," Ms. Hogan said.

"This is borrring," Camille contended. "All we do is listen to you taaalk." She rolled her eyes, laid back, and rested her elbows on the ground. Ms. Hogan was done. "Go to the Think Spot. You can make this up for homework." Camille's eyes lit up. She promptly stood up and went to the desk just outside the classroom. Ms. Hogan felt a sense of relief as she got back to the lesson. Little did she know, so did Camille.

Physical Space

_____

_____

Expectations

_____

_____

Routines

_____

_____

Schedules

_____

_____

(continued)

Applied Practice: Direct Instruction Disaster (*continued*)

Instructional Practices

_____

Reinforcement of Desirable Behavior

_____

Responses to Challenging Behavior

_____

Take Two:

   Ms. Hogan stood at the front of the room as her third graders cleaned up their desks after snack. She felt pretty tired, but she reserved her energy for the upcoming lesson. Her students started trickling over to the carpet. She did a quick headcount as they walked to make sure all were accounted for.

   Thomas quickly cut a corner and nearly collided with Ms. Hogan on his way to his spot. "Thomas. . .," she started slowly, giving him some time to self-evaluate. Thomas got up, walked back, placed the water bottle back on the table, and went to sit down at this desk. He looked at Ms. Hogan. She nodded, and he got up and transitioned once again.

   Ms. Hogan didn't need to do much direct correcting any more at this point in the year. Her students knew that if a transition did not meet the agreed-upon criteria that they would simply try it again. She cocked her head and made a half-serious, half-silly face once he returned to the carpet. He knew this was her signal to tell her why he was rushing. "I didn't want to sit next to Peter, so I was trying to get a different spot before someone else," he whispered. She whispered back, "And why don't you prefer to sit next to Peter, may I ask?" "He called me a mean name in Music class this morning," he said. "Understood. Let's table this and we will problem-solve with Peter during lunch today. You may go sit next to Sarah," Ms. Hogan replied. Thomas went to sit down.

   She made her way around the maze of children and sat down. Suddenly, she sprang back up, acted as if she were putting on a hat, and grabbed her fake microphone. She led with a voice like that of Bruce Buffer, the great UFC Octagon Announcer. "Boys and girls. . .WELCOME. . .to another lesson on. . .," she paused and raised her hands in the air. "GRAMMMMARRRR." Her students' eyes widened. "But FIRST, a quick review of our EXPECTATIONS!" She quickly sat back down, pretended to remove her hat, and put on another hat (her teacher hat). In a more serious tone, Ms. Hogan took a moment to review the expectations for the instructional block of the lesson. After checking for understanding, she pretended to put her announcer hat back on and jumped back up.

With a click of a button she projected two photos up on the board: one of a pack of dogs, the other of a pack of wolves. In her announcer voice she asked the students to silently look at the two photos and think about the differences between the two. She told them there was something special that made them different, but it was up to them to try and figure out what it was. She then had the students turn to their shoulder partner and discuss the potential differences. Ms. Hogan had one member of each pair share out one key difference they came up with. "You all came up with many fantastic differences, but still not the secret difference I'm looking for. She then clicked to a new slide with the words, "Dog→Dogs" and "Wolf→Wolves." She kept silent and watched as her students' brains tried to track where she was going with this. Malik's hand shot up in the air. "I think I know!!" he exclaimed. "Give it a go!" Ms. Hogan said. "'Dogs' adds an 's' to the end without changing the word, but 'wolves' changes the spelling and doesn't follow the 's' or 'es' rule," he explained. "BINGO," she said as she pointed to him. The word "wolves" is what we call an irregular plural noun." She leaned and extended her arm to point to a list of words on the board. "These are different than our regular plural nouns – they don't follow the same rule. We can't just add an -s or -es at the end. . ."

Before Mr. Gabriel reviews our agenda for us, I would like to tell you what a fantastic job you are doing following our classroom expectations for instruction time. You are listening to the speaker, you are turning and talking when asked, your arms and legs are staying in your own space on the carpet. "Air bumps" (she double-fist-bumped the air as her students did the same).

After Gabriel helped her review the lesson agenda, she continued on with the mini-lesson around irregular plural nouns. For the next 15 minutes she had her students moving about the room, clapping, pointing, writing, choral responding, popcorn responding, and using their response cards every minute. Kai and Isla (two students the other teachers labeled as "Chatty Cathies") were most definitionally chatting, but their chatter was about irregular plural nouns.

Camille, whom other teachers struggled with when it came to her excessive blurting of off-topic comments, was on-task and beaming. Mr. Carpenter, the principal, popped his head in, "Got a moment?" he said. "Actually, Mr. Carpenter, may I come see you later? I'd like to keep this engagement train chugging along," Ms. Hogan advocated. "You got it, conductor," he said, and carried on his way.

CHAPTER 8

Problem-Solving Barriers

Fidelity of Implementation

In our experience with dozens of schools and programs across the country, one of the biggest reasons students and staff continue to struggle is that universal supports aren't implemented effectively or with fidelity. And because of this, student behavior doesn't improve. We then think, "Well, this strategy doesn't work. . .," and we throw it out with all the other universal supports that "didn't work."

As a result, we are left feeling as if we have no other options than to use punishment procedures after challenging behaviors as a means of deterring students from engaging in challenging behavior in the future. Using punitive practices might make us, the adults, feel better in the moment, but they certainly aren't effective long-term and will not improve a student's quality of education (or life for that matter).

Considerations to increase the effectiveness of universal supports:

Train and coach all team members: Ensure everyone interacting with the class or student is using the strategy at the right times. This can be difficult when working at the secondary level because students don't just have one primary teacher any longer. But this is where we must put awkwardness aside and start advocating for what our students need and deserve. The schools we've observed that prioritized training and coaching their staff significantly decrease office referrals and increase engagement, participation, and time in class. They have been creative in how they build capacity and confidence among their school team. Creating a school Google Drive with Tier 1 folders of each strategy, along with related visuals supports, implementation checklists, and short videos not only explaining the strategy but showing video models of teachers using the practice in real time, is a great way to *supplement* in-class training and coaching.

Implement across the entire day: These supports are intended to be utilized across the entire day, period, or specific times throughout the day. These are not intended to be implemented just for a challenging routine (though they absolutely can and should be in place during challenging routines). Universal supports are intended to be in place for all students all the time. For example, if positive feedback is only given during a 20-minute period in which a student struggles, we are falling short. Positive feedback is necessary throughout the day. We want our students to *want* to come to class, stay in class, and persist through difficult situations and tasks because good things happen in class.

Reflect on implementation: Build metacognition and continuously evaluate performance as it relates to each strategy. How did it go? How did students respond? How did I feel implementing it? Do I need more practice? What can I do to increase the effectiveness? We preach a growth mindset to kids; we need to be using a growth mindset ourselves!

Ask for student feedback: It is rare that students are given the opportunity to provide feedback to staff on the supports, strategies, and instructional practices they use. Yet, our practices directly impact them. If they aren't asked for feedback, their motivation may tank. Doing things *with* students rather than *to* them increases motivation. In the behavior analytic world, we refer to this as social validity, examining stakeholders' views and opinions about a procedure. If something about it wasn't helpful, we need to know, and the students are usually the best people to ask!

Questions to ask:

- Did you appreciate (insert strategy, e.g., behavior-specific praise)
- Do you think (insert strategy) helped you?
- What was helpful about it? How did it help?
- Was there anything about (insert strategy) that was unhelpful?

Make needed adjustments: Rather than immediately moving to try another strategy, consider things that can be tweaked to increase its effectiveness. If it's not "working," we need to look at what we can tweak or adjust within this strategy to make it more likely we will observe positive behavior change.

Gaining Buy-In and Advocating for Change

As the manager of your classroom, you have the power to implement the strategies outlined in this book throughout your students' day, some of which may require some outside support at times (this should be minimal if the recommendations outlined in this book have been implemented). However, as you watch your students succeed within your classroom environment, there will likely come a time when you worry when they leave your room. Perhaps you'll wish for other teachers to implement the same strategies so that your students can be equally successful within their classrooms. Or maybe you will want to support your fellow teachers in implementing school-wide expectations, active supervision on the playground, and behavior-specific praise in the lunchroom, just to name a few.

As you know, shifting one's mindset and behavior is hard. It's hard to make these shifts alone, and it's just as hard to help *someone else* make the shift. We are not going to sit here and tell you that you can single-handedly achieve schoolwide change in 100% of cases. However, advocating for change is one thing; taking specific, actionable steps to initiate that change and gain buy-in is another. Think back to the first chapter of this book when we learned about Danielle's own shift. She and I had many conversations about what she could do to extend best practice outside the walls of her room. It took time. It took persistence. It also took empathy, flexibility, and the willingness and creativity to do the work with others.

Whether you are a classroom teacher or you fill a role outside of the classroom, such as an administrator, instructional coach, school psychologist, behavior specialist, or related service personnel, you may want to implement the strategies outlined within this book in your school. The following are evidence-based strategies you can utilize to increase staff buy-in and acceptance of universal supports with an individual or groups of staff.

Pair yourself: Before you approach others with a hard pitch, take the time to get to know others professionally and personally. Part of building rapport with someone involves associating (pairing) yourself with things that person values. Spend time asking them about the things that bring them joy. Why did they become an educator? What are their values? Find out what you have in common. Gift them that Golden Retriever magnet you saw at the store because you know how much they love their "Good boy." Invite them to join the running club because you noticed their impressive selection of Hokas. The goal is for your sheer presence to give them the same positive feelings they get when they think about the things that interest them. Jumping in and immediately making recommendations or asking for help without solidifying a connection is likely only going to cause the other staff member to view you as a source of frustration and inconvenience.

Get in the mix: Nobody likes to listen to people who aren't in the trenches with them or, better yet, in their specific trench. Spend time in their classroom or in the environment where you'd like specific supports implemented. And we don't just mean sitting back to observe. Even the playing field and show them that you empathize with how difficult it is to manage 24 energetic kindergarteners or those six high schoolers who won't stop passing notes in the back of the class. Run a small group. Cover snack time. Do a read-aloud. Help them make copies. Let them take a 10-minute break. This not only goes a long way for overwhelmed staff, but it helps you gain credibility when they know you can walk the walk, and you aren't just there to tell them what to do having never walked in their shoes. Many times, this will also allow you to pinpoint where the root of the issue might be. It may be difficult for staff to get a bird's-eye view of what's really going on all the time. You'll strike out if you come onto the field swinging with recommendations without being present to see what's going on.

Hold proactive meetings: We know there isn't time for more meetings. Constant emergency meetings about students' challenging behavior are likely frequent anyway. The idea is to replace a large majority of those discussions with proactive check-ins or meetings that are lower stakes – meetings where all brains are more rational and available because emotions are not yet heightened!

- How are things going?
- What is going well?
- What are they proud of?

- At what point in the day do they notice things aren't going as smoothly?
- Are there situations in which students are showing signs of struggling?
- Is there anything that has popped up that can be nipped in the bud?

These meetings can be weekly or bi-weekly, but recognize that the more time passes, the more likely that both student and staff behaviors (desirable and challenging) will become routine, engrained, and harder to change. Like any meeting, they should be highly structured and purposeful. Create an agenda and set meeting norms to ensure that the meeting focuses on problem-solving staff and student needs, rather than "admiration" of the problems. Keep some scripts in your back pocket for how you will redirect and keep conversations solution focused. We recommend reviewing these expectations at the start of each meeting (e.g., "If at any point during this check-in one of us notices we aren't speaking about students in a dignified way, we have permission to pause and remind one another of our goal here today").

Give them the mic: While you've already brainstormed potential areas of need, it's important to ensure that the teacher or team you are meeting with have a voice. Actively listening (relatedness) to their concerns, while being careful not to wallow in the problem, is one of the most important factors and first steps in motivating someone to change for the right reasons. If their behavior is to change, they need to feel like they are part of the decision-making process (autonomy). Ask probing questions to gather more information about their perspective of any issues brought to the table. Get in the habit of paraphrasing (e.g., "I want to make sure I heard you correctly" or "Let me make sure I understand.") and become comfortable with validating and empathizing (e.g., "That is tough," "I can see how that causes a lot of frustration," "Yes, that is a difficult situation indeed"). Two things can be true at once: you can internally disagree, but you can externally empathize with their very real emotions and validate their own personal experience. It will also behoove you to ask what solutions and insights they have to offer. Though it can be an unpleasant truth, you may have to change course in terms of what you are hoping the other person can do. "If they would only implement (insert universal support), students would benefit!" Students will not benefit, however, if you push too much change on this staff member too soon.

Take your buy-in where you can get it and go forward from there; being rigid and insisting on a particular change they are reluctant to make at this moment in time won't be effective. The micro-changes are the key to large-scale changes. Lastly, during these conversations it's important to remind yourself that this staff member has their own learning history, their own sources of motivation, and their own underdeveloped skills, and they likely feel just as stressed as you do.

Identify the rationale or "why": It's time to target motivation. You can use their pain points in combination with the things that they value to identify supports that are most meaningful. What are students doing that makes teaching difficult? What tends to interrupt their instruction? If only their class would just _____, they would feel better. What keeps them up at night? Then, how can changes to organization, physical layout, or visual supports be made to reduce frustration? Are there instructional practices like precorrection or active student response methods that would increase engagement during lessons? Could reinforcement be embedded by increasing opportunities for autonomy during small group work to increase motivation? Identify two or three potential pain points and possible solutions to propose and clearly explain how the strategy will help the teacher ultimately reach their previously discussed goals. To do this, it's important you know what you're talking about and *why* this strategy has the potential to be so darn effective. Discuss the risks versus the benefits of what you are recommending versus the thing they want to be implementing.

Teach 'em: This is the "theory" piece of the puzzle. Just as we need to explicitly teach our students the behaviors and skills they need to meet expectations, we need to also provide instruction for staff. We cannot simply assume they know what to do or how to do it. This starts with first clearly describing the skill or strategy you want them to implement. Describe what it looks like and sounds like, as well as what it does not look like or sound like. This is also where staff job aids come into play (think written descriptions and flow-charts they can hang up that tell them exactly what to do and when to do it). You might include scripts of what to say to implement precorrection, behavior-specific praise, or instructional choice. Provide them with the resources to simplify implementation of the strategy and make their life easier.

Step onto the runway: Instruction followed by modeling is key in skills transference. Ask them if it's okay if you can set up a time to model what you would like to happen. Make sure you kindly let them know the expectation is that they watch you and write down any questions so your conversation afterward is solution-oriented and productive. Setting this expectation also discourages staff from going off and doing something else; the whole point is for them to watch and learn through modeling.

Follow up with feedback: Feedback is a crucial part of the learning process. Ask them what their preferred method of feedback is (e.g., in the moment? Immediately after? Via email?) Be sure to provide feedback as soon as possible after they implement the strategy so you can help them make any needed adjustments. We recommend seeking feedback from them as well. This isn't necessarily an invitation for them to find an "out," but rather an opportunity to discuss how you can better assist them in the implementation of the identified supports. Are they feeling adequately supported in this area? Is there anything they would like you to do more, less, or differently?

Wash, rinse, repeat: If you want to be *deliberate* in gaining buy-in, you cannot pull the infamous disappearing act. If we don't return to provide additional modeling, rehearsal, and feedback to help correct performance errors, staff will likely fall short of mastering the skill you have worked so hard to teach. What do we know about ongoing failure? It decreases human motivation! We also need to be considering motivation from the "won't do" side of things; if the teacher was resistant in the first place and they know you will never return, check in, or progress monitor from time to time, they are likely to avoid implementing the skill at all (escape). So, schedule times to return, check in by email or phone, create simple data sheets for them to track the progress and share via Google Drive, and make your presence known. Show them they can trust in your continued support.

Gaining buy-in from others can be daunting, but it is not impossible. Start small, lead by example, consider their needs, show them how, and keep your frustration in check. This will all assist you in moving forward, even if that movement is slower than you'd like.

It's still forward movement! Schools are complex systems, and change doesn't occur overnight. Likewise, your forward movement individually in implementing universal supports may move inconsistently at times. When you find yourself stuck, give yourself grace, reflect on the educator you want to be, and continue to move toward your goals and values. You're doing an awesome job and should be proud of the work you are doing for yourself and your students!

Appendix

Reproducible Forms

Form 1.1   Executive Functioning Skills

Executive functions: The cognitive processes that enable us to regulate and direct our behavior in order to begin tasks and achieve goals	**Planning:** The ability to create a roadmap to complete a task or navigate a routine
Response inhibition: The ability to think before you act, to resist the urge to do something	**Organization:** The ability to create and maintain systems to keep track of information and materials
Emotional control: The ability to manage your behaviors under stressful circumstances	**Time management:** The ability to accurately estimate the time one has to complete a task and then allocate that time accordingly
Working memory: The ability to retain and draw upon information when needed	**Persistence:** The ability to follow through on the completion of a task or goal
Attention control: The ability to attend to relevant stimuli despite distraction or a decrease in motivation	**Flexibility:** The ability to revise a plan and adapt to changing conditions
Task initiation: The ability to begin tasks efficiently and in a timely manner	**Metacognition:** The ability to self-monitor and self-evaluate one's own behaviors

Form 1.2   Executive Function Skills Self-Planning Guide

Read through the following executive function skills and determine which areas may be impacting your ability to effectively implement universal supports. Next, brainstorm some possible strategies to employ that can help you improve the identified skills.

Executive Function Skill	Area of Focus?	Strategies to Support Myself
Response Inhibition: The ability to think before you act, to resist the urge to do something	Yes / No	
Emotional Control: The ability to manage your behaviors under stressful circumstances	Yes / No	
Working Memory: The ability to retain and draw upon information when needed	Yes / No	
Attention Control: The ability to attend to relevant stimuli despite distraction or a decrease in motivation	Yes / No	
Task Initiation: The ability to begin tasks efficiently and in a timely manner	Yes / No	
Planning: The ability to create a roadmap to complete a task or navigate a routine	Yes / No	
Organization: The ability to create and maintain systems to keep track of information and materials	Yes / No	
Time Management: The ability to accurately estimate the time to complete a task and then allocate that time accordingly	Yes / No	
Persistence: The ability to follow through on the completion of a task or goal	Yes / No	
Flexibility: The ability to revise a plan and adapt to changing conditions	Yes / No	
Metacognition: The ability to self-monitor and self-evaluate one's own behaviors	Yes / No	

Form 2.1   Universal Supports Core Components Checklist

Rater: _____   Date: _____

No = not in place **Partial** = somewhat or inconsistently in place **Yes** = consistently in place

Physical Space	No	Partial	Yes
Instructional spaces are clearly defined			
Allows for ease of movement and limited crowding			
Students can be seen at all times			
Furniture arrangement matches instructional approaches			
Students have clear view of the source of instruction			
Materials are organized, labeled, and easily accessible			
Wall displays support instruction and promote a positive culture			
Distractions are minimized			

Expectations	No	Partial	Yes
Developed with students			
Between 3 and 5			
Aligned to school-wide expectations (if applicable)			
Positively stated			
Equitable (reflective of student culture, needs, characteristics)			
Supported by visual cues			
Posted within clear view			
Explicitly taught across common routines			
Reviewed prior to routines and activities (precorrection)			

Routines	No	Partial	Yes
Critical routines (e.g., attention signal, entry/exit routine, transitions) are established			
Routines are supported by step-by-step visual cues			
Explicitly taught			

Schedules	No	Partial	Yes
Posted in clear view			
Consistently followed			
Advance notice is given when changes are made			
Referenced throughout the day			
Lesson agendas are posted and reviewed			
High allocation of instructional time (minimal downtime)			

Instructional practices	No	Partial	Yes
Curriculum is differentiated and appropriate for ability level			
Materials are prepared and ready to go			
Teaching method is varied (discussions, partner work, project-based learning, independent, etc.)			
Lesson length is appropriate for age and ability			
Lesson includes a discussion about the rationale (the "why")			
Lesson targets and success criteria are reviewed			
Active supervision is used (moving, scanning, interacting)			
Students are provided frequent opportunities to respond (ASRs)			
Student interests and experiences are tied directly to lessons			
Instruction is delivered at a brisk pace			
Students are given frequent checks for understanding			
Instructional choice is provided when possible			
Skills are taught explicitly (instruct, model, practice, feedback)			
Lesson is closed out			
Reinforcing Desirable Behaviors	No	Partial	Yes
Behavior-specific praise is utilized following target behaviors			
4:1 ratio of positive to corrective interactions			
A variety of strategies are used to meet students' basic needs to the maximum extent possible			
A variety of strategies are used to help students feel connected to and related to staff, their peers, and activities			
A variety of strategies are used to help students increase their skillset and feel competent			
A variety of strategies are used to meet students' need for freedom and choice			
Responses to Undesirable Behaviors	No	Partial	Yes
Pre-determined			
Explicitly taught			
Calm, brief, private, and unemotional			
Applied responsively and with flexibility as needed			
Void of the following: threats, lectures, sarcasm, inappropriate gestures, raised voice			

Form 3.1   **Visual Checklist**

	Notes	Yes	No
1. Identify the situation or challenging routine where you believe visuals may be of benefit.			
2. When considering the underlying reason the students are struggling, determine the behavior or skills students should engage in.			
3. Identify what type of visual would increase success.			
4. Create the visual support.			
4a. Age appropriate			
4b. Reflective of student culture			
4c. Functional			
4d. Visible and accessible			
4e. Legible			
4f. Limited number of colors and fonts			
5. Explicitly teach the visual			
6. Reference the visual			

Form 3.2   Lesson Agenda Implementation Checklist

	Notes	Complete
1. Identify and make a list of times and/ or activities during the day when you give multi-step directions.		
2. Determine if you will be using a lesson agenda for a large group, small group, or individual student.		
3. Determine what presentation format students will benefit from (written, pictorial, object, etc.).		
4. Gather necessary materials needed to create the lesson agenda.		
5. Create and display the lesson agenda in advance or upon the start of the activity.		
6. Review the lesson agenda with the student(s) prior to the activity.		
7. Cross off or remove each task as the student(s) complete(s) it (if applicable).		
8. Refer to and direct student(s) to the lesson agenda throughout the activities.		
9. Provide positive feedback to students actively utilizing the lesson agenda to move through each task.		

Form 3.3   Expectation Implementation Checklist

	Notes	Yes	No
1. Identify the times or days you will set aside to develop and/or teach the expectations.			
2. Define and discuss the rationale behind expectations, ensuring you are showing how they benefit the students.			
3. Develop no more than 3–5 class-wide expectations (ideally as a group).			
4. Ensure expectations and are phrased positively.			
5. Provide instruction around examples and non-examples of the expectations (what it looks like/sounds like vs. what it doesn't look like/sound like.			
6. Demonstrate the expectation or expected behaviors through modeling.			
7. Provide opportunities for students to practice the expected behaviors.			
8. Provide positive and, as necessary, corrective feedback during practice sessions.			

Form 3.4   Steps to Classroom Routines and Procedures

Using your pregenerated list of routines, list the duration the routine is expected to take, as well as the procedural steps the students must take to successfully complete each routine. Steps should be positively stated, observable behaviors.

Routine		Duration	
Procedure/success criteria			
1.			
2.			
3.			
4.			
5.			
6.			

Routine		Duration	
Procedure/success criteria			
1.			
2.			
3.			
4.			
5.			
6.			

Routine		Duration	
Procedure/success criteria			
1.			
2.			
3.			
4.			
5.			
6.			

Form 3.5   Routine Task Analysis

Routine:	
Steps:	
1.	
2.	
3.	
4.	
5.	
6.	
7.	
8.	
9.	
10.	
11.	
12.	
13.	
14.	
15.	

Form 4.1 Precorrection Implementation Checklist

	Notes	Yes	No
1. Determine the contexts, activities, settings, and times that occasion challenging behavior.			
2. Identify and operationally define the challenging behaviors that occur during these times.			
3. Identify and operationally define the behaviors/skills that you are looking for during these times.			
4. Provide opportunities for students to practice the expected behaviors/skills outside of the moment (during a structured lesson).			
5. Review the expected behaviors and outcomes prior to the activity or routine starting.			
6. Acknowledge the behaviors/skills when students engage in them.			
7. Reflect if students do not engage in the behaviors/skills.			

Form 4.2   Instructional Choice Implementation Checklist

	Notes	Yes	No
1. Identify the challenging activity, routine, or demand for which you will use instructional choice.			
2. Determine whether you will provide instructional choice within the activity or across the activities.			
3. Create a running list of choices you feel comfortable giving.			
4. Determine what modality the choices will be delivered in (vocal, pictorial, written words, a combination, etc.)			
5. When it comes time, present the choices to the student(s).			
6. Ask the student(s) to make a choice.			
7. Provide time for the student(s) to process the choices and make a selection.			
8. Provide positive feedback for making a choice.			
9. Provide the student(s) with their selected choice.			

Form 4.3   Active Student Responding Implementation Checklist

	Notes	Complete
1. Determine for which lessons and content you will incorporate opportunities to respond (OTR).		
2. Create a list of questions or prompts related to instructional content.		
3. Identify instruction modality (how will you present the content?)		
4. Identify which response methods you want to utilize for each lesson/activity (you might also choose to have your students pick their favorite response methods).		
5. Gather and create ASR materials if necessary.		
6. Determine where you will keep ASR materials for easy access. Consider assigning a student to pass out the materials when the time comes.		
7. Set aside time to explicitly teach and practice chosen ASRs. This should be outside of the actual lesson and include student feedback.		
8. Introduce the lesson and ASR being used (or let students choose).		
9. When it comes time, pose the question/prompt.		
10. Give students time to process and generate a response yet keep a brisk instructional pace.		
11. Cue response.		
12. Scan student responses and assess.		
13. Provide positive and/or corrective feedback.		
14. Repeat steps 8–12 a minimum of 3 times per minute (simple responses) and 1 per minute (complex).		

Form 4.4   Active Student Response Methods

Preprinted Response Cards: Students hold up a preprinted card that corresponds to their answer (true/false, yes/no, agree/disagree, numbers, letters, story elements, etc.). When cued, students hold up their card to display their response.

Whiteboard Write: Each student has a personal whiteboard to write down their answers. Responses may include letters, words, numbers, symbols, solving problems, etc. When cued, students hold up their board to display their response. Students then use an eraser to erase their answer and wait for the next question.

Time Trials: The instructor describes the task and tells students how much time they will have to respond (roughly 30–60 seconds). Students are then signaled to write their response and stop when the time is up. This strategy is also known as "stop and jot."

Gestures: Students show their response by using hand signals or gestures. Gestures may include thumbs up/down, holding up a certain number of fingers, pointing, etc.

Stand Up, Sit Down: The teacher will pose a question and ask students to either sit down or stand up in response (e.g., Stand up if you think this statement is true).

Whip Around: The instructor poses a question or statement. When given the cue, students quickly go around the class and answer out loud in sequence or popcorn fashion.

Round Robin: Students are placed into small groups of no more than 6. The instructor presents a topic and students are required to brainstorm ideas related to it. Students go around in a circle voicing a single word or phrase about the topic, careful to avoid repeating; the goal is for the students to generate as many details and ideas about the concept or topic as possible.

Guided Notes: This strategy, used during lectures and videos, requires students to fill in an instructor-prepared handout with concepts, key facts, and other fill-in-the-blank responses.

Numbered Heads: Students are placed in small groups and each student is assigned a number. A question is posed, and the students are required to discuss the answer within their group. When the class comes back together, the instructor calls out a number and the student in each group with the corresponding number shares their group's response.

Inside-Outside Circle: Students form two circles around one another – one facing inward, the other facing outward. On cue, students take turns talking to their partner. Discussions may include asking one another questions from pre-prepared index cards, discussing certain topics, quizzing one another, etc. The instructor then signals one circle to rotate and students repeat the activity with their new partner.

Four Corners: Also known as "move the room," students move to a certain corner or area of the room that corresponds to their response to the question or statement. Students then discuss their answer as a small group before coming back together.

Write the Room: Students move about writing responses to various questions and prompts posted about the room.

Think-Pair-Share: This strategy is also known as a "turn and talk." When given the cue by the instructor, students think about their response to the question or prompt. Next, students are paired up and instructed to share their response with a peer. Instructors may choose to expand student sharing to the class as a whole-group.

Think-Write-Pair-Share: Similar to think-pair-share, students first think about their response before writing it down. Next, students are paired up and instructed to share their response with a peer. Instructors may choose to expand student sharing to the class as a whole-group.

Choral Responding: All students verbally respond to the question in unison. Responses are meant to be brief and fast-paced, leaving more time for a large series of questions.

Cloze Reading: Similar to choral responding, all students fill in the blanks to a reading passage by responding in unison.

Snowballs: The instructor poses a question to which students are required to write the answer on a piece of paper. Students are then instructed to crumble up the piece of paper into a "snow-ball." Instructors may have students throw them to specific areas of the room that represent the answer options or choose to have students throw them into one designated area such as a basket. The instructor then reads through each paper while discussing the response.

Round Table: Students are placed in small groups and given a piece of paper. Each group is given a topic or question. One student writes a brief response to the question or prompt (sentence, phrase, or word). Instructors may choose to have students read their response out loud after they write it. The student then passes the paper to the next student to write their response. Students continue writing and passing until the designated time has elapsed.

Class-wide Peer Tutoring: Students are paired up for a "tutoring session." Students are provided with the materials necessary to quiz and practice concepts with one another. The "tutor" quizzes their partner by asking pre-printed questions. When their partner responds, students are taught to give both positive and corrective feedback before moving on to the next question. When given the cue or when finished, the students then switch roles. Instructors may also choose to have students track their progress during these sessions.

High-Tech Response: Students respond to instruction using a clicker, iPad, keypad, computer, etc. Consider commercially available software to assist with polls, questions, and response collection.

Jigsaw: Select material you want students to explore or learn about. Separate the class into small groups. Each group will be required to become the "expert" on their specific material, concept, or topic. It can be helpful to provide guiding questions, so students know what information they are responsible for presenting. After each group has a solid understanding of their content, create new groups containing one or two members of each expert group. Students (or "experts") are then required to present their information they learned to the group. Requiring students to take notes as their peers share can help increase engagement.

Form 4.5   Active Supervision Implementation Checklist

	Notes	Complete
1. Identify the activity or setting that would benefit from active supervision.		
2. Identify and explicitly teach the expected behaviors/skills for the activity or setting.		
3. Explicitly teach the corresponding routines and procedures.		
4. Arrange the physical environment in a way that students can always be seen and easily accessed.		
5. Position staff (or self) in a purposeful way throughout the setting.		
6. Review expectations (precorrection) prior to the activity.		
7. Provided a clear cue to signal the start of the activity.		
8. Consistently look, listen, and move throughout the setting making your presence known.		
9. Consistently interact with students utilizing a variety of engagement strategies to include: prompts, modeling, proactive check-ins, and task assistance.		
10. Provide positive feedback for desirable behaviors.		
11. Ratio of positive to corrective interactions should be at least 4:1.		
12. Respond to undesirable behavior quickly, calmly, and privately.		

Form 4.6 Lesson Delivery Guide

Research shows there are effective ways to package and deliver lessons, and less effective ways that impact the behavior and academic success of our students. When we shift our focus to making sure we include the components of effective lesson delivery, rather than solely focusing on how we are going to respond when they are off-task, we will naturally see engagement increase and disruptive behavior decrease.

Opening (quickly engage students)
1. Hook students with starter activity
2. Identify the topic, skill, or concept
3. Review learning targets
4. Review lesson agenda
5. Precorrection

Body (maintain attention and active involvement)
1. Discuss the rationale
2. Provide instruction
3. Guided release (I do, we do, you do)
4. Discuss success criteria
5. Provide ongoing feedback
6. Check for understanding

Closing (review, reflect, and prepare for transition)
1. Give advance notice of time left or time until the next activity
2. Brief review of content
3. Reflection (lesson itself, student behavior, teacher behavior)
4. Prepare for transition

From start to finish:

- *Verify the vibes:* Make sure students are in a space to learn (to the best of your ability).
- *Sell it so they'll buy it:* If you aren't having fun, they aren't, either.
- *Embody "the power walk;"* Move around, keep a brisk pace, and do less talking.
- *Incorporate OTRs:* Create many opportunities for all students to respond.
- *Connect the content:* Focus on the "why" to increase motivation.
- *Live the lesson:* Bring concepts to life with videos, photos, and objects.
- *Beat the behaviors:* Provide positive feedback sooner rather than later.

Lesson Delivery Guide

Starter activity: A brief, stand-alone activity (ideally related to lesson content) that all students can independently achieve, regardless of prior content knowledge.

Topic: A label that clearly identifies the skill, concept, or idea you are teaching about.

Learning targets: Also referred to as "learning objectives," "learning aims," or "learning intentions." Outcomes that state what you want students to know, understand, or be able to do by the end of the lesson. Identify 1–3 clear intentions in student-friendly language.

Resources: The materials and supplies necessary to help students meet the learning objectives. Consider materials that will help bring the skill or concept to life (videos, photos, objects, etc.). Additionally, think about scaffolds that can be used such as a visual representation of success criteria, sentence starters, graphic organizers, prompts, etc.

Lesson agenda: A list of the activities in the lesson. What are the students going to do to master the learning objectives? Agendas should include the following:

- **Rationale:** A discussion about the relevance to students' lives. Why should it matter? Where is this skill or concept used or experienced in the real world? How will learning this skill or concept benefit them? What will the positive outcomes be? (Tie it to their goals/values/things that are important to them).

- **Instruction:** A clear explanation of the topic, skill, or concept. Include examples (and non-examples when applicable). Break it down into sequenced, teachable steps (success criteria).

- **Guided release and feedback:** A demonstration of the skill or activity (I do). Should also include guided practice (we do), and independent practice (you do). Be sure to include frequent positive feedback (and corrective as necessary) as part of this step.

Closing activity: A brief description of how you will have students review the content (exit slip, summary, etc.).

Notes: May include important information such as accommodations, modifications, or specific behavior support strategies.

Form 5.1   Behavior-Specific Praise Samples

Sample Remarks			
Wonderful	Awesome	Wow	Hooray
Nice	Excellent	Hot dog	Brilliant
Impressive	Great	Right on	You got it
Outstanding	Marvelous	Incredible	Super
Fantastic	Terrific	That's it	Magnificent
Amazing	Superb	Remarkable	Phenomenal

Sample Skills			
Attention control	Planning	Persistence	Communication
Initiation	Organization	Monitoring	Cooperation
Emotional control	Time management	Evaluation	Self-advocacy
Impulse control	Flexibility	Toleration	Staying calm

Sample Adjectives			
Courageous	Respectful	Generous	Assertive
Thoughtful	Friendly	Sincere	Amicable
Thorough	Hardworking	Resourceful	Ingenious
Patient	Clever	Reliable	Resilient
Admirable	Honest	Courteous	Positive
Considerate	Efficient	Flexible	Proactive

Sample Statements

- Gabriel, look at you taking turns with the markers. Camden, how does it make you feel when Gabriel takes turns with you?
- Leah, you made a respectful choice just now when you gave Andy personal space. I'm sure he appreciated that.
- Class, you all are showing great persistence through this assignment by using your resources and problem-solving difficult questions. Kiss your brain!
- Paul, you put it back without me even reminding you. Way to self-monitor.
- Yes, Allie, you may absolutely take a break. Great self-advocacy.
- That's walking! (Said while smiling and nodding).
- Cate, you must be very proud of how much you participated today in math block – you gave your brain muscles a great workout.
- Ian, you stayed so calm and came up with a resolution to that issue. And look, now Jamie is willing to continue working with you.
- Class, let's pause and reflect on that transition. How would you rate it? Yes, I would give it a thumbs up for sure! And what was the outcome of having such a smooth transition?
- Class, you know what I just noticed? I noticed you just followed all the steps of the entry routine calmly and independently. How responsible of you. Air five!

Form 5.2   Positive Feedback Preferences

How I Prefer Positive Feedback

Student: _____

_____ In front of the class _____ In private _____doesn't matter

_____ verbally   _____ gesture _____ sticky note

_____ fist bump   _____ smile   _____ thumbs up

_____ other: _____

Permission to call/text/email parents or guardians to share? Yes / No

How I Prefer Positive Feedback

Student: _____

_____ In front of the class _____ In private _____doesn't matter

_____ verbally   _____ gesture _____ sticky note

_____ fist bump   _____ smile   _____ thumbs up

_____ other: _____

Permission to call/text/email parents or guardians to share? Yes / No

Form 5.3 Behavior-Specific Praise Implementation Checklist

	Notes	Complete
1. Assess your current average ratio of positive to corrective feedback statements given.		
2. Identify a list of specific behaviors to target using BSP.		
3. Determine statement phrasing according to student need.		
4. Seek student input on how they would prefer to receive positive feedback.		
5. Determine and gather additional reinforcers or materials to be utilized along with BSP (if applicable).		
6. Observe student behavior, watching for target behavior.		
7. Gain student attention.		
8. Immediately following the target behavior, specifically state what the student(s) did well.		
9. Connect the behavior to positive outcomes when possible.		
10. Evaluate your rate of positive feedback as you go.		

Form 6.1   Staff Regulation Plan

Describe certain life events or stressors that contribute to your underlying feelings of anxiety or stress in the classroom (e.g., lack of sleep, too much caffeine, arguments with spouse, late to work, feeling sick, etc.).

I notice I am more likely to struggle to maintain regulation when:

These are the things I will do to minimize/eliminate the above events or at minimum, reduce the stress as a result of them (e.g., set an alarm on your phone as a reminder it's time for bed, make a morning checklist to help get out the door in time so you aren't late, etc.).

Stressor	Plan to address it

List any particular student behaviors that make it difficult to stay regulated (e.g., bullying, work refusal, homophobic comments, etc.). It's important to recognize these triggers so you can better prepare yourself to stay regulated if they occur:

-
-
-
-

These are the steps of the strategy I will use in these moments to ensure I can effectively help my student(s) regulate and get back on track:

1.
2.
3.
4.
5.

Form 6.2   Response Continuum

Mild "Distracting" Behavior	Immediate Response	Follow-Up Response
Moderate "Disruptive" Behavior	Immediate Response	Follow-Up Response
High-Magnitude "Dangerous" Behavior	Immediate Response	Follow-Up Response

Form 6.3 Student Staff Reflection Form A

Student: _____ Date: _____ Staff reflecting with: _____

The hurdle: What happened that made it difficult to stay calm? Did someone say or do something? Did something happen earlier? Did you want or need something?

Your behaviors: What did your body feel like? What were you thinking to yourself? What emotions were you feeling? What did you say? What did you do?

Outcomes: What happened after? What did adults do or say? What did peers do or say? Did you get what you wanted or needed? Did the outcomes make things better or worse short-term? Long-term? Did this get you closer or further away from your goals? Values?

Alternative solutions or strategies: Do you have any ideas that might prevent this hurdle from popping up again? If this hurdle *does* pop up again, what can *you* do differently that might help you work through it or get a better outcome? What can *adults* do the same/differently next time that would help you work through this?

Resolution plan: Was anyone impacted by your actions? Did an activity get missed? Was the physical environment damaged? Do you feel impacted by anyone else's actions? What do you need from them to help you move on?

Form 6.4   Student Staff Reflection Form B

Name: _____
Date: _____

Name of adult you are filling this out with: _____

What happened first?	What happened next?	What happened last?

It would be better if next time I. . .	It would be helpful if next time adult(s)/peers. . .	Some skills I'd like help with are. . .

I can make it right by. . .Others can make it right by. . .

References

Dawson, P., & Guare, R. (2018). *Executive skills in children and adolescents: A practical guide to assessment and Intervention*. Guilford Press.

Greene, R. W. (2014). *Lost at school: Why our kids with behavioral challenges are falling through the cracks and how we can help them*. Scribner.

Hanley, G. (2024). Today's ABA: An effective and humane approach for addressing PB. FTF Behavioral Consulting. **https://ftfbc.com/courses/todays-aba-an-effective-and-humane-approach-for-addressing-problem-behavior/**

Kolu, C. (2017, August 25). Part 7 in Trauma-informed behavior analysis: When praise doesn't work. **Cuspemergence.com**. **https://cuspemergence.com/2017/08/**

Kolu, C. (2024). Reflections on choice and control, informed by lessons in parenting. *Operants, Double Issue, IV*/2023(1/2024), 24–27. **https://cuspemergence.com/resources/**

Maslow, A. H. (1943). A theory of human motivation. *Psychological Review, 50*(4), 370–396. **https://doi.org/10.1037/h0054346**

Niemiec, C. P., & Ryan, R. M. (2009). Autonomy, competence, and relatedness in the classroom. *Theory and Research in Education, 7*(2), 133–144. **https://doi.org/10.1177/1477878509104318**

Professional, C. C. medical. (2024, September 1). *Brain: How it works, function, parts & conditions*. Cleveland Clinic. **https://my.clevelandclinic.org/health/body/22638-brain**

Weeks, M. R., Sullivan, A. L., & Nguyen, T. (2019). *Universal supports/ prevention services and student rights. Equity by Design*. Indianapolis, IN: Midwest & Plains Equity Assistance Center (MAP EAC)

Winston, M. (n.d.). Breakin' the law! Ways to increase compliance with rules and expectations. BehaviorLive. **https://behaviorlive.com/courses/breakin-the-law-ways-to-increase-compliance-with-rules-and-expectations**

Glossary

Active student responding: When students make an *observable* response that you can see or hear to an instructional question or prompt.

Active supervision: A proactive strategy to prevent challenging behavior through the continuous monitoring of students with strategic movement, scanning, and interactions.

Behavior: Anything a person thinks, says, or does. Behaviors can be external (observable) or internal (private).

Behavior-specific praise (BSP): A statement that clearly points out the desirable behavior or skill that has been performed.

Challenging behavior: Distracting, disruptive, or dangerous behavior that interferes with the student's learning or the learning of others.

Challenging routine: A routine within the day you can reliably predict a student or group of students will struggle to complete the procedure of a routine or will engage in challenging behavior.

Consequence: An event or stimulus occurring immediately after a behavior that increases or decreases the behavior over time. This can be considered the immediate outcome.

Contrived reinforcement: Rewards or incentives provided contingent upon engagement in targeted behaviors with the goal of increasing the behavior.

Effective lesson design and delivery: A three-part lesson structure containing an opening, body, and closing. Each section includes several components to keep students engaged, maximize motivation, and pace instruction appropriately.

Executive functions: The cognitive processes that enable us to regulate and direct our behavior in order to begin tasks and achieve goals.

Expectations: The broad, general guidelines of how one is to act within the environment.

Expected behaviors: The specific, observable behaviors that describe the broad expectation they fall under.

Fundamental needs: Basic, innate human psychological needs, which, when met, ensure optimal functioning.

Instructional choice: Providing opportunities for students to independently make selections from two or more options, either across activities or within activities. Instructional choice is ideally embedded throughout the day and is provided prior to engagement in challenging behaviors, not in response to.

Lesson agenda: A type of schedule that outlines the sequence of tasks to be achieved during a lesson or instructional block.

Motivation: The underlying want or need to get or get away from something. This can be an immediate or a delayed want or need.

Natural reinforcement: Outcomes that occur naturally within the environment that pay off use of a targeted behavior (i.e., the behavior worked to meet a need).

Precorrection: A meaningful review of the expected behaviors prior to a routine.

Procedure: The specific steps necessary to engage in or complete a routine.

Reinforcement: The outcome that occurs after the behavior that increases the likelihood the behavior will be used again in the future to meet the same or similar need.

Routine: A general task or activity to be completed – one that is typically done on a consistent basis (daily or weekly).

Schedule: A sequenced list of events according to the date and time they will happen.

Universal Tier 1 Supports (AKA Universal Supports or Tier 1 Strategies): Universal supports are free, low-to-no-prep, time-efficient evidence-based strategies that should be implemented across all ages, grades, abilities, settings, and subjects. They include strategies for the following: physical space, expectations, routines, schedules, instructional practices, reinforcement of desirable behaviors, and responses to challenging behaviors.

Visual support: A concrete object, such as a photo, graphic, written word, or combination, that gives information about an activity, routine, expectation, or skill to be demonstrated.

Index